THE STUDENT'S

COMPREHENSIVE GUIDE

TO THE

Canterbury Tales

ALLAN H. MACLAINE

Professor of English
University of Rhode Island

BARRON'S EDUCATIONAL SERIES, INC.

WOODBURY, NEW YORK

TO

MY BELOVED WIFE

AND

FELLOW CHAUCERIAN,

SARA BRIDEN HURDIS MACLAINE

Preface

The germinal idea for this handbook first came to me in 1947 while studying Chaucer as a graduate student at Brown University under the stimulating guidance of Professor George K. Anderson. Not until 1954, however, when I began teaching the Chaucer course myself at Texas Christian University, did the original notion of the need for and usefulness of such a guide begin to take definite shape. In its final form, the book owes much to the students in my Chaucer classes whose enthusiastic response to the general idea and practical advice on specific features have been most helpful. My huge debt to the scores of Chaucer scholars whose work is represented in the notes and lists of commentaries is obvious enough and is here gratefully acknowledged.

Several individuals have contributed significantly to whatever merit the book may have. The following of my recent graduate students have given substantial help in the preliminary spade-work on parts of the commentary, in checking the manuscript, or both: Mrs. Jeanne D. Ford, Mrs. Bobbie Simms, Mr. R. B. Reaves, Jr., Mr. Mark M. Loftin, and Mr. C. Pruitt Davis. My thanks are also due to my father, Mr. Allan MacLaine of Montreal, for much careful proof-reading and assistance with the notes, and to my typists, Miss Beth Hunt and Miss Paulette Allen, for skilled and faithful work on a difficult manuscript. Above all, I am indebted to my wife Sara who, besides her firm faith in the project and her steady encouragement, has been of enormous help in relieving me of other duties, and has herself compiled most of the raw material for the notes on several tales; to her this book is gratefully inscribed.

Whatever shortcomings the handbook may prove to have are, of course, my responsibility. In any attempt to survey (even partially) the vast and complex mass of Chaucerian scholarship sins of omission and commission are virtually inevitable; I can only ask to share in Chaucer's own request for the indulgence of readers:

> *And if ther be any thyng that displese hem, I preye hem*
> *also that they arrette it to the defaute of myn unkonnynge,*
> *and nat to my wyl, that wolde ful fayn have seyd bettre*
> *if I hadde had konnynge.*

University of Rhode Island, June, 1964   A.H.M.

Contents

INTRODUCTION

TABLE OF ABBREVIATIONS

THE CANTERBURY TALES

   The General Prologue 11
   The Knight's Tale 43
   The Miller's Tale 63
   The Reeve's Tale 76
   The Cook's Tale 84
   The Man of Law's Tale 87
   The Wife of Bath's Tale 101
   The Friar's Tale 122
   The Summoner's Tale 130
   The Clerk's Tale 138
   The Merchant's Tale 153
   The Squire's Tale 169
   The Franklin's Tale 176
   The Physician's Tale 190
   The Pardoner's Tale 193
   The Shipman's Tale 210
   The Prioress's Tale 217
   Sir Thopas 224
   The Tale of Melibee 232
   The Monk's Tale 240
   The Nun's Priest's Tale 252
   The Second Nun's Tale 263
   The Canon's Yeoman's Tale 271
   The Manciple's Tale 280
   The Parson's Tale 286

Introduction

The purpose of this handbook is to provide a legitimate study aid for the serious student of Chaucer who reads *The Canterbury Tales* in Middle English. To this end, the book supplies for the *General Prologue* and for each of the tales the following practical helps: 1] a selective list of the principal commentaries, together with concise data on genre, sources and/or analogues, date of composition, and verse form (when other than the usual pentameter couplets); 2] a summary of the text; 3] a selective gloss of the particularly troublesome or difficult words and phrases; and 4] a comprehensive digest of the significant critical pronouncements and interpretations by Chaucer scholars. A word of explanation here of the arrangement and purpose of each of these features will make it easier for the student to use the guide intelligently and profitably.

LISTS OF COMMENTARIES

These lists, which are in highly abbreviated form (see the explanatory note prefixed to the table of abbreviations), are not intended as exhaustive bibliographies. Rather they are limited in scope by two considerations: 1] they include only those critical and interpretive commentaries which, in the author's opinion, are particularly helpful; and 2], generally speaking, they exclude the more complex and detailed technical studies of language, meters, order of the tales, manuscripts, and sources, except where these seem of special importance. Among source studies, for example, the pertinent chapter in *Sources and Analogues* is regularly listed for each tale; otherwise, only a few source studies of paramount interest are included. The commentaries on each tale are arranged in four groups, each in alphabetical order, as follows: 1] the two standard bibliographies, Griffith and Hammond, which the student may consult for complete listings up to 1953; 2] the pertinent sections in the four basic editions—Donaldson, Manly, Robinson, and Skeat; 3] the pertinent sections in standard critical books on Chaucer; and 4] separate articles in periodicals or compilations. Additional notations are given for articles reprinted in any of the three paperback collections of critical essays on *The Canterbury Tales,* edited by Wagenknecht (W), Owen (O), and Schoeck and Taylor (ST). Altogether, the lists of commentaries are meant to give the student a good start in locating the most useful criticism on each tale.

SUMMARIES OF THE TEXT

The tales are broken down into logical narrative units with line numbers indicated, and a brief summary of each unit is provided. (In the line numbering, order of the tales, and spellings in the gloss, Robinson's second edition of Chaucer is followed throughout, since this is the most widely used text.) The aim of these summaries is twofold: to assist the student in grasping the narrative structure of the whole tale, and to help him in reviewing for examinations when he needs to refresh his memory of the contents of a larger number of separate tales.

SELECTIVE GLOSSES

For each unit of each tale a gloss is provided which is limited to the difficult words and phrases and does not include the basic Middle English vocabulary except for those few troublesome words with multiple meanings. These glosses are intended to function in two ways. First, they will greatly facilitate reading speed once the student has learned the basic vocabulary and has to look up only the hard or unusual words; with the handbook at his side, he will not have to go through the time-consuming process of consulting the large glossary (which is usually at the back of his textbook) every time he comes to a difficult word. Second, these selective word-lists will be of great value for review purposes.

NOTES

The notes, which are perhaps the most valuable and unique feature of this handbook, record in very condensed form the most important or controversial comments by Chaucer critics on each tale. A few notes by the author are also included. Generally speaking, the notes are subject to the same limitations in scope as are the lists of commentaries. Many excellent technical studies of manuscripts, order of the tales, sources, etc., have had to be omitted, not because they are unimportant, but simply because they do not lend themselves to brief summary and their inclusion would swell this book beyond all bounds. As a rule, the notes are restricted to critical and interpretive comments, with only occasional excursions into other phases of Chaucer scholarship. The comments are arranged in two ways as follows: Those which apply to a tale as whole and cannot logically be attached to any specific passage in it are all grouped together near the beginning of the section on that tale under the heading of GENERAL CRITICISM, and are arranged there in *chronological* order. This chronological arrangement helps to reveal developing tendencies in Chaucer criticism, as later critics have built upon the work of earlier ones; insofar as possible new critical approaches have been credited to the critics who first conceived them. Notes which apply to particular lines or passages within a tale are attached to the appropriate narrative units and placed immediately after the glosses. The notes are not, of course, meant to take the place of full reading of original sources in any kind of detailed study or in the preparation of papers. The fact is that a summary, no matter how skillful, can never do full justice to the original; by its very nature the summary must leave out what may be significant qualifications and subtleties of argument; it can present only central ideas in concise, but bald and unadorned, statements. With these limitations understood, however, the notes should prove of great value to the student in providing him with a highly condensed overview of the most important critical opinions on each tale, directing his attention to the major emphases, controversial points, and special problems of Chaucerian scholarship on *The Canterbury Tales* for the last half century.

This guide may be used in a variety of ways which will be obvious enough to the intelligent reader. On many pages there is sufficient blank space opposite the glosses to allow the student to write in additional notes of his own or comments of his professor. A student who is having trouble with vocabulary, for instance, may read through concentrating on the glosses alone. A similar method may be followed with the general data and criticism on each tale, or with the summaries of the text.

Though Chaucer is, or at least should be, among the most exciting and rewarding of all literary studies, experience has shown that most students find him rather difficult, especially at first. This book has, therefore, been designed throughout to provide the most practical aids possible within a relatively small space for the student struggling with Middle English and with vast welter of Chaucer scholarship. The author's earnest hope is that this handbook will contribute to the removal of some of the barriers, and will make more accessible to many readers the rich delights of *The Canterbury Tales*.

Table of Abbreviations

EXPLANATORY NOTE:

In this guide every effort has been made to save space, without sacrificing clarity or exactness, in the bibliographical references. In the lists of COMMENTARIES for each tale, references to standard books and editions have been reduced to an abbreviated form of the author's or editor's last name, with terminal page numbers for the passage cited. Similarly, in citations of articles only the author's last name (in full), title of periodical (abbreviated), the *year* of the volume (last two digits only), and terminal page numbers are given. The volume years rather than volume numbers have been used because they are equally helpful in locating the material and supply the added information as to when the articles appeared. In the notes, the author's last name (short form) and exact page numbers are provided for references to books, the author's last name alone for articles (to find the rest of the data the reader has only to consult the list of COMMENTARIES on that tale).

EXAMPLES:

For a passage in a book in the list of COMMENTARIES:

Man 31-9 = John M. Manly, *Some New Light on Chaucer* (New York, 1926), pp. 31-9. A note from this passage might be headed: Man 35 (exact page of material cited).

For an article in the list of COMMENTARIES:

Manly, *PBA,* 26, 95-113 = John M. Manly, "Chaucer and the Rhetoricians," *Proceedings of the British Academy,* 1926 volume, pp. 95-113. In the notes, this article would be cited simply as: Manly (unless more than one article by Manly were listed for that tale, in which case the abbreviated title of the periodical would be added).

Other space-saving devices are self-explanatory. The following abbreviations are used throughout:

AHM	Author's note
Bald	Baldwin, Ralph. *The Unity of the Canterbury Tales.* (Anglistica V). Copenhagen, 1955.
Baugh	*Studies in Medieval Literature in Honor of A. C. Baugh.* Philadelphia, 1961.
Baum	Baum, Paull F. *Chaucer: A Critical Appreciation.* Durham, North Carolina, 1958.
Bow	Bowden, Muriel. *A Commentary on the General Prologue to the Canterbury Tales.* New York, 1948.
Brew	Brewer, D. S. *Chaucer.* London, 1953.
Bron	Bronson, Bertrand H. *In Search of Chaucer.* Toronto, 1960.
Brown	*Essays and Studies in Honor of Carleton Brown.* New York, 1940.
BUSE	Boston University Studies in English.
CE	College English
Ch	Chaucer
Ches	Chesterton, Gilbert Keith. *Chaucer.* 2nd ed. New York, 1948.
CkT	The Cook's Tale
CL	Comparative Literature
ClT	The Clerk's Tale
Cog	Coghill, Neville. *The Poet Chaucer.* London, 1949.
Cow	Cowling, G. H. *Chaucer.* London, 1927.
CritQ	Critical Quarterly
CT	The Canterbury Tales
Cur	Curry, Walter Clyde. *Chaucer and the Medieval Sciences.* 2nd ed. New York, 1960.
Cweal	Commonweal
CYT	The Canon's Yeoman's Tale
DA	Dissertation Abstracts
Dem	Dempster, Germaine. *Dramatic Irony in Chaucer.* Palo Alto, California, 1932. Reprinted New York, 1959.
Dodd	Dodd, William G. *Courtly Love in Chaucer and Gower.* Boston, 1913. Reprinted Gloucester, Mass., 1959.

Don	Donaldson, E. T., ed. *Chaucer's Poetry: An Anthology for the Modern Reader.* New York, 1958.
EIE	English Institute Essays
ELH	Journal of English Literary History
EM	English Miscellany
ES	English Studies
ESt	Englische Studien
Ev	Everett, Dorothy. *Essays on Middle English Literature.* Oxford, 1955.
Expl	Explicator
Flügel	*Flügel Memorial Volume.* Palo Alto, California, 1916.
FranklT	The Franklin's Tale
Fr	French, Robert Dudley. *A Chaucer Handbook.* 2nd ed. New York, 1947.
FrT	The Friar's Tale
FSUS	Florida State University Studies
Gen Prol	The General Prologue
Ger	Gerould, Gordon Hall. *Chaucerian Essays.* Princeton, New Jersey, 1952.
Giff	Giffin, Mary. *Studies on Chaucer and His Audience.* Quebec, 1956.
Gr	Griffith, Dudley D. *Bibliography, of Chaucer, 1908-1953.* Seattle, 1955.
Ham	Hammond, Eleanor P. *Chaucer: A Bibliographical Manual.* New York, 1908.
Hin	Hinckley, Henry B. *Notes on Chaucer: A Commentary on the Prologue and Six Canterbury Tales.* Northampton, Mass., 1907.
JEGP	Journal of English and Germanic Philology
Kit	Kittredge, George Lyman. *Chaucer and His Poetry.* Cambridge, Mass., 1915. Reprinted 1956.
KnT	The Knight's Tale
Lang	Language
Law	Lawrence, William Witherle. *Chaucer and the Canterbury Tales.* New York, 1950.
Leg	Legouis, Emile. *Geoffrey Chaucer.* Trans. L. Lailavoix. London and New York, 1928.

Low	Lowes, John Livingstone. *Geoffrey Chaucer and the Development of His Genius*. Boston 1934. Reprinted 1958.
LGW	Legend of Good Women
Lum	Lumiansky, Robert M. *Of Sondry Folk: The Dramatic Principle in the Canterbury Tales*. Austin, 1955.
Mad	Madeleva, Sister Mary (Mary Evaline Wolff). *A Lost Language*. New York, 1951. (Originally published as *Chaucer's Nuns and Other Essays*. New York, 1925.)
MÆ	Medium Ævum
Mal	Malone, Kemp. *Chapters on Chaucer*. Baltimore, 1951.
Man	Manly, John Matthews. *Some New Light on Chaucer*. New York, 1926.
ManCT	Manly, John Matthews, ed. *Canterbury Tales*. New York, 1928.
MancT	The Manciple's Tale
Mel	Tale of Melibee
MerchT	The Merchant's Tale
MillT	The Miller's Tale
MissQ	Mississippi Quarterly
MkT	The Monk's Tale
MLN	Modern Language Notes
MLQ	Modern Language Quarterly
MLR	Modern Language Review
MLT	The Man of Law's Tale
MP	Modern Philology
MS	Mediaeval Studies (Toronto)
Mus	Muscatine, Charles. *Chaucer and the French Tradition, a Study in Style and Meaning*. Berkeley, 1957.
Neophil	Neophilologus
NPT	The Nun's Priest's Tale
N&Q	Notes and Queries
O	Owen, Charles A., Jr., ed. *Discussions of the Canterbury Tales*. Boston, 1961.
PardT	The Pardoner's Tale
ParsT	The Parson's Tale

Pat	Patch, Howard Rollin. *On Rereading Chaucer*. Cambridge, Mass., 1939.
PBA	Proceedings of the British Academy
PhysT	The Physician's Tale
PMLA	Publications of the Modern Language Association of America.
PQ	Philological Quarterly
Pres	Preston, Raymond. *Chaucer*. New York and London, 1952.
PrT	The Prioress's Tale
REL	Review of English Literature
RES	Review of English Studies
Rob	Robinson, Fred N., ed. *The Works of Geoffrey Chaucer*. Second ed. Cambridge, Mass., 1957.
Root	Root, Robert K. *The Poetry of Chaucer*. Revised ed. Boston, 1922. Reprinted Gloucester, Mass., 1957.
RR	Romanic Review, also Roman de la Rose
RvT	The Reeve's Tale
SA	*Sources and Analogues of Chaucer's Canterbury Tales*. Ed. William F. Bryan and Germaine Dempster. Chicago, 1941.
SecNT	The Second Nun's Tale
Sedg	Sedgwick, Henry Dwight. *Dan Chaucer*. Indianapolis and New York, 1934.
SFQ	Southern Folklore Quarterly
Shan	Shannon, Edgar Finley. *Chaucer and the Roman Poets*. Cambridge, Mass., 1929.
Shel	Shelly, Percy Van Dyke. *The Living Chaucer*. Philadelphia, 1940.
ShipT	The Shipman's Tale
Sk 5	Skeat, Walter W., ed. *The Complete Works of Geoffrey Chaucer*. Oxford, 1894-97. 6 vols. Vol. V.
Sp	Speirs, John. *Chaucer the Maker*. London, 1951.
SP	Studies in Philology
Spec	Speculum
SqT	The Squire's Tale

ST	Schoeck, Richard J., and Jerome Taylor, eds. *Chaucer Criticism, The Canterbury Tales: An Anthology.* Notre Dame, Ind., 1960.
SumT	The Summoner's Tale
Tat	Tatlock, John S. P. *The Mind and Art of Chaucer.* Syracuse, 1950.
TatDC	Tatlock, John S. P. *Development and Chronology of Chaucer's Work.* Chaucer Society, 1907.
Tho	Thomas, Mary Edith. *Medieval Skepticism and Chaucer.* New York, 1950.
Thop	The Tale of Sir Thopas
TLS	Times Literary Supplement
TSE	Tulane Studies in English
Tup	Tupper, Frederick. *Types of Society in Medieval Literature.* New York, 1926.
TWA	Transactions of the Wisconsin Academy of Sciences, Arts, and Letters
UMCMP	University of Michigan Contributions in Modern Philology
UTQ	University of Toronto Quarterly
UTSE	University of Texas Studies in English
W	Wagenknecht, Edward C., ed. *Chaucer: Modern Essays in Criticism.* New York, 1959.
WBT	The Wife of Bath's Tale
Wells	Wells, J. E. *Manual of Writings in Middle English.* New Haven, 1916.

The General Prologue

COMMENTARIES: Gr 163-84; Ham 265-70;/ Don 873-901; ManCT 495-539; Rob 650-69; Sk 5, 1-59;/ Bald 19-64; Baum 60-73; Bow (entire book); Brew 132-9; Bron 63-9; Cog 113-26; Cow 147-53; Cur 3-118; Fr 202-9; Ger 33-54; Hin 1-49; Law 41-61; Leg 143-52, 162-77; Lum 15-27; Mad 27-60; Mal 144-209; Man 70-234; Pat 154-85; E. Power, *Medieval People* (London, 1924; N.Y., 1954), 73-97; Pres 147-80; Root 160-3; Sedg 240-55; Shel 309-23; Sp 99-121;/ Aiken, *SP*, 36, 40-4, and 56, 22-4; Barnouw, *Nation,* Dec., 1916, 540; Baum, *PMLA,* 56, 225-46; Beichner, *Spec,* 59, 611-9 (ST); Birney, *N&Q,* 59, 345-7, and *REL,* 60, iii, 9-18; Blenner-Hassett, *Spec,* 53, 791-800; Block, *Spec,* 54, 239-43; Bloomfield, *PQ,* 49, 503-7, and *MLN,* 55, 559-65; Braddy, *MLQ,* 46, 265-7; Bressie, *MLN,* 39, 477-90; Brown, *MLN,* 34, 216-22, and *SP,* 37, 8-35; Bryant, *MLN,* 48, 318-25; Camden, *PQ,* 28, 314-7, and *MLN,* 32, 360-2; Cook, *JEGP,* 15, 375-88, and *Tr. Conn. Acad. of Arts and Sc.,* 16, 161-240; Cunningham, *MP,* 52, 172-81; Curry, *JEGP,* 19, 593-606; Drennan, *N&Q,* 14, 365; Duncan, *Ess. in Honor of W. C. Curry* (1955), 77-101; Eliason, *MLQ,* 42, 9-16; Emerson, *PQ,* 23, 81-96; Fink, *PQ,* 38, 321-30; Forehand, *PMLA,* 54, 984-9; Fullerton, *MLN,* 46, 515-23; Galway, *MLR,* 39, 497-514; Garbaty, *JEGP,* 60, 691-709; Hamilton, *JEGP,* 41, 48-72; Haselmayer, *Spec,* 37, 43-57; Hendrickson, *MLN,* 51, 328-9; Herndon, *FSUS,* 52, 33-44; Hoffman, *ELH,* 54, 1-16 (W, O); Horrell, *Spec,* 39, 82-92 (ST); Horton, *MLN,* 33, 31-4; Hostia, *CE,* 53, 351-2; Hulbert, *PMLA,* 49, 823-8 (W); Ives *MLR,* 32, 144-8; Johnson, *JEGP,* 53, 50-7; Jones, *MLQ,* 55, 3-15; Kaske, *ELH,* 57, 249-68, and *MLN,* 59, 481-4; Kellogg and Haselmayer, *PMLA,* 51, 251-77; Kimpel, *ELH,* 53, 77-86; Kittredge, *MP,* 10, 475; Kuhl, *TWA,* 16, 652-75; Law, *PMLA,* 22, 208-15; Lisca *MLN,* 55, 321-4; Loomis, *Brown,* 129-48; Lowes, *Anglia,* 10, 440-51, and *RR,* 14, 368-85; Major, *PMLA,* 60, 160-2; Malone, *ELH,* 46, 38-45; Manly, *Tr. Am. Philol. Assoc.,* 07,

89-107 (W); McCutchan, *PMLA*, 59, 313-7; Moffett, *PQ*, 25, 208-23; Moore, *PQ*, 47, 307-12; Muscatine, *MLN*, 55, 169-72; Nicholls, *Dalhousie Rev*, 32, 218-30; Patch, *MLN*, 25, 1-14; Powley, *TLS*, 32, 516; Pratt and Young, *SA*, 1-81; Richardson, *TLS*, 32, 331, 390; Rickert, *MP*, 26, 249-56; Rockwell, *N&Q*, 57, 84; Schoeck, *ST*, 245-58; Steadman, *MP*, 57, 1-6, and *Neophil*, 59, 49-57; Stillwell, *JEGP*, 58, 192-6; Stillwell and Webb, *MLN*, 44, 45-7; Stobie, *PMLA*, 49, 565-9; Tatlock, *MP*, 16, 257-68, and *Flügel*, 228-32, and *MLN*, 40, 350-4; Tupper, *Nation*, June, 1913, 640-1, and *JEGP*, 15, 256-70; Wainwright, *MLN*, 33, 34-7; Walker, *MLN*, 23, 314; Willard, *UTSE*, 47, 209-51; Williams, *Spec*, 53, 499-513 (ST); White, *MP*, 28, 249-55, and 29, 379-84, 123-8; Wood-Legh, *RES*, 28, 145-51; Woolf, *MLN*, 53, 118-21, and *CritQ*, 59, 150-7; Wretlind, *MLN*, 48, 381-2.

GENRE: Gallery of character portraits used to introduce narrative framework for tales told by pilgrims.

ANALOGUES: No direct source is known; 14th-century analogues of the frame story idea are Boccaccio's *Decameron* and Giovanni Sercambi's *Novelle* (tales told on pilgrimage with links between them, but author is sole teller), though Ch is not likely to have known either.

DATE: About 1387.

GENERAL CRITICISM: Kit 154-5: Prol is first act of drama, setting group of vital characters in motion; tales exist for sake of the pilgrims as "long speeches" characterizing each. Root 160-1: brilliant blending of abstract types and real individuals in portraits. Patch: Ch's technique in portraits, drawn largely from life with many personal and local allusions, is new and revolutionary. Man 70-6: Ch did not aim at systematic cross-section of society, chose pilgrims according to his own interests and prejudices; many are more individuals than types, probably taken from life with identifying traits that would be obvious and amusing to small court audience. Leg 164-5: unforgettably colorful portraits, "as good as illuminated miniatures." Low 163-4: static portraits become dramatic and dynamic as pilgrimage starts; "long before Balzac Ch conceived and executed the Human Comedy." Shel 194-8: a triumph of realistic, descriptive verse unequaled in literature before or since; homely, matter-of-fact technique gives freshness, variety, intensity, amazing sense of life. Malone, *ELH*: well distributed use of personal pronouns (*I gesse,* etc.) gives informal, conversational effect. Cog 124-5: Ch's effortless, homely "imagery of common sight and sense" makes prosaic statements "gleam and glow as they never do in prose" (see 267-8, 287, 332, 626). Hulbert: no known source for portrait gallery which is clearly result of "inspiration." Law 53-5: portraits are "subtly varied" to avoid monotony, with stress on more picturesque pilgrims. Mal 152, 167: heavy stress on 7 church representatives (320 lines, with 349 lines for other 19 pilgrims); Ch uses traditional story-telling device of describing in superlatives, making pilgrims as striking as possible to interest readers. Cunningham: Prol is special realization of dream-vision prologue as in *RR, House of Fame, LGW,* etc., where author falls asleep, dreams of spring scene, meets group of characters, describes them in catalogue fashion. Brew 133: haphazard impression conceals brilliant significance of details in portraits ("that supreme art which conceals art"). Kimpel: Ch was probably not conscious of whether comments on pilgrims were his own or narrator's; narrator is not vividly portrayed, is no more important than is necessary for narration. Hoffman: whole Prol shows pilgrims affected by various destructive and restorative kinds of love; duality of motive appears in opening lines, in relative idealism or perversion of first group of pilgrims (descending from Kn, Sq, Pr, to Monk and Friar), in mixtures of natural and divine loves. Duncan: narrator repeatedly shifts back and forth from limited, personal point of view to one of omniscience. Lum 20: devices for realism in portraits are conversational style, colloquial exaggeration, insertion of personal comments, combination of expected and unexpected traits in pilgrims. Baum 60-6: subtle blending of formal and casual (seemingly careless) styles; brilliant portraits, but pace is so fast that final effect may be blurred; Ch alternates realistic reporting and literary convention, point of view of narrator and that of omniscient author. Don 874-81: Ch, keenly aware of dangers of static portraiture (characteristic medieval device), does all he can to avoid dullness, creates pilgrims who "are at once perfect types and perfect individuals"; he achieves ironic satire, telling but not "emotionally scathing," through difference between sophisticated poet Ch and naive pilgrim Ch ("almost unfailingly simple-minded") who admires Monk, observes keenly but indiscriminately, thus ironically condemns by his very admiration; pilgrim Ch is fictional character. Woolf, *CritQ*: pilgrim Ch is obtuse, fictional character who accepts vicious pilgrims uncritically, sharing "the immoral premises from which they speak," though Ch's own voice can occasionally be heard in images which imply censure or ridicule and in portraits of virtuous pilgrims (also in satirist's choice of detail); individuality of pilgrims is artistic illusion—all are types. Bron 25-33, 68-9: theory that pilgrim Ch is fictional *persona* is unsound—Ch is simply showing distorted picture of himself for amusement of listening audience; Manly's attempts to identify pilgrims with actual persons is misleading—Ch the artist, even when working from real models, would surely "take care to falsify the record significantly as he worked" (Man's strongest cases are probably his weakest). Major disagrees with Don—narrator is not presented consistently as fictional *persona;* rather "the point of view shifts back and forth quite unrealistically" from narrator to omniscient author to suit Ch's needs.

THE GENERAL PROLOGUE

I, 1-42

In April folk love to go on pilgrimages, especially to Canterbury. I was about to do so when I was joined by 29 other pilgrims at the Tabard Inn, Southwark. I shall describe them.

3	*veyne* sap vessel	14	*ferne halwes* distant shrines
5	*Zephyrus* west wind	18	*seeke* sick
6	*inspired* quickened	33	*forward* agreement
7	*croppes* shoots, buds	34	*devyse* describe, relate
11	*corages* spirits, feelings	40	*degree* rank

1-18 Malone, *ELH*: Ch begins sentence in "high style," but gradually descends, beginning at line 12, to easy conversational level. Sp 99-101: "superb expression of a sense of harmony between man and nature" (contrast conscious disharmony of opening of Eliot's

Waste Land). Hoffman: sentence moves from phallic symbolism at start (natural love) to sacred image at end (divine love); whole Prol is organized around tension between these "two voices." Bald 19, 27-8: Ch adds homely touch in line 10 to ritualized "nature-introduction"; surge of springtime becomes metaphor for religious awakening. Lum 16-7: sentence effectively relates man to natural world at springtime, suggests both social and religious motives for pilgrimage. Baum 60: "nothing could be finer"—both conventional and fresh, well balanced, with formality relieved by brief "asides." Don 876-7: sentence suggests mixed motives for pilgrimage, implies "that the divine love that revives the dead world annually is large enough to countenance the whole paradox of man's nature."

1-4 Pat 154: spring sap suggests restlessness of season, later reflected in "emotional turbulence" of pilgrims themselves.

5 Brew 132-3: a magical line, with *Zephirus* (fanciful and musical word) reinforcing "sensuous realism" of *sweete breeth*.

15-8 Ches 149: despite holiday spirit, Ch carefully establishes fact of religious motive which was actually paramount in many of his pilgrims.

19-26 Lum 19-20: lines set tone of "pleasant, everyday informality."

30-2 Kit 184: "This, beyond question, is the real Ch"—sociable, agreeable, etc.

34 Mal 147: the *yow* "adds to the easy, chatty stylistic effect," introducing Ch's intimate "tête-à-tête with his readers" which follows.

37-41 Baum 43: Ch will describe pilgrims' *condicioun* under general character, rank, physical appearance

42 Tup 33: Ch puts chivalry and church first. Bald 35: a "reasonable class beginning"; Ch was very conscious of conventions of his age.

THE KNIGHT

43-78

He was honorable, chivalrous man and fine soldier. Had fought at Alexandria, in Russia, Spain, North Africa, etc. He was modest, well spoken, a true gentleman, just returned from wars.

46 *fredom* generosity
48 *ferre* farther
52 *bord bigonne* sat at head of table
54 *reysed* campaigned
60 *armee* armada

67 *sovereyn prys* high reputation
72 *verray* true
74 *hors* horses (pl.)
75 *gypon* tunic
76 *bismotered* stained. *habergeon* coat of mail

43-78 Cow 152: an idealized portrait, "viewed in the radiance of the light that never was." Loomis: ideal portrait shows resemblances to Ch's friends the "Lollard Knights"; Ch perhaps a Wycliffite, or at least very sympathetic. Cog 128: dignified, humble, kindly Kn reflects "long tradition of militant Christianity." Bald 45: Kn combines military and Christian virtues, is "idealized to the point of complete depersonalization," reflects an already vanished chivalric ideal. Don 881: with Kn Ch sets up ideal "against which all the other pilgrims may be measured."

43-68 Tup 33: *worthy,* used 5 times of Kn, means having prowess ("chief badge of knighthood"), in loftier sense than when applied to Friar, Merchant, Franklin, Wife of B. Camden, *MLN: worthy* in Ch means having qualities suited to social position or function whatever it may be (see *WBT* 8).

47-66 ManCT 499: Kn's wars were almost all crusades against heathens on fringes of Christendom; they fall into 3 groups: (1) against Moors at west end of Mediterranean, (2) against Turks at east end, (3) against Lithuanians and Tartars on Russian border. Fink: attempts by Manly and Cook to identify Kn with real knights (2 members of Scrope family and Earl of Derby) is futile since many knights clearly had similar careers. Stillwell and Webb: Loomis's view that Ch disapproved of war with France is unconvincing, since Sq fought in France, probably with Kn, and Kn is also said to have fought in Christendom. Mal 199: catalogue of battles gives Kn heroic stature—"a fighting-man bigger than life."

52 Cook, *JEGP:* refers to "table of honor" established by Teutonic Knights to attract famed foreign knights to their service; table was reserved for small, distinguished group of 10-14.

68-9 Lum 33-4: Kn's courtesy and piety are unexpected traits in soldier.

69 Pat 155: in Ch's time meekness did not have today's insipid connotation.

70-1 Pres 155: "a safely negative virtue."

72 Sp 103: line expresses Kn's "inner beauty of life beneath his battered exterior."

THE SQUIRE

79-100

Son of Knight was gaily dressed lover, age 20, well built, soldierly. He could sing, ride well, write songs, dance, etc., was courteous and dutiful.

80 *lovyere* lover. *bachelor* aspirant to knighthood
81 *crulle* curly
83 *evene* medium
84 *delyvere* agile
85 *chyvachie* cavalry raids

89 *embrouded* embroidered
95 *endite* compose words (for songs)
96 *purtreye* draw
00 *carf biforn* carved in front of

79-00 Brown, *MLN:* Sq was later addition to Ch's list of pilgrims, with *he* in 101 referring to Kn, not to Sq; this would make Ch's original total of 29 pilgrims accurate. Sedg 241: charming picture of English youth, with gentlemanly modesty despite abundant zest for life. Shel 196: delightful example of Ch's skill in building up vital impression through series of specific details. Sp 103: "extravagant spring-like figure" contrasts with "external fadedness" of Kn. Bow 74-5: Ch "speaks to youth in youth's language" (light, swift style contrasting with measured language of Kn's portrait), reflecting his own youth as page and squire.

97-8 Shel 199: touch of poetry in basically realistic passage saves it from monotony.

THE YEOMAN

101-117

Servant of Knight, he was dressed in green, with bow and arrows of expert archer, doubtless a forester.

04 *pecok arwes* arrows with
peacock feathers
06 *dresse takel* prepare tackle
09 *not* knot, close-cropped

11 *bracer* armguard
16 *bawdryk* baldric (belt passing over shoulder, under opposite arm)

01-17 Sedg 241: interesting example of world famous English archer. Birney, *REL:* Yeoman is Sq's servant, not Kn's; like Sq, he is gaily decked with accoutrements less for military use than for show (peacock feathers were handsome but impractical on arrows), has probably come with Sq to join Kn for pilgrimage; portrait has quiet irony, helps illuminate gay Sq, contrasting with Spartan Kn. 17 Bow 85: *forster* was gamekeeper in Middle Ages; this one also acts as "sound and likable" attendant to Kn.

THE PRIORESS

118-164

Madame Eglentyne was modest, sang well, spoke French, had very dainty table manners, imitating court behavior. She was soft hearted about her dogs. A large handsome woman, she was well dressed, had gold brooch, A nun and 3 priests rode with her.

19 *coy* modest
24 *fetisly* elegantly
32 *lest* pleasure
34 *ferthyng* tiny drop
36 *raughte* reached
39 *countrefete* imitate. *cheere* behavior

47 *wastel-breed* fine white bread
49 *smerte* sharply
51 *pynched* pleated
55 *spanne* hand breadth
59 *gauded* with large beads between groups of 10 small ones

18-64 Lowes, *Anglia:* Ch includes touches which suggest "delightfully imperfect submergence of the woman in the nun." Kit 175-6: sympathetic, delicate portrait of amiable, gentle, sweetly dignified woman. Root 161: a type similar to modern mistress of girls' school. Power 73-97: being a nun was only career for well-born medieval spinster; going on pilgrimage, owning dogs and brooch were all against rules for nuns. Man 202-20: Pr may have been modeled on nun of St. Leonard's convent at Stratford-Bow, to which Queen Philippa's sister

Elizabeth of Hainaut belonged. Cow 148: refined lady with traces of worldly affectation. Wainwright refutes Mad's view of Pr's total purity; humanizing touches make her religious dedication "more significant and perhaps more heroic." Sedg 242: Pr's affectations (her sentimentality, French, mild oath) make her very distinct. Bow 93-5: "sharp colours of irony combined with the gold of humour and sympathy"; Ch gives Pr traits of worldly romance heroine, but keeps portrait dignified. Mal 181: "most delicately, daintily humorous passage in *CT*." Sp 104: "most delicately poised irony." Hostia: Pr is worldly, vain, insincere—contrasts with truly religious Second Nun. Schoeck: Pr is warped character who weeps over dogs or mice but ignores human suffering (torture of Jews in *PrT*); portrait drawn with "superbly controlled irony and devastating tact," leaving many shadows of doubt. Woolf, *CritQ:* pilgrim Ch, ignorant of distinction between worldly lady and nun, "records all the details sweetly, as though there were no matter here for blame."

19 Lowes, *Anglia: symple and coy* was conventional phrase in description of mistresses in 14th-century French love poetry. Mad 35: *smylyng* was sign of hospitable spirit expected of nuns.

20 Lowes, *RR:* St. Eligius (Loy) was 6th-century French saint, famous as goldsmith, artificer of beautiful church decorations, also very handsome—thus fitting as favorite saint of Pr. Steadman, *Neophil:* beyond Lowes' reasons, there was famous episode in which St. Loy refused to swear at all; hence irony of saying Pr's greatest oath was by him.

21 Mal 181: *Eglentyne* has no religious associations, derives from *chansons de geste,* fits lady perfectly.

22-3 Law 60-1: though nasal intonation was customary, this is surely "a sly dig." Sp 104: *in hir nose* "gently discomposes the propriety, upsets the solemnity."

24-6 Sk 5, 15: no satire here; king himself spoke Anglo-French. Hin 10: "exceedingly delicate little thrust" at provincial Anglo-French dialect. ManCT 504-5: Sk is wrong in thinking Anglo-French was regarded as equally good as Parisian; French of Stratford was probably Hainaut dialect of Elizabeth (king's sister) and of Ch's wife.

27-36 Sk 5, 16: passage on table manners drawn from *RR,* ultimately from Ovid's *Ars Amatoria*. Mad 39-40: on a journey nun was expected to wear new habit, be extra careful not to spill food; hence Pr's dainty manners (no affectation). Don 875: Pr's table manners artfully "convey the very essence of the courteous, misdirected lady."

36 Drennan: *raughte* means retched (OE *hraecan*), not reached (OE *raecan*); "this little Rabelaisian touch has more of the true Chaucerian ring than the tame anticlimax of 'She reached for her meat in seemly wise.' "

38-41 Kit 176: Pr simply had exquisite manners befitting her position—no satire on affectation intended. Sp 105: Pr is more anxious to be respected for affected courtly manners than for holiness.

42-50 Bow 99-100: harshest criticism in portrait, suggesting Pr's charity is aroused more easily for animals than for human beings, as her tale confirms.

46 Mad 47: Pr probably middle aged; nuns over 50 were allowed pets. Steadman, *MP:* Pr's pity was misdirected, especially since she was supposed to enforce rule against pets.

52-6 Lowes, *Anglia:* every detail echoes conventional lover's description of his mistress. Lum 80: Ch describes Pr as romance heroine, then makes fun of all this in 156 with mention of her incongruous largeness ("brilliant use of understatement").

52 Moore: *greye* probably means gray, not blue (Man, Rob).

57 Mad 41-2: not vanity but duty causes Pr to wear her habit becomingly.

58-62 Manly: coral beads and *Amor* motto are both ambiguous; coral was both a defense against worldly temptation and an earthly love charm.

60-2 Mad 43: a typical motto on what was undoubtedly a sacred medal, inspiration to virtue. Mal 206: brooch is outward sign of worldliness. Lum 80: motto refers to divine love.

63-4 Emerson: *preestes thre* is meant to include Monk and Friar. Eliason: both lines may have been added by scribes to account for *SecNT* (which Ch perhaps meant as second tale of Pr). Bow 104: prioresses were required to take one nun as chaplain on travels, possibly one priest but not three; probably scribe filled out incomplete line with *preestes thre* for rime.

THE MONK

165-207

He loved horses and hunting, cared nothing for strict monastic rules against such sports. He was richly dressed, bald, fat, with glowing eyes.

65 *a fair for the maistrie* a most excellent one
66 *outridere* one who rode out to supervise estates
72 *celle* subordinate monastery
76 *the space* meanwhile
79 *recchelees* careless
87 *Austyn bit* St. Augustine bids
89 *prikasour* hard rider
91 *prikyng* tracking by footprints (pricks)
93 *purfiled* trimmed
94 *grys* gray fur
01 *stepe* prominent
02 *leed* lead cauldron

65-07 Sedg 242: amazingly exact picture of forerunner of English sporting parson. Pat 159: this *manly man,* fond of comfort, hunting, self-indulgence, with bells on his horse, really has "the heart of a child." Shel 197: portrait is "as full of easy tolerance and hearty, unaffected admiration as it is of sly satire." Tatlock, *MLN:* Monk must belong to important house, since he is described as impressive prelate, is apparently a prior (172), but not abbot. Ches 239: sketch is "protest against the decline of monastic discipline." Mal 174-5: Monk, far from being a misfit, is "perfect picture of a successful man." Don 885: Ch satirizes Monk's "brute force" more sharply than Pr's "charm." Woolf, *CritQ:* pilgrim Ch's approval of Monk shows narrator must be clearly distinguished from poet; it is incredible that Ch would reject authority of St. Augustine.
65-6 Kaske, *ELH* (also Don 886): lines echo description of Kn in 43-5, pointing up contrast between ideal Kn and corrupt "hunting" Monk; Monk rebels against ideals of his calling (173-7, 182, 188), whereas Kn is loyal to his (45-50); Monk hunts rabbits (189-92), whereas Kn does God's work fighting heathens (61-6); Monk's dress and horses are extravagant (193-7, 203), but Kn's are conservative and well used (74-6).

72 Beichner doubts that line means Monk was prior; if so, Ch would have called him prior.

77-8 Willard copiously documents canon law rulings against hunting by clergy.

83-7 Cog 120: opinion given in "Ch's accent of sardonic innocence." Sp 108: unmistakable irony; argument really undermines Monk's position rather than supporting it. Lum 98: narrator's opinion "probably refers to his approval of the Monk's making his way in the world."

87 Don 885: basic premise of monasticism is that God is to be served, not the world.

97 Sp 109: unlike Pr's motto, meaning of Monk's love-knot is unambiguous.

99-00 Sp 109: *as he hadde been enoynt* contrasts holy oil with Monk's "greasy fatness"; *in good poynt* (often used of horse or dog) "implies his animality."

THE FRIAR

208-269

He was gay blade, had found husbands for girls he had seduced. He gave easy penances in return for money. He could sing well, knew taverns, was skilled at begging. He was well dressed, had lisp, was called Hubert.

09 *lymytour* one licensed to beg in certain district. *solempne* gay, festive

19 *curat* parish priest

26 *yshryve* shriven

27 *make avaunt* assert

33 *typet* loose hood used as pocket. *farsed* stuffed

36 *rote* fiddle with 3 strings

37 *yeddynges* ballads

41 *tappestere* barmaid

42 *bet* better. *lazar* leper. *beggestere* beggar-woman

47 *poraille* poor folk

51 *vertuous* capable

56 *purchas* what he picked up. *rente* income

57 *rage* play wantonly

63 *presse* mold

08-69 Leg 168: "delicate yet slashing irony" pervades portrait. Sedg 243-4: popular idea of friars demands satire in portrait. Pat 160: Fr has vitality and outgoing charm which Ch relishes. Bow 137-9:

Fr resembles False-Seeming in *RR,* but is probably also modeled on actual contemporary; he is both type and individual through "arrogant strength of his personality." Sp 111: Fr is triumphantly guilty of fleshy sins and avarice. Pres 149-55: Fr, based on Ch's observation and reading, is superb reanimation of type shown allegorically in *RR,* presented in "irony with the right degree of sharpness to clean the system and leave it sweet"; Fr is climax of "ecclesiastical sequence" in Prol. Williams: Fr perhaps not typical, reflects attitude of secular party (dominant in government circles) which opposed friars, attacking their confessional powers, worldly possessions, catering to rich. Don 887: abusive practices in portrait, stressed by narrator's praise of Fr's efficiency, define "by inversion" the ideal of mendicant friars.

12-3 Don 887: "a kind of parody of an act of charity."

35-7 Don 887: St. Francis's cheerfulness has become "gaiety of an accomplished ballad-singer and flirt, an intimate of barmaids, and a seducer of maidens."

38 Horton: in medieval physiognomy, white neck means moral depravity.

53-5 Law: *In principio,* favorite text of Fr, refers to John i, 1-14. Bloomfield, *MLN: In principio* passage was believed to have magic power to exorcise demons; friars specialized in this (see *WBT* 864-81).

69 Muscatine: Ch took name Hubert from rascally clerics in French poems of *Renart* tradition, especially from *Roman de Renart* used in *NPT.*

THE MERCHANT

270-284
He was fashionably dressed, spoke always of his profits so no one would guess he was in debt. I don't know his name.

74	*resons* opinions	78	*sheeldes* French crowns	
75	*sownynge* proclaiming		(coins)	
76	*for any thyng* at all costs	79	*bisette* used	
		82	*chevyssaunce* loans (illegal)	

70-84 Man 181-200: merchants, wholesale importers and/or exporters, were organized in 2 groups—Merchants of Staple (wool) and Merchant Adventurers; Ch's Merchant probably one of latter group; historically, merchants were also money lenders, dealers in foreign currency (illegal), anxious to keep sea free of pirates between Middelburg and Orwell. Rickert identifies Merchant conjecturally with Gilbert Maghfeld. Sedg 245-6: Merchant is shy, narrow-minded, lacking in wit (his tale makes different point from what he intends), "with nothing to recommend him." Bow 151-3 agrees with Rickert—Merchant was probably Maghfeld whom Ch surely knew; Merchant was actually in debt. Sp 112: "keeping up appearances" is keynote of portrait. Pres 154: composite portrait with effective (not haphazard) order of details—visual image as well as suggestion of character. Bald 24-9: dominant trait of portrait is Merchant's "facade." Don 887-8: with impressive clothes and pose of financial success to inspire confidence in clients, Merchant is perhaps leaving town anonymously because of debts.

75 Sp 112: "monotony of the Marchant's conversation is wonderfully conveyed" here.

76-7 Walker: these lines and hence whole Prol probably written in 1385-6 when piracy between Middelburg and Orwell was at height.

80 Johnson opposes usual interpretation that Merchant was in debt; line means rather that he was "decidedly not in debt." Stillwell: line means "If he was in debt, certainly no one knew it."—consistent with ironic treatment of other middle-class characters (Lawyer, Physician, etc.).

84 Baum 64: line means "I'd better not name him."

THE CLERK

285-308

He had long studied logic at Oxford, was thin, poorly dressed, and sober. He loved books, learning, and teaching, had little money. His speech was concise and edifying.

86	*ygo* proceeded	96	*fithele* fiddle. *sautrie* psaltery
90	*overeste courtepy* short outer coat	97	*philosophre* (pun on "alchemist")
92	*office* secular job	02	*scoleye* study
93	*hym was levere* he would rather	06	*sentence* meaning

85-08 Man 261 suggests portrait "began with a real person even if it ended in the ideal." Richardson: Clerk may have been Waultier Dissy (or Dysse), well known at court, unbeneficed confessor to John of Gaunt. Pat 168-9: perhaps most congenial of pilgrims to Ch, but "too exclusively Aristotelian" (no romances, no nonsense) to resemble Ch himself. Cog 139: unworldly Clerk seems "lost cause among the ecclesiastical successes of his fellow-pilgrims." Law 139-40: one of most attractive of pilgrims, reflecting Ch's own interest in youth, books, *moral vertu*. Mal 156: Ch probably placed virtuous Clerk between Merchant and Lawyer for contrast. Pres 160: "an Oxford man who slept by Aristotle and not with Alison" (unlike clerk in *Mill'T*). Bron 64: Clerk (*sownynge in moral vertu*) makes perfect contrast to worldly Merchant (*sownynge alwey th'encrees of his wynnyng*).

08 Lum 141: shows Ch's appreciation for "contemplative, humanistic, intellectual, and spiritual values."

THE SERGEANT OF THE LAW

309-330

He was sly and learned, often served as judge, bought many properties. He knew law thoroughly.

09	*war* wary	20	*infect* defective
10	*Parvys* porch of St. Paul's	23	*doomes* judgments
19	*fee symple* absolute possession	28	*medlee* motley
		29	*ceint* girdle

09-30 Man 131-57: Sergeant probably modeled on Thos. Pynchbek of Lincolnshire, only one of few sergeants active in 1380's who fits description, was surely known to Ch; possible pun on his name in 326. Bow 168: portrait is "consistently ironic," as Ch reports Lawyer's traits "in outward praise and inward condemnation." Brew 136: Ch dislikes *nouveau-riche* Lawyer. Don 889-90: despite exalted position, Lawyer's real interest is in money; "all the skill that might be directed toward settling problems of right and wrong is used instead to make the Sergeant rich."

21-2 Tat 91: brilliant use of "closed and balanced couplet," probably learned from Ovid. Bald 45: "devastating couplet," adding to "smack of professionalism, of guile" in portrait.

THE FRANKLIN

331-360

He had white beard, loved pleasure. He served the best food and drink in his district, and took great pride in his hospitality, keeping a table always set. He had served as judge, sheriff, member of Parliament.

32	*dayesye* daisy (eye of day)	52	*geere* utensils
33	*complexioun* temperament	53	*dormant* fixed in place
35	*wone* custom	57	*anlaas* short knife. *gipser*
41	*after oon* same quality		purse
42	*envyned* stocked with wine	59	*contour* auditor
49	*muwe* coop	60	*vavasour* landowner
50	*stuwe* fishpond		

31-60 Man 157-68: Franklin probably modeled on Sir John Bussy, near neighbor of Thos. Pynchbek (Lawyer) and often associated with him in Lincolnshire business. Wood-Legh thinks Stephen de Hales, who also knew Pynchbek, fits better than Bussy; but since such country gentlemen were always on public business, list of Franklin's jobs is inconclusive. Leg 149: portrait attests to "growing prosperity of commoners." Ger 33-54: Franklins were already untitled members of gentry, often served as Knights of Shire, judges, etc.; Ch's Franklin is "true gentleman," among most appealing of pilgrims. Blenner-Hassett: portrait suggests Ch himself had legal training and drew on own experience as Knight of Shire (1385-6) and justice of the peace. Lum 183-4: Franklin's Epicureanism conflicts with high offices; perhaps lavish hospitality is partly play acting, imitation of nobility. Don 890: portrait combines "deep-rooted materialism" (appetite) with more liberal values of aristocracy (public offices).

31-52 Bryant: Franklin's diet a healthful one (in medieval theory) for sanguine temperament and advanced age—all *drying* foods and drink (*sop in wyn*).

34 Birney, *N&Q:* *sop in wyn* was not luxurious breakfast (as Bow suggests), but common remedy for morning-after indigestion.

37-8 Sp 113: contrast between *pleyn delit* (gluttony) and *felicitee parfit* points up Franklin's confusion of values.

55-60 Don 891: no suggestion of self-interest; Franklin one of "few pilgrims who are capable of disinterested conduct."

THE FIVE GUILDSMEN

361-378

A haberdasher, carpenter, weaver, dyer, and tapestry-maker traveled in group, were prosperous guildsmen.

65 *apiked* adorned
66 *chaped* mounted
70 *yeldehalle* guildhall. *deys* dais
72 *shaply* fit

73 *catel* property
77 *vigilies* vigils (services on eve of festival). *al bifore* before all others

61-78 Kuhl: in choice of guilds, Ch avoided any victualling and non-victualling guilds involved in bitter political struggle in 1386; of 30 others he chose 5 of most prominent which had had no members in Aldermancy. Camden, *PQ:* probably a later addition to Prol (Cook was originally meant to accompany rich Lawyer and Franklin), added after 1391 when political fight had died down. Sedg 250: Guildsmen are "shy, conscious of lack of breeding but proud withal." Fullerton: Guildsmen must have been of 5 different trade guilds, but were members of same *parish* guild (socio-religious fraternity) and wore that livery. Mal 148-9: stress on wealth, dignity, social pretensions ("which our court poet evidently regards as amusing"). Herndon: Ch declined to develop this group further perhaps because they were under suspicion of subversive activities (complicity in Peasants' Revolt), were subjects of parliamentary investigation in 1388-9. Pres 167: Guildsmen "exhibit their own careful bourgeois pride." McCutchan: *greet fraternitee* was probably powerful and affluent Drapers' Guild (or Brotherhood of St. Mary of Bethlehem), which fits description best; some mild satire on pretentiousness. Garbáty: Ch's Guildsmen most likely belonged to powerful parish guild of St. Fabian and St. Sebastian of St. Botolph's Church, Aldersgate, which included many cloth workers (4 of Ch's 5 men are in cloth work).

66-7 Don 891: silver mounting shows prosperity, but legally was reserved to aristocracy.

71-4 Lisca: "mordant irony" in suggestion that wealth constitutes wisdom needed by aldermen.

73-8 Sp 114: these wives are "just as sinfully proud" as Wife of Bath.

THE COOK

379-387

With guildsmen was cook who was very skillful at his trade but had ulcer on shin.

79	*for the nones* for the occasion	84	*mortreux* thick soups
81	*pouder-marchant* flavoring powder. *galyngale* a spice	86	*mormal* ulcer
		87	*blankmanger* meat in white cream sauce

79-87 Bow 186: Cook enhances prestige of Guildsmen who have employed him as specialist for their comfort; his vices "do not interfere with his skill" in making exotic dishes. Don 891-2: portrait is "concoction of culinary superlatives," suggests nothing of Cook's character except fondness for ale.

82 Sk 5, 37: London ale was very famous, higher priced than other ales.

85-6 Hin 3: *mormal* adds nothing to artistry of portrait. Cur 48: *mormal* is dry ulcer from skin disease *malum mortuum,* caused by faulty diet, uncleanliness, intercourse with unclean women; thus Cook's disease becomes clear index of character (compare Summoner). Braddy: *mormal* not dry, but probably wet or running ulcer, giving point to following line on *blankmanger*. Lisca: *mormal* suggests dissolute living; Cook's defects may explain how Guildsmen can afford him (cooks usually very expensive), and may be part of satire on their pretentiousness. Don 892: narrator seems unaware of shocking effect; "he is sorry about the Cook's ulcer, not disgusted by it."

86-7 Bald 51-2: this "glaring couplet" is startlingly effective use of "contrapuntal detail," or Ch's technique of achieving "collusion of impression from collision of detail."

THE SHIPMAN

388-410

He was from Dartmouth, had often stolen from wine cargoes. Ruthless in sea fights, he was also a skillful navigator of his ship, the *Maudelayne*.

88	*wonyng* living	97	*chapman* merchant
90	*rouncy* strong horse. *as he*	98	*nyce* tender. *keep* heed
	kouthe as well as he could	00	*by water* by drowning
91	*faldyng* coarse wool cloth	03	*lodemenage* pilotage
95	*good felawe* merry companion (as in 648)		

88-10 Man 169-81: Shipman's barge *Maudelayne* of Dartmouth was owned by notorious privateer John Hawley whose men were noted for kind of behavior Ch's Shipman was guilty of; barge's master at time of writing was either Geo. Cowntree or Peter Risshenden, probably latter. Low 163: fine example of Ch's "delicate balance" between type and individual character; line 406 alone "sets him, like the Flying Dutchman and the Ancient Mariner, among the immortals who in their spheres are every one and no one." Galway argues strongly that Shipman was based not on Risshenden but on Basque sailor John Piers of Teignmouth, an unscrupulous rascal. Ches 255-6: Shipman is pirate, but "Ch is not to be shaken out of his geniality by trifles like that." Mal 206: Shipman one of few pilgrims who bear arms. Lum 71-2: Shipman's presence hardest to account for among pilgrims; he is not devout, would be unlikely to choose pilgrimage for vacation. Don 892: portrait of occupation rather than of man.

89 ManCT 523: Dartmouth noted for piracy at the time. Bow 193:

fact that Shipman is from Dartmouth marks him as recognizable and notorious type.

96-7 Bow 193-4: in this petty thievery, Shipman is "particularly fond of Bordeaux wine." Stobie: wine merchants usually supplied master and crew of ship with "courtesy wine" for their drinking; probably it was this that Shipman stole in large quantities, requiring merchants to supply more for crew.

98-00 Ches 256: Ch is casual about murder here because writing on lower comic level; in tales on high moral plane (*PrT*) he takes it seriously.

10 Bow 194-5: *barge* meant trading vessel of under 200 tons with broad beam, unwieldy.

THE DOCTOR OF PHYSIC

411-444

He was expert in medicine, surgery, astrology, knew all medical texts. He was very richly dressed and mercenary.

16	*houres* favorable hours for treatment	39	*sangwyn* red cloth. *pers* Persian blue
18	*ymages* astrological emblems to aid patient	40	*sendal* fine silk
		41	*esy of dispence* slow to spend money
24	*boote* remedy		
26	*letuaries* medicaments		

11-44 Tup 45: a stock character without a single personal touch. Cur 27-36: portrait is satire not on medieval medicine but on contemporary doctors; Ch leaves sketch ambiguous, with some intentionally vague suggestions of charlatanism which cast doubts upon doctor's impressive learning, honesty; a complex and "tantalizing figure." Sp 115: Avarice is keynote of "somewhat sinister figure." Pres 170: doctor's impressive qualifications are slightly stained by Ch's acid satire in 425-8, 435-44. Bald 45: portrait is mainly impersonal doctor of folklore, with miserliness as added touch. Lum 195: a "society doctor," impressive but mainly interested in fat fees. Don 892: medieval doctors (and lawyers) were constantly satirized;

this doctor "is unusually well treated, for he is said actually to be able to heal the sick."

14-6 Low 18-9: knowledge of astronomically favorable *houres* for treatment was as indispensable then as surgeon's knowledge of anatomy today. Aiken, *SP,* 56: *houres* refers to *hora,* technical term for each stage in development of a disease (does not mean astronomical hours).

38 Tupper, *Nation:* doctor's study was but little on the Bible because he was expert in Arabic medical lore, the study of which was popularly supposed to lead to disbelief in Christian faith.

39-40 Mal 203: usual dress for rich doctors.

41-4 Don 893: "he hoards his money as he hoards his skill," with medicinal gold as symbol of his practice.

43-4 Bald 50: good example of Ch's unexpected thrusts, giving "quick glimpse at the interior man."

THE WIFE OF BATH

445-476

She was slightly deaf, good at weaving, gaudily dressed, and aggressive. She had had 5 husbands, had gone on many pilgrimages. She was very sociable, knew much about love.

46	*scathe* a pity		68	*gat-tothed* with teeth set
47	*haunt* skill			wide apart
53	*ground* texture		70	*ywympled* covered with
61	*withouten* besides			wimple
62	*as nowthe* at present		71	*targe* shield
			74	*carpe* talk

45-76 Cur 91-118: portrait reflects conflicting astral influences of Venus and Mars [see note on *WBT* 603-20]. Man 225-34: probably based on actual woman of St. Michael's parish, suburb of Bath, noted for weaving. Ches 197: W is "an amusing monster to be stared at." Pres 171: W gives first impression of Pride (in weaving, in precedence at offering, in clothes); like Falstaff, she can be admired, but is more "'useful as a scarecrow'" [quoting Blake]. Hoffman: W on pilgrimage is "impelled so powerfully and frankly by St. Venus rather than drawn by St. Thomas, and goaded by a Martian desire to acquire and dominate another husband." Don 893-4: 2 chief traits in portrait are independence and sexuality.

47-8 Lum 119-20: no irony intended—W is fiercely competitive. Don 893: for Ch's audience weaving shows W as independent middle class type, also links her with Eve (the first weaver) whom she resembles in all ways.

49-52 Sp 115: W typifies Pride "in her own unique way."

52 Baum: pun on *charitee* (the Christian virtue, but also generosity or alms in this context).

53-7, 70-3 Don 894: W's clothes are elegant ("she is intensely feminine") and extreme ("she is flamboyantly unconventional").

53-5 Tup 119: hat is "outward and visible sign of feminine pride of heart." Wretlind disagrees with Man 230-1 that W's hat was out of style; heavy hats were introduced by Queen Anne in 1382.

60 Ches 72-3 notes much remarrying in Ch's own family, "a household somewhat haunted by widows."

61 Sk 5, 44-5: line from sketch of La Vieille in *RR;* also line 476. Tatlock, *Flügel:* pun on *withouten* (not having any, and not to mention)—deliberate ambiguity.

63-7 Ger 78: W's love of adventure fits in with her marital experiments. Don 894: W's many pilgrimages "emphasize her sexual aberrancy."

67 Sp 116: phrase includes subtle allusion to "errant soul."

68 Barnouw: in primitive peoples 1 or 2 front teeth were often removed from girls at puberty to allow passage for magic fluid supposed to be real cause of procreation; thus, a woman gap-toothed by nature was "believed to be predestined for the office of love." Don 894: a sign of "both lust and *wanderlust.*"

72 Mal 203: *foot-mantel* to shield clothes from mud.

75 Bow 220: allusion to Ovid's *Remedia Amoris.*

THE PARSON

477-528

A poor priest of small village, he was learned, diligent, patient; he helped and visited his people, set a noble example. Unlike many, he did not neglect humble duties, but tried to live by Christ's example.

78 *persoun of a toun* village priest

82 *parisshens* parishioners

86 *cursen* excommunicate

94 *muche and lite* great and small

04 *shiten* befouled

10 *chaunterie* endowment to sing masses for dead

11 *bretherhed* guild. *withholde* retained (as chaplain)

23 *snybben* rebuke

26 *spiced* too fastidious

77-541 Sp 103: these 2 share "inner beauty of life" like Kn's. Brew 136: 2 most idealized, least vivid of all pilgrims—"theories rather than persons," but with great poetic beauty.

77-28 Root 284-5: "one of the loveliest bits of Ch's poetry." Cow 152: an artistic triumph in making a wholly good man appealing. Leg 151, 169: only Christ-like pilgrim (contrasting sharply with church "degenerates and parasites"), portrayed touchingly but without sentimentality. Ives: Parson is Wyclif himself—learned, from farming family, insistent on importance of gospel; everything here and in tale fits Wyclif's theological views. Loomis: stress on gospels links Parson with Lollard movement; Ch himself perhaps a Lollard. Mal 184-5: notable length of sketch (62 lines) and stress on Parson's learning and poverty—"Ch seems to have taken poverty for an outward sign of holiness." Bald 46: portrait is a "rebuke to the ecclesiastical worldling." Don 894: like Kn, ideal Parson contrasts with baser pilgrims who follow.

86 Tatlock, *MP:* "Ch clearly felt the sordidness of using so solemn a spiritual weapon for such mundane reasons."

95 Don 895: staff symbolizes both support and chastisement.

26 Rockwell: *spiced conscience,* meaning peppery, easily aroused indignation, contrasts with *sweete spiced conscience* (*WBT* 435), meaning bland, gentle disposition.

THE PLOWMAN

529-541
With Parson was his brother the Plowman, an honest worker who loved God and was charitable.

30 *fother* load
34 *thogh him gamed or smerte*
whether it gave him pleasure
or pain

38 *hire* wages
41 *tabard* worker's smock

29-41 Leg 166: Plowman represents "perfect charity in the poor." Pat 156: Ch seems to view Plowman from distance, with "startling touch of something like nineteenth-century romanticism." Horrell: sympathetic portrait in which "Ch crowned this lowliest of the pilgrims with the highest Christian virtues." Loomis: ideal picture, amazing only 6 years after Peasants' Revolt, perhaps shows Ch's sympathy for peasantry. Bow 238-42; portrait lacks vitality and warmth of Parson's. Cog 117: nearest lay pilgrim to Kn in "generous Christianity." Mal 166: portrait typifies Ch's use of superlatives in Prol. Bald 46: Plowman is "almost unbelievable perfection of a disappearing convention" of Christian peasant.

32 Sp 103: Plowman shares this trait with Kn; "they are blood-brothers in Christ."

THE MILLER

542-566

He was brawny, good at wrestling and butting with his head. He had red beard, wart on nose, large mouth, liked to tell coarse tales. He led pilgrimage, playing bagpipe.

49 *thikke knarre* thickly
knotted, or muscular fellow
50 *heve of harre* heave off
hinges
54 *cop right* right on top
57 *nosethirles* nostrils

60 *goliardeys* coarse joker
61 *harlotries* rascalities
62 *tollen thries* take 3 times
legal toll
65 *sowne* play

42-66 Cur 79-90: all Miller's features are physiognomical signs which build up unified picture of character—stocky build, round face, red beard, large mouth, flat nose, wide nostrils, wart on nose show he is shameless, irrascible, deceitful, garrulous, lustful, gross, gluttonous, lying, loudmouthed, etc. Leg 170: "one of the most vigorous sketches of an unmitigated brute ever drawn by poet or painter." Cog 116: grandest, most independent of churls. Sp 117: dishonesty and ribaldry are "both grounded in his total coarseness of texture." Mal 199-201: rich, realistic detail stresses "grossness and dynamic force" of character. Jones: portrait shows not individual (as Man and Bow think), but popular view of miller type—socially aggressive, presumptuous in carrying arms, drunken, dishonest, etc.

42-4 Baum 66: Ch probably added last 5 rascals to introduce lively quarrels.

54-6 Shel 197: "incomparably forceful" simile, even though we don't really know what the bristles of sows' ears are like. Don 875: wart helps sum up Miller—"ugly and crude, yet vital and unabashed."

57 Jones: wide, black nostrils (also flat noses, etc.) had long been traditional traits of serfs from whom millers were recruited.

58 Mal 205: Miller's weapons symbolize his aggressiveness. Jones: carrying weapons was illegal for lower classes—satire on Miller's presumptuousness.

59-61 Don 896: gross body matched by gross speech "that belches from his huge furnace of a mouth."

64 Mal 201: white coat is mark of Miller's trade. Jones: *blew hood* was theoretically illegal for lower classes, shows Miller's typical arrogance in overstepping social barriers in clothing.

65-6 Block: bagpipes in medieval literature commonly symbolized gluttony and lust (belly and male organs).

THE MANCIPLE

567-586

He was expert in buying food, getting bargains. Though employed by a college of learned lawyers, he managed to cheat them all.

68	*achatours* buyers	77	*curious* skillful
70	*by taille* on credit	81	*propre good* own income
71	*wayted* was cautious. *achaat* buying	86	*sette hir aller cappe* made fools of them all
74	*pace* surpass		

67-86 Bald 46: Manciple is "negative figure—the menial in position who is master by craft." Don 874: Manciple is "epitomized as an exclamation mark punctuating his talent for cheating his masters."

THE REEVE

587-622

He was slender, choleric, close shaven, and skilled at managing grain and livestock for his lord while slyly feathering his own nest. He came from Norfolk, had been carpenter, rode last of pilgrims.

93	*gerner* granary	04	*covyne* deceit
97	*neet* cattle. *dayerye* dairy-cows	13	*myster* trade
		14	*wrighte* workman
98	*stoor* live-stock	15	*stot* stallion
02	*brynge* prove. *arrerage* arrears	16	*pomely* dapple
		21	*tukked* with coat tucked under girdle
03	*hierde* herdsman. *hyne* worker		

87-22 Moffett: portrait and later characterization in *RvT* show Ch's intimate, accurate knowledge of rural life. Man 84-94: Reeve probably modeled on real person; Ch knew Baldeswelle, Norfolk, through his part in legal actions over Pembroke estates there. Powley: Ch probably chose Baldeswelle because his patron Prince Lionel held land there. Mal 198 disagrees with Man—realistic detail does *not* mean Ch must have had actual reeve in mind. Cur 71-9: physiognomical traits here—shaved beard and cropped hair (low caste), choleric type (lean, light, dry, given to wrath, sharp-witted, vengeful, with good memory, unduly amorous), thin legs (lustful)—all imply character traits made explicit in Prol to *RvT*.

87-92 Pat 159: Reeve's thinness "suits his meager spirit."

93-05 Tupper, *JEGP:* Reeve was evidently a bailiff, general manager of whole manor.

06-7 Don 897: Reeve's house, away from huddle of village houses, shows his unusual status.

09-12 Leg 149: Reeve's independent wealth reflects economic flux of the times.

18 Bow 249-55: rusty sword indicates low class. Forehand: rusty sword suggests old age, is carried as symbol of lost youth.

22 Forehand: Reeve rides last because he is old and tires easily.

Don 897: Reeve rides last to avoid enemy Miller (at front) or merely because it is best place to watch other pilgrims.

THE SUMMONER

623-668

He had red, diseased face, loved rich food and wine, spoke Latin when drunk. He employed informers, extorted money by blackmail, was lecherous himself.

25	*saucefleem* pimply	63	*in daunger* in his power.
27	*scalled* scabby. *piled* scraggy		*gise* way
44	*grope* test	64	*girles* young people of either
47	*harlot* rascal		sex
52	*fynch koude he pulle* engage in illicit love	67	*ale-stake* stick holding sign of tavern
53	*owher* anywhere		

23-68 Cur 37-47: Sum suffers from *alopicia,* a kind of leprosy developing out of skin disease *gutta rosacea* (a type of morphea); symptoms are inflamed eyes, loss of hair in eyebrows and beard, small red pimples, infected white pustules, etc.; 2 main causes are lechery (relations with infected woman) and gluttony (especially eating of onions, garlic, leeks, and drinking of strong, heating red wines); whole picture fits medieval medical theory exactly. Aiken, *Sp,* 36: Sum has not *alopicia* but *scabies* (skin disease), as exactly described by Vincent of Beauvais, accounting for *all* his symptoms. Haselmayer: Sum, probably modeled on actual corrupt and revolting individual (harshest portrait in Prol), is perhaps not a fair representative of summoners as a whole. Cog 117: Sum and Pard, both laymen, were hated church parasites. Sp 117-8: "The serene Chaucerian scrutiny certainly never rested on objects more grotesquely repellent" than Sum and Pard, most degraded of pilgrims, arrogant "arch-cheats." Lum 137: least attractive of pilgrims. Don 898: physical repulsiveness symbolizes "his diseased spirit and gross appetites"; narrator's "surprising geniality" reflects common fear of summoners.

24-8 Sp 118: "visible bestiality confronts us in repulsive details."

34 Kaske, *MLN:* Sum's perverse love of very foods that aggravate

his disease provides suggestive parallel to his depraved state of soul.
36-8 Sp 119: Sum's Latin intensifies drunken, unnatural, blasphemous effect.
49-52 Kittredge: "pull a finch" means fornicate, also defraud or gull.
Woolf, *MLN:* probably means Sum gave up own concubine for
year to *felawe* for quart of wine, then secretly continued to visit her
(this would give "pull a finch" both meanings—fornicate and defraud); *excuse hym* may be reflexive—Sum maintains own innocence.
Lum 137: for wine Sum will refrain from reporting *felawe.*
53-8 Sp 119: Sum has contempt for both church law and divine
law.
59-62 Lum 137-9: narrator's comment implies total corruption of
church law system. Rob 667: doubt as to efficacy of absolution is "a
hint which perhaps comes as close to downright heresy as anything
in Ch."
62 Tatlock, *MP: Significavit* was writ to imprison one who had been
excommunicated for 40 days until he was absolved; suggests Ch had
doubts as to eternal consequences of excommunication—but look out
for temporal results anyway.
63-5 Bloomfield, *PQ:* here *girles* means girls in female sense, loose
women or prostitutes (see *MillT* 3769).
66-8 Sp 119: "a revelling buffoon . . . wantonly fantastical." Lum
137: Sum's drinking symbolized by garland, gluttony by loaf.

THE PARDONER

669-714

Fresh from Rome, he rode with friend Summoner, had thin hair,
glaring eyes, squeaky voice, was probably eunuch. He carried false
relics, cheated folk with flattery and tricks, was clever preacher.

73	*stif burdoun* strong bass		87	*bretful* brimful
77	*ounces* thin clusters		94	*pilwe-beer* pillow-case
79	*colpons* shreds		99	*latoun* brass
82	*jet* fashion		02	*upon lond* in the country
83	*dischevelee* with hair loose		12	*affile* polish
85	*verncyle* copy of St. Veron- ica's handerkerchief			

69-14 Kit 180: "the one lost soul" among pilgrims. Curry: eunuch Pard seeks to hide handicap—sings lovesong with Sum (672), brags of wenches (*PardT* 453), applauds Wife of Bath (*WBT* 164) whose physical stamina he admires—is almost as pathetic a character as January in *MerchT*. Cur 54-70: Pard was born eunuch, as Ch shows by signs of physiognomy that would be clear to his audience—glaring eyes (shameless libertine, drunkard), long yellow hair (effeminate, cunning), goat-like voice (impotent). Man 122-30: Pard probably based on real person, a legitimate pardoner of St. Mary Rouncival hospital at Charing Cross which was much in the news in 1380's and of which Ch's friend John of Gaunt was a patron. Kellogg and Haselmayer: Ch's satire is not so much on Pard as on system which made him possible; he probably used Rouncival (notoriously corrupt) to give specific connotation to satire on "a generic corruption." Mal 177: Ch perhaps put Pard last to symbolize his opinion of this most contemptible of clerics on pilgrimage. Brew 137: Pard is "mercilessly exposed for a lying, fraudulent, grasping, conceited eunuch." Don 900: physical handicap symbolizes Pard's moral depravity.

70 Hamilton: Ch probably linked Pard with Rouncival hospital because it was very unpopular for money scandals and for connection with main house in Navarre (Spain).

72-3 Cur 68: sheer bravado by eunuch Pard. Pat 164: Pard's joining horrible Sum in lovesong is "most violent satire in all of Ch's poetry." Hoffman: song is both "perverted invitation and an unconscious symbolic acknowledgement of the absence of and need for love" (of God)—"superb dramatic irony." Lum 205: Pard joins Sum in lewd song to test reactions and tolerance of pilgrims he plans to cheat.

75-9 Hamilton: Pard's long hair was violation of clerical rule of tonsure; he wished to look like fashionable layman. Hendrickson: Pard's hair not long (ManCT) but sparse, as *his lokkes that he hadde* implies.

88 Ger 60: inconsistent with *PardT* 330-1 where Pard is shown as powerful speaker.

91 Ger 59: *mare* suggests homosexual. Bald 51: a brilliant "flash framing of the individual," hinting at Pard's whole nature.

07-10 Hamilton: Pard's officiating at mass suggests he was in major orders, probably an Augustinian canon regular of Rouncival hospital. Sp 120: Pard's pulpit impression is "cunning theatrical illusion."

715-746
Now I have described pilgrims at Tabard and will go on to tell of journey. Please excuse any rudeness; I must report truthfully.

19	*faste* close	26	*arette* impute. *vileynye* bad
21	*baren us* behaved. *ilke* same		manners

15-24 Mal 152-3: lines beautifully balance passage introducing pilgrims (35-42), with same friendly style.
25-42 Mal 157: tongue-in-cheek apology for humorous effect, since reader knows that whole *CT* is fiction, "that every word spoken by every pilgrim was put in his mouth by Ch himself"; Ch poses as historian in playful game with readers. Bald 59-60: apology is clever hoax, a fiction in itself, a humorous wink, relieving artist of "moral onus"; absurd citing of Plato (implying comparison of his philosophical dialogues with Ch's fabliaux) adds spice to irony. Lum 24: mock apology cleverly whets reader's appetite.
43-6 Law 81: Ch "threw a sop to aristocratic feelings." Mal 153-5: another joke; Ch is actually careful about rank, but does not want to cramp his style.

THE HOST

747-858
He serves us well, is portly, talkative, knowing, and good natured. After supper he offers plan to pass time on trip if pilgrims agree to accept his judgment. We agree. Host suggests each pilgrim tell 2 tales going and 2 more on return trip. He will accompany group and choose best tale, winner to get free supper at Tabard. All agree. Next morning, outside town, pilgrims draw lots for first tale, Knight wins.

50 *us leste* it pleased us
60 *maad rekenynges* paid bills
70 *quite* pay. *meede* reward
72 *shapen* plan. *talen* tell tales
75 *disport* entertainment
78 *stonden at* abide by
84 *seche* seek
85 *make it wys* deliberate about it
87 *voirdit* verdict
09 *shape* prepare

14 *reportour* umpire
16 *devys* will
25 *paas* foot-pace
26 *wateryng* place to water horses
27 *areste* stop
29 *foreward* agreement
35 *twynne* depart, go
38 *accord* agreement
39 *neer* nearer

47-58 Kit 161-2: big, merry, loud Host is well suited as leader; his hearty manner is "partly temperament, partly professional technique." Man 77-83: Host almost certainly modeled on real Harry Bailly (see *CkT* 4358), innkeeper of Southwark, who appears in many official records for 1367-93. Leg 175-7: Host is "king of innkeepers," clear-headed, practical, cordial, skilled in handling men; "he has no sooner received his money than he forgets his dependence and assumes the manner of a rich burgher treating his friends" (761-83). Cog 120: character of Host, like that of Pandarus in *Troilus,* is "miracle of clarity and fullness." Mal 187-96: Host is not actual innkeeper of Southwark (Man) but a fictional type, "one of the great comic characters of English literature," incredibly impudent (bullying gentleman as no real innkeeper would, asking pilgrims to sign blank check), but ideal instrument for Ch's artistic purposes in *CT*. Bald 72, 62: Host is "cohesive inner voice" of pilgrimage, Ch's comic alter ego, directing whole action; Ch delights in Host's mercenary self-interest in agreement with pilgrims (note *money* and *mirth* motifs of passage).

47 Bald 61: Ch skillfully introduces Host apart from original pilgrims (he claims no religious motive).

51-7 Mal 159: Ch, anxious to get on with tales, gives Host ("his most important character") only 7 lines of direct description.

59-60 Bald 62: here money and mirth motifs are "strikingly juxtaposed" (also in 767-8).

61-83 Mal 159: Host's speech begins solicitously, ends domineeringly. Lum 25: drama of *CT* begins here with first speech.

63-5 Bald 62: Host's hearty welcome is "appallingly, and skillfully, typical."

66-8 Bald 63: idea comes to Host with "rote spontaneity of a sideshow barker," with *it shal coste noght* as "unrefusable come-on."

77-83 Mal 194: "What are they to vote for?" (Host asks for blank check).

84-7 Bow 294: pilgrims agree because Host "has the kind of presence that demands acceptance." Mal 194: pilgrims' acceptance is comic, not realistic. Bald 62: Host, once again, "has put over a deal."

89 Bald 62: Host seems to apologize, but from here on he dominates pilgrims.

05-6 Mal 195: huge fine typifies comic exaggeration in Host's behavior.

10-8 Bald 63: pilgrims give Host absolute authority, including right to set menu and price of supper. Lum 26: pilgrims' warm reaction to Host's second speech contrasts with coolness after first—they are relieved Host's idea involves no expense.

40-1 Mal 207-9: Host has been polite to Kn and Pr, but here is mildly baiting Clerk; thus Ch shows both Host's impudence and Clerk's quiet seriousness.

54 Tup 50: innkeepers were notable blasphemers.

56-8 Lum 27: Ch makes clear that tale to follow is to be viewed as recital by Kn.

The Knight's Tale

COMMENTARIES: Gr 184-92; Ham 270-4;/ Don 901-5; ManCT 539-58; Rob 669-83; Sk 5, 60-95;/ Baum 84-104; Brew 88-94; Bron 17-8, 22-4; Ches 156; Cog 128-31; Cow 153-5; Cummings, *Indebtedness of Ch's Works to Italian Works of Boccaccio* (Cincinnati, 1916); Cur 119-63; Dem 89-91; Dodd 234-46; Ev 140-2, 164-9; Fr 210-5; Ger 88-9; Hin 50-120; Kit 19; Leg 119-21; Lum 29-49; Mal 231; Mather ed. *The Prologue, KnT, and NPT* (Boston, 1899); Mus 175-90 (W); Pat 85, 109-10, 178-9, 200-10; Pres 183-90; Root 163-73; Shel 228-41; Sp 121-6; Tat 95-6; TatDC 45, 66-7, 231-2; Tho 126-8;/ Aiken, *PMLA*, 36, 361-9; Baker, *MLN*, 30, 460-2; Baum, *MLN*, 31, 302-4, and *PMLA*, 56, 225-46; Brown, *MLN*, 08, 53-4; Curry, *Anglia*, 23, 213-43, and *JEGP*, 30, 83-99; Dustoor, *MLR*, 27, 438-41; Emerson, *MP*, 19, 287-91, and *PQ*, 23, 81-96; Fairchild, *JEGP*, 27, 285-93; French, *JEGP*, 49, 320-8; Frost, *RES*, 49, 289-304 (ST); Gibbs, *MLN*, 09, 197-8; Ham, *ELH*, 50, 252-61; Herben, *MLN*, 38, 595; Hibbard, *PQ*, 22, 222-5; Hulbert, *SP*, 29, 375-85; Kovetz, *N&Q*, 58, 236-7; Lloyd, *EM*, 59, 11-25; Lowes, *MP*, 14, 491-546; Marckwardt, *UMCMP*, 47, No. 5; Moore, *CL*, 51, 32-46; Muscatine, *PMLA*, 50, 911-29 (W); Owen, *ES*, 54, 49-56; Parr, *PMLA*, 45, 307-24; Pratt, *SA*, 82-105, and *PMLA*, 47, 598-621, and 48, 726-36, and *JEGP*, 58, 416-23; Robertson, *JEGP*, 15, 226-55, and *MLN*, 28, 234-6; Ruggiers, *CE*, 58, 296-302; Underwood, *ELH*, 59, 455-69(O); Webb, *RES*, 47, 289-96; Wilson, *UTQ*, 49, 131-46.

GENRE: Romance.

SOURCE: Giovanni Boccaccio's epic poem *Il Teseida*, or story of Theseus (1339-40), which Ch reduced to about ⅕ of length of Italian poem; with minor influence from the *Thebaid* of Statius (Boccaccio's source), and perhaps also from *Le Roman de Thèbes;* for philosophical passages, important influence of Boethius' *Consolation of Philosophy.*

DATE: First version, referred to in *LGW* as *Palamon and Arcite*, probably dates 1382-5 (before *Troilus*); this version was later adapted slightly to fit *CT*, probably in late 1380's.

GENERAL CRITICISM: TatDC 66-7: brilliant romance of picturesque incident, weak emotional interest, subtle satire; no signs of revision beyond addition of 875-92, 3108, to earlier version. Hin 52-3: "poem of burning youth," almost Ch's finest, highly original, superior to Boccaccio, tempered by satire and philosophy; "madcap" Pal wins lady, but more rational Arc wins our sympathy. Kit 19: marvelous condensation of Boccaccio. Dodd 234-46: Ch's purpose to show conflict between love and friendship; hence he abridged Boccaccio, built up Pal to equal Arc, made Emily characterless to throw spotlight on 2 heroes. Robertson, *JEGP:* tale gives realistic picture of chivalric world of England and Europe (not of Greece) in 14th century, as shown by parallel incidents in Froissart's *Chronicles;* least realistic parts taken from Boccaccio; Ch's changes all in direction of realism. Root 169-72: tale conceived in spirit of romance, "a web of splendidly pictured tapestry"; its greatness lies not in characterization but in description; Pal is dreamer who drifts with circumstances, Arc is man of action; Theseus, "most actual personage," is motive power of plot; Ch wisely kept Emily a mere vision which we see only in effect upon others. Cur 119-63: astrological conflict between Saturn and Mars under surface, used by Ch to aid primary interest in action and conflicting passions of characters. Fairchild: Pal and Arc stand for opposed ideals of Contemplative and Active Life in God's service; such allegory essentially medieval, though Ch may not have had it specifically in mind. Cow 153-5: theme is honor among friends, shown in Arc's noble renunciation; characterization indefinite, Pal and Arc "as alike as Rosencranz and Guildenstern"; style pictorial, not analytic as in *Troilus,* succeeds by magnificent description; "genial cynicism" of Theseus probably Ch's own. Leg 119-21: Ch's huge debt to Boccaccio; value of tale not in psychology but in great scenes which all come straight from *Teseida.* Hulbert: tale intended as problem in courtly love—which of 2 almost equal knights should win lady; this explains Ch's changes in Boccaccio, reducing characters to conventional types, stripping away epic machinery, etc. Baker: Pal's love (*affectioun of hoolynesse*) more deserving than Arc's selfish passion. Baum, *MLN,* disagrees with Baker, no clear distinction between Pal and Arc; Ch weakens Boccaccio's characterization, but compensates with stress on necessitarian element, shows characters as types in "highly picturesque and amusing game" filled with touches of Ch's humor. Dem 89-91 agrees with Hulbert's view; Ch purposely plays down characterization, avoids chances for irony that would distract from theme. Pat 109-10 refutes idea Ch was determinist—Boethian Destiny is instrument of God's providence, does not affect man's free will; Ch departs from Boccaccio to show poetic justice (Arc defied oath of brotherhood); 178-9 —humor all through tale, but satire not destructive, is like "amused tolerance" of Theseus; 205-10—Ch enriches characterization at expense of chivalric fights, makes heroes seem alive (Arc more manly, Pal more intent on love, less scrupulous) and sympathetic, was attracted by chances for dramatic and humorous reflections in tale. Shel 228-41: finest verse romance in English, has realism (cp. Froissart) without losing romantic atmosphere; characters subordinated to action; Theseus most vivid, typical feudal lord at his best, nearly steals show; Pal and Arc rather blurred, much alike, though Pal's love seems deeper; Emily negative, but still seems "winsome and desirable." Parr: tale substantally revised after mid 1390, with 2461-2 referring to astronomical configuration and troubled times of 1388-9, 884 and 2568 suggested by "tempest" of revelry at Queen Isabella's entry into Paris in 1389, and by great tournament in London in May, 1390; all these passages mainly original with Ch. Pratt, *PMLA,* 48 refutes Parr mainly on grounds that most of passages *do* have counterparts in Boccaccio. Marckwardt rejects Fairchild's view of contemplative Pal, active Arc; actually Pal is more positively active; Arc more profound thinker, a realist, not extravagant idealist. Webb: Theseus kindly but also cruel at times (destroying Thebes *after* Creon's death, pillaging, refusing ransom, harsh treatment of noble prisoners, etc.); even kindly acts seem selfish (desire to curry popular favor, increase honor); repeated epithet *noble* may be ironical. Pratt, *PMLA,* 47: by careful selection Ch reduced Boccaccio's plot to central theme of lovers' rivalry; since outcome depends on destiny, he subordinated characterization—Emily merely "beautiful prize," Pal (devoted to love) slightly more attractive than Arc; though Ch medievalized tale, he never destroyed illusion of remoteness.

Ches 156: "a tapestry of heroes clad in gold," with sustained nobility. French: Ch's audience would understand clearly that chivalric lover was expected to serve lady in 2 ways, as lover and as winner of military glory; Pal stresses first kind of service, Arc second—this is *only* real distinction between them. Wilson: Ch makes knights equal, since tale is exemplum of power of love overruling all fellowship, shows vanity of human aims, with central theme of Divine Love working through imperfect human love to a higher end. Frost: 3 themes in tale—rivalry for Emily, conflict between love and friendship, establishment of divine order out of "disintegrating human situation"; Pal more idealistic, Arc more practical, with Pal winning because more worthy; Theseus central character, "executant of destiny"; tragic view of universe, with man as victim of cruel and ironic mischance; important function of tale to show mind and heart of teller, whose idealism is burlesqued in *MillT*. Muscatine: tale is "poetic pageant" of nature of the noble life, stressing through its symmetry the principle of order in life (central figure of Theseus) and in universe, conflicting with forces of chaos (erratic fates of Pal and Arc who struggle nobly); long, stately descriptions and speeches express order principle, with touches of irony showing conflict between noble designs and forces of disorder. Tat 95-6: many touches of "delicate ridicule" typical of Ch's unique literary personality; tale well proportioned, satisfying, with Theseus as true hero—virile, humane, adult, contrasting with 2 boys; Pal and Arc individualized, with Pal less masculine. Mal 231: tale fits teller as knight but not as individual; from *Gen Prol* we expect tale of his campaigns, not of love. Sp 121-6: though tale remains romance, it is full of vivid realistic passages, conversational tones, comic touches, sharp images even in allegorical personifications. Pres 183-90: tale taken too solemnly; seen in relation to *MillT* and *RvT*, it is "bold combination of mockery and pathos," truth and nonsense. Brew 88-94: tale about love rather than lovers (not much individualized), with great merit in description; has humor (mostly in Theseus), some jarring flippancy. Owen: outcome gives victory to thoughtful Arc, reward to impetuous Pal—irony. Lum 29-49: philosophical theme from Boethius dominates tale, with Boethian terms (Providence, Destiny, Fortune, Nature, *cas, aventure*) used to explain almost all important events. Ev 166 disagrees with Frost; rivalry in love rather than love-friendship theme is emotional focus; very doubtful that tale shows mind of Knight, since it was written before *CT* were conceived. Pratt, *JEGP:* in addition to unity of action and philosophic theme (Boethian Providence), tale has 3rd unifying idea of joy after woe; after sufferings Arc finds *welfare* (3063), honor, end of pain, Pal finds *wele* (3101) in marriage. Don 901-5: like Boethius, tale strongly stoic with Theseus as spokesman for belief in and acceptance of divine plan; Pal and Arc about equal; not much characterization except for Theseus; tale fits Knight in showing restraint, teaching that "excessive emotion is an enslavement of the spirit and a threat to order." Baum 84-104: tale early, imperfect, full of inconsistencies, but with fine passages, symmetry, romantic appeal tempered by Ch's humor (often clashing with other elements); no attempt at realism in characterization; not especially suited to Knight, better for Squire. Kovetz: mythological figures mere masks for Christian concepts, instruments of Divine Providence. Lloyd refutes Frost's view of Pal as worthier; Arc represents Ch's idealization of love, with Pal only interested in *possession* of Emily.

THE KNIGHT'S TALE, PART I

I, 859-974

Theseus of Athens returns from victory over Amazons, accompanied by their queen, Hippolyta, now his wife, and her sister Emily. I do not have time to describe their array and feast at homecoming. On way into city, Theseus is met by weeping widows of Thebes. They beg him for vengeance against Creon who, having killed their husbands in battle, refuses to let them be buried. Theseus leads army to Thebes.

59	*whilom* once	87	*wayke* weak
60	*highte* was called	89	*letten* hinder
66	*regne* kingdom	02	*waymentynge* lamentation
79	*for the nones* for this pur-	09	*mysboden* insulted
	pose (conquest of *Femenye*)	13	*cheere* look
81	*asseged* besieged	24	*caytyves* wretched ones
86	*ere* plow	33	*starf* died

43	*yslawe* slain	65	*abood* delay
49	*gruf* face downward	72	*sheene* bright
55	*maat* dejected	74	*rit* rides
61	*wreke* avenge		

85-92 Lum 31: such comments make dramatic situation clear; Knight talks directly to pilgrims.

24-6 Lum 35: reference to Boethian *Fortune.*

34 Baum, *PMLA,* notes pun on *array* (condition, situation and mourning garments).

975-1032

Theseus defeats and kills Creon, takes Thebes. On battlefield two Theban knights, Palamon and Arcite, are found still alive. They are cousins, of royal blood. Theseus condemns them to life imprisonment in tower at Athens.

78	*penoun* pennon	10	*thurgh-girt* pierced through
93	*gyse* fashion		
04	*hym leste* it pleased him	11	*by and by* side by side
05	*taas* heap	12	*oon armes* same coat of arms
06	*wede* clothing		
07	*pilours* pillagers	32	*quite* ransom

77 Hin 57-8: *feeldes* means plains, not armorial fields; glittering of army marching is almost commonplace in medieval literature. Gibbs agrees, citing parallels in Chrétien de Troie.

79 Emerson, *PQ:* *ybete* means embroidered with gold thread.

13-4 Hin 59-60: names Arc and Pal probably taken by Boccaccio from Greek philosophers Archytas of Tarentum and Polemon of Athens. ManCT 543 thinks this derivation improbable.

1033-1186

One May morning Emily, Theseus' sister-in-law, walks in garden beneath prison tower. Palamon sees her, is instantly smitten with love, and tells Arcite. Arcite then looks for himself and falls likewise in love. The two knights argue long and fruitlessly over who shall have first claim.

38	*stroof* vied	24	*dispitously* angrily
40	*wone* custom	27	*me list ful yvele pleye* I
41	*dight* dressed		have little desire to jest
48	*devyse* describe	55	*paramour* in the way of
60	*joynant* adjoining		passionate love
74	*aventure or cas* luck or	62	*pose* suppose
	chance	65	*pan* brain-pan
78	*bleynte* started back	69	*maugree his heed* in spite
89	*it sworn* sworn to contrary		of himself
20	*but* unless		

35-55 Sp 122: freshness and naturalness of Emily, not a personification but a young English girl.

74 Lum 36: use of Boethian terms *aventure* or *cas*.

78 Sp 122-3: exclamation "dramatically (and humorously) natural and right."

92-86 Root 170: debate shows Pal dreamer, Arc man of action; Pal drifts with circumstances, Arc determines both their fates. Cog 129: "deliciously absurd debate" original with Ch.

01-2 Fairchild: Pal takes attitude of contemplative visionary; Arc (1118-22) speaks language of courtly love; Arc (Active Life) relies on facts, Pal (Contemplative Life) on theory.

29-39 Baker: Arc's deliberate breaking of covenant shows unworthiness, compared to Pal, as knightly lover.

65-8 Lum 42-3: Arc's patient Boethian resignation vanishes in face of new desire for Emily.

81-6 Lum 43: Arc feels controlled by 2 forces—Love and Fortune, will serve Love but realizes imprisonment part of established plan.

1187-1218

One day Perotheus, old friend of Theseus and of Arcite, comes to Athens and persuades Theseus to change Arcite's imprisonment to exile.

92 *felawe* friend
93 *lite* little
01 *write* (error—should be "tell")

09 *forward* agreement
12 *oo stounde* one moment
16 *reed* advice
18 *to wedde* for a pledge

01 Hin 67: good evidence tale not originally written for *CT*.

1219-1354

Arcite, now home in Thebes, bewails his fate, envies Palamon who at least has sight of Emily. Meanwhile, Palamon tears his hair in prison, envies Arcite who is free and may be able to get Emily by war or stratagem. Who has the worse situation?

25 *is me shape* am I destined
36 *dure* stay
38 '*dys* dice
49 *wanhope* despair
52 *purveiaunce* providence
58 *meynee* servants
64 *slider* slippery
71 *heele* health

79 *pure* very
01 *woodly* madly
05 *atthamaunt* adamant
08 *rouketh* huddles
17 *letten* refrain
23 *dyvynys* theologians
40 *mester* occupation

38-43 Lum 36: reference to Boethian *Fortune*.

51-4 Lum 38: Arc takes blame for own misery and, like Boethius, acknowledges God's inscrutable providence.

51-60 Owen: ironically Arc here foreshadows own fate, not Pal's; his prayer will be granted to his own harm.

60-5 Sp 123: comedy in such passages, when "colloquial element, concrete, commonsensical, in Ch's English asserts itself" (see also 1530-3, 1809-10, 2835-6).

03-33 Tho 126-8: Pal's, and perhaps Ch's, despair over "wilful punishment of guiltless men" who suffer more keenly in this world and next than beasts; "Pal could give the riddle of life over to the theologians, but he could not believe in a just providence." Lum 39: Pal cries out against cruelty of gods as Boethius does at beginning of *Consolation*.

28 Owen: ironically Saturn, whom Pal here blames, finally slays Pal's rival, makes possible his marriage.

31 Baum 88: "bit of rum-ram-ruf."

32-3 Lloyd: Pal driven less by desire for Emily than by jealousy of Arc, who shows no jealousy.

PART II

1355-1450

Arcite endures lovesickness a year or two; then, prompted by vision of Mercury, he goes to Athens in disguise as servant ("Philostrate"), is hired as page to Emily, later as squire to Theseus.

56 *swelte* swooned	89 *took keep* noticed
64 *falow* yellow	98 *recche* care. *to sterve* if I
72 *geere* changing mood	die
74 *Hereos* lovesickness. *manye*	13 *nexte* nearest
mania	16 *drugge* drudge
80 *endite* (error—should be	23 *for the nones* at that time
"tell")	48 *derre* dearer
87 *slepy yerde* caduceus	

74 See Lowes on *Hereos*.

85-6 Lum 44: Arc "seems to have conjured up Mercury to instruct him as he wants to be instructed."

28 Hin 70: Boccaccio took name from Philostratus, father of Greek philosopher Polemon, also used it as title of epic *Filostrato* (source of *Troilus*).

1451-1622

One May night Palamon escapes after 7 years in prison, hides in grove outside city. Next day Theseus and Arcite go hunting; Arcite chances to enter grove (where Palamon hides) and bewails his fate aloud. Palamon accosts him; they argue fiercely over Emily, and agree to fight duel next day.

53 *forpyned* in torment	79 *dredeful* fearful
71 *clarree* sweet liquor	84 *werreye* make war
77 *nedes cost* of necessity	95 *greves* thickets

09 *ayeyn* in response to
24 *unset stevene* unappointed time
32 *crope* heights
36 *geery* changeable
66 *erst than* before

70 *sette* value
81 *hent* caught
95 *asterte* escape
09 *darreyne* decide the right to
22 *to borwe as* a pledge

51-87 Fairchild: in escaping Pal combines for moment ideals of Active and Contemplative Life, becomes "working dreamer."

65-6 Lum 36: reference to Boethian *destynee;* also to *Fortune* in 1488-90, and *aventure* in 1516.

72 Emerson, *MP:* opium from Thebes, Egypt, widely used in medieval Europe (along with other narcotics) as remedy for love-melancholy; Pal would thus have it for himself, used it for other purpose in drugging jailer.

91-6 Bron 17-8: miraculously suggestive description, unusually full for Ch, "sheer legerdemain."

10-2 Moore: fragment of roundel probably known in full to Ch's audience, serves to heighten Arc's spirit of gaiety.

66 Hibbard: in folk belief a man's shirt (close to body) came to symbolize his fate.

1623-1747

Next day Arcite brings armor and weapons and he and Palamon attack each other fiercely. The duel is broken up by Theseus who is hunting with his wife and Emily. Palamon reveals their identities and love for Emily. Theseus condemns both to death.

24 *regne* power
26 *his thankes* willingly
30 *dight* prepared
46 *me myshappe* I am unfortunate
48 *as fer as* as soon as
75 *hert* hart (stag)
78 *hunte* huntsman
81 *bane* killer

91 *launde* clearing (mod. Eng. "lawn" is later form)
97 *under the sonne* shielding eyes from sun
99 *breme* furiously
10 *myster* kind of
39 *juwise* sentence
46 *pyne* torture

23 Baum, *PMLA:* pun on *charitee* (sensual love and human kindness).

60-2 Baum 88: example of Ch's unfelicitous sinking from high style.

63-74 Lum 35: "Boethian Destiny causes Theseus to go hunting."

42-1880 Baum 91: whole scene in Ch's best comic manner.

1748-1880

The ladies weep and beg mercy for the knights. Theseus softens and comments on the absurdities of lovers: Palamon and Arcite have been suffering for years over woman whom neither has met. Since only one may wed Emily, Theseus revokes death sentence and orders a tournament. Two knights agree to appear one year later with 100 men apiece to fight for Emily.

60	*aslaked* softened	14	*servant* (of love)	
62	*sterte* started	17	*laas* snare	
80	*kan* knows. *divisioun* distinction	22	*dere* hurt	
81	*after oon* equally	41	*forthy* therefore	
84	*on highte* aloud	45	*plat* flat	
92	*quitly* scot-free	46	*repplicacioun* reply	
96	*maugree* despite	50	*fer ne ner* farther nor nearer (exactly)	
07	*jolitee* sport	77	*namely* especially. *sithe* times	
09	*fare* goings-on			

48-69 Robertson, *JEGP:* Ch makes clear Theseus agrees to mercy because it pleases him, will help his reputation; he sees humor, sees chance for tournament, is more typically medieval character than in Boccaccio.

85-25 Muscatine: Theseus' speech is "mature appraisal, not an adverse criticism, of courtly love"; sees paradox of love as both laughable and admirable.

06-10 Dem 90: reader enjoys speech for irony and because Theseus' smile brings "welcome change of atmosphere." Tat 95: fine humorous touch. Brew 90-1: Ch not ridiculing love, but showing that looked at from outside it often seems absurd.

60-1 Lum 37: use of Boethian term *Fortune.*

PART III

1881-2094

Theseus builds a magnificent amphitheater for the tournament. Over the gate at east end is temple of Venus, decorated with murals showing joys, sorrows, deceits, and fickleness of love. Over west gate is temple of Mars, with pictures of war, murder, strife, etc. In north wall is temple of Diana, with murals showing hunting, chastity, moon, etc.

90	*degrees* tiers. *pas* feet	85	*veze* blast
92	*letted* hindered	86	*rese* shake
98	*ars-metrike* arithmetic	94	*tonne-greet* large as wine
05	*auter* altar		cask
08	*fother* load	00	*shepne* stable
21	*waymentynge* lamentation	03	*contek* strife
26	*Bauderie* jollity, mirth	07	*shode* temple
29	*gooldes* marigolds	12	*Outhees* outcry
49	*champartie* equal authority	13	*careyne* carrion
50	*gye* govern	17	*hoppesteres* dancing
71	*estres* interior	26	*styth* anvil
77	*knarry* gnarled	68	*freeten* devoured
79	*swough* groaning	79	*gaude* bright
81	*bente* slope		

81-92 Herben: Ch reduced number of tiers from Boccaccio's 500 to 60, but even so, given circumference of 1 mile, such a stadium would seat 180,000 people, 4½ times population of London, obviously absurd.

67-50 Hin 83-4: Mars shown more as malign planet than as God of War; hunter, sow and child, barber, butcher, smith—all added by Ch (not in Boccaccio).

71 Hin 81 disagrees with interpretation of *estres* as interior; word has various meanings; here context (especially 1975-2004) suggests meaning of "surroundings" or "exterior."

95-23 Sp 124-5: "Shakespearean vividness and immediacy" in solid, sharp images of universal violence; Ch's intense vision comparable, on smaller scale, to Dante's *Inferno;* similarly powerful effect in 2456-69.

17-30 Curry, *Anglia:* here Ch shifts from Mars the god to power of Mars the planet, stressing astrological influence which later in tale is to replace that of divinities.

2095-2208

When day of tournament approaches, Palamon and Arcite arrive in Athens with their followers. Palamon's 100 supporters are led by King Lycurgus of Thrace, a fierce fighter; Arcite's troop is led by King Emetreus of India. Theseus entertains all of the warriors at a great feast.

00	*at alle rightes* in all respects	51	*mosel* muzzle
03	*of hir hond* of their deeds	52	*tourettes* rings on collar for leash
07	*passant* surpassing		
19	*som* one	58	*dyapred* decorated with small pattern
21	*som* another		
34	*kempe* coarse	67	*citryn* citron-colored
35	*brawnes* muscles	69	*frakenes* freckles
39	*trays* traces	70	*ymeynd* mixed
42	*for old* because of age	72	*caste* reckon
48	*alauntz* hunting dogs	77	*deduyt* pleasure

30-44 Curry, *Anglia:* Lycurgus represents Saturn and is Saturn's man in physique.
69-74 Curry, *Anglia:* Emetreus is representative of Mars and is in body a product of Martian influence.
00-6 Baum 88: passage of obvious burlesque, "astonishing anti-climax" which clashes with style of preceding lines.

2209-2270

On night before battle Palamon prays in temple of Venus that he may win Emily. Statue of Venus shakes—prayer granted.

29	*biwreye* reveal	38	*kepe* care. *yelpe* boast
35	*emforth* to the limit of	52	*go* walk
36	*holden werre* make war	53	*beete* kindle

09-2437 Hin 98 and Curry, *Anglia:* Ch shifted Boccaccio's order of prayers in order to assign astrologically accurate *houres* to Venus, Mars, Diana. Fairchild: "Pal thinks of ends; Arc, of instruments" (medieval ideals of Contemplative and Active Life).

13-5 Baum 88: playful echo of opening lines of *Gen Prol.*

38-44 French: shows Pal clearly prefers boudoir duty of knight to lady to duty of glory in arms.

42-7 Lloyd: shows Pal's unscrupulous desire for possession of Emily, no ideal love-service as in Arc's devotion.

2271-2366

On same night Emily goes to temple of Diana and prays that two knights cease to love her so that she will not have to marry either. Emily sees blood dripping from logs in fire; then she is told by Diana that she must wed one of them.

78	*longen* belong	90	*cerial* evergreen
79	*meeth* mead	08	*venerye* the chase
81	*smokynge* burning incense	33	*queynte* strange
	in. *clothes* hangings	34	*queynte* went out
89	*untressed* loose	58	*caas* quiver

71-66 Fairchild: Emily wishes to be contemplative nun, but is fated to serve God in Active Life; Venus and Diana in Pal's and Emily's prayers are 2 different images of Virgin Mary (to Pal she is Queen of Love, to Emily Virgin); Mars simply represents Arc's craving for practical success.

84-6 Tat 95: Knight's roguishness—he dare not describe Emily's bathing, but it would be fun to do so.

49-52 Kovetz: Diana's words premature, since strife and decision between Mars and Venus has not yet happened; this results from Ch's shifting order of prayers to fit astrological hours.

2367-2437

Next, Arcite goes to temple of Mars, prays for victory in battle. Statue of Mars murmurs "Victory!"

70 *payen wyse* pagan custom
88 *mysfille* had bad luck
89 *las* net
97 *wher* whether. *fleete* float

98 *heete* promise
13 *fynde* provide
28 *haf* heaved

67-37 Root 170: Arc prays for definite, practical means to attain desires.

2438-2482
Argument follows in heaven between Venus and Mars over these promises. Saturn is called in and settles dispute by arranging for prayers of both Palamon and Arcite to be fulfilled.

41 *stierne* stern. *armypotente* powerful in arms
49 *atrenne* outrun. *atrede* outwit
54 *cours* orbit
57 *cote* dungeon

60 *groynynge* murmuring
65 *mynour* sapper
68 *castes* plots
75 *compleccioun* temperament
77 *aiel* grandfather

43-69 Curry, *Anglia:* Ch's Saturn is entirely the planet, not the god.

PART IV

2483-2598
On day of tournament all the knights put on armor. Theseus announces rules for battle, and the whole company proceeds to the arena.

97 *unkouth* strange
98 *browdynge* embroidery
99 *testeres* head armor for war horses. *trappures* trappings
00 *hauberkes* mail plates
01 *parementz* rich clothing
04 *giggynge* fitting arm-straps. *layneres* straps

08 *prikynge* riding
11 *nakers* kettle-drums
20 *sparth* battle-ax
41 *shapen* contrive
44 *shot* arrow, dart
50 *foyne* parry. *were* defend
68 *sarge* serge
94 *renges* ranks

2599-2675

Tournament begins, both sides fighting furiously. Finally, Palamon is overwhelmed by Arcite, Emetreus and others, and taken prisoner. At this point Theseus declares Arcite the winner of Emily. The goddess Venus weeps for Palamon, is consoled by Saturn.

02   *in arrest* in the rests (spears couched)

06, 12   *he . . . he* this man . . . that man. *herte-spoon* depression at base of breastbone

15   *tronchoun* broken spear-shaft

71   *trompours* trumpeters

02-16 Robertson, *MLN:* several lines (02, 3, 5, 11, 12, 16) scan better as OE 4-stress verse with alliteration than as iambic pentameter; perhaps Ch here recalls some OE battle scene such as in *Maldon* or *Brunnanburh* and slides into its rhythm. Ev 140-2: whole passage has authentic "feel" of alliterative verse.

25 Dustoor: "Each had unhorsed the other twice." (Day, *MLR,* 28, 208 rejects "twice"—*tweye* never means this—but otherwise agrees with Dustoor).

64-6 Tat 95: delightfully humorous touch in Venus letting tears fall in very lists.

2676-2816

As Arcite parades in arena his horse shies at a Fury sent by Pluto at request of Saturn. Arcite is thrown and badly hurt, his chest shattered by his saddle-bow. After 3 days other warriors leave. Physicians struggle to save Arcite, but in vain. He calls Emily and Palamon to bedside, says farewell to Emily and recommends Palamon to her. Arcite dies.

89   *pighte* pitched. *pomel* top

97   *blyve* soon

10   *thirled* pierced

29   *arretted* imputed

38   *journee largely* day's march fully

45   *for lechecraft* despite medical skill

47 *veyne-blood* bleeding.   91 *longeth* belongs
    ventusynge cupping   11 *divinistre* divine
53 *lacerte* muscle
54 *shent* defiled

84-91 Brown: accurate astrology; Saturn could act on Tues. only during his 3 hours (6th, 13th, 20th); 6th hour (noon) too early, fight not decided; 13th hour at sunset (see 2637) is just right, Saturn's hour has come, Arc's horse is frightened.

00-60 Aiken: shows Ch's remarkably accurate knowledge of medieval medicine; Arc dies from abcess rising out of putrified blood near heart (result of wound) which spreads infection through lungs and chest; extreme measures (deep cutting and *ventusynge*) by doctors fail to expel venom, breathing becomes difficult, nature fails; whole treatment fits exactly instructions in encyclopedic *Speculum Majus* by Vincent of Beauvais, with even some verbal parallels—probably Ch's direct source.

11-4 Robertson, *JEGP:* realistic details expanded from brief mention in Boccaccio.

40-16 Tat 96: passage is touching but detached; Ch "has not surrendered to his imagination but holds on to reality." Bron 22-4: passage illustrates Ch's perplexing shifts in style, reversals of tone, "apparent sacrifice of achieved effects," which baffle modern readers.

43-56 Curry, *Anglia:* Arc's injury made incurable by Saturn, who governs retentive powers in the body, prevents expulsion of poisons and hot humors from Arc's breast.

43-08 Shel 237: scene one of "most affecting in all Ch," as Arc dies with love and forgiveness on tongue.

43-26 Pat 85: Ch reduced pathos of scene from Boccaccio, "increased the touches of something very close to humor."

58-60 Lum 37: reference to Boethian *Nature*. Ger 88-9: lines intended as pedestrian to counteract pathos which would clash with romantic spirit of tale; Ch aims at non-personal tone, not flippancy (see also 2809-10). Baum 90: these lines and 2809-15 are "extraordinary lapses into facetiousness" in serious context, unhappy examples of "fault into which Ch's cheerfulness may at any moment betray him."

65-97 Fairchild: Arc's final bewilderment shows inadequacy of his ideals; he has been too exclusively devoted to Active Life, just as Pal is too wholly fixed on Contemplative Life.

65-12 Cog 131: Arc, doomed by betrayal of code (in claiming Emily after Pal declared love), here shows real magnanimity in speech which is "among the finest things in Ch," followed by Ch's witty comment lest speech "overbalance our feelings" in favor of Arc.

77-9 Root 172: "terrible reality of the mystery of life, its tragedy and its pathos" are here vividly but lightly suggested by Ch. Lum 47: bewildered by fate, Arc dies without finding satisfactory solution.

09-15 Curry, *JEGP:* Ch's flippancy here may be attack on smugness and futility of scholastic dialectic in arguments about nature of soul. Lum 48-9: Boccaccio gave Arc philosophic solution (from heaven he laughs at folly of seeking earthly happiness), but Ch left Arc's questions unanswered.

2817-2966

Emily, Palamon, Theseus, and the whole city mourn the death of Arcite. Theseus is given philosophic comfort by his father Egeus. Arcite's funeral is ordered with great pomp and his body is burned on a pyre.

20	*tarien* delay, waste		15	*raughte* reached
34	*cracchynge* scratching		18	*stree* straw
60	*selve* same		21	*holm* evergreen oak
67	*colpons* strips		22	*wylugh* willow. *chasteyn*
83	*ruggy* rough			chestnut
95	*Turkeys* Turkish		28	*amadrides* hamadryads
02	*maister* main		62	*disjoynt* evil plight
04	*ywrye* draped			

17 ManCT 557: "no modern poet would use such words as *shrieked* and *howled* in a serious passage like this, but earlier writers and readers seem to have felt no comic effects from them."

22-6 Hin 113: such satiric passages, certainly out of place, probably prompted Arnold's charge that Ch lacked high seriousness. Frost disagrees, Knight is here neither insincere nor satirical; but Ch's very irony is what gives him "in our eyes, his seriousness as a poet and as a critic of life."

35-6 Pres 189 notes Pope's parody of these lines in letter referring to death of Lord Orrery's dog:

> Ah Bounce! Ah gentle beast, why wouldst thou die
> When thou hadst meat enough, and Orrery?

42-9 Tat 95: satire in absurd obviousness of old Egeus's sententious consolation.

19-24 Tat 95: mild humor in Knight's listing what he is *not* going to tell, also in sylvan gods panicking at loss of habitation (2925-8).

2967-3108
After several years Theseus sends for Palamon (still in mourning) and Emily. He tells them that excessive grief is pointless, life must go on, that all of nature is tied to God (Jupiter) in a "bond of love." Arcite is not to be pitied; he died at height of his honor and fame. Theseus orders mourning to cease, and gives Emily to Palamon in marriage. They live happily ever after.

71	*caas* matters (plural)	16	*at ye* at a glance	
79	*hye* haste	54	*vassellage* prowess	
81	*hust* hushed	66	*lustes* desires	
85	*siked* sighed	67	*serye* argument	
99	*al* although	89	*passen* prevail over	
08	*cantel* portion	00	*aboght* paid for	
10	*corrumpable* corruptible	06	*teene* trouble	

67-3108 Fairchild: Pal prevails at end because he has prayed for a more enduring thing than victory. Tat 96: "ironic reality in the reward going to the less worthy lover." Baum 95: marriage appears to be "political maneuver" by Theseus to confirm his domination of Thebes (possibly oblique allusion to marriage of Richard II and Anne), distorts tale's ending by unhappy mixture of politics and love story.

87-3089 Muscatine: orderly speech with general principles first, then examples from nature, finally the matter at hand; Theseus symbolizes order, earthly king interpreting will of divine one. Brew 93-4: speech has "authentic poetic blend of thought and feeling in musical verse," expressing "exalted conception of life."

3099-08 Lum 40-1: after death of Arc, Pal gives up pursuit of false felicity, accepts Boethian view of ordered universe, is deserving of Emily's hand.

The Miller's Tale

COMMENTARIES: Gr 192-5; Ham 275;/ Don 905-9; ManCT 558-60; Rob 683-6; Sk 5, 95-112;/ Brew 141-5; Ches 156; Cog 131-2; Cow 155; Cur 71-90; Dem 35-8; Ev 164; Law 65-89; Low 176-81; Lum 51-3; Mal 228-30; Man 94-101; Mus 223-30; Pat 181; Pres 190-4; Root 173-9; Shel 244-7; Sp 126-31; Tat 98; Tillyard, *Poetry Direct and Oblique*, rev. ed. (London, 1945), (O); Tup 52-5;/ Albrecht, *Expl*, 51, item 25; Beichner, *MS*, 50, 222-33, and 52, 151-3; Brown, *MLN*, 33, 369-70; Bühler, *Spec*, 49, 410-2; Cline, *MLN*, 45, 480-2; Coffman, *MLN*, 35, 311-2, and 52, 329-31; Collins, *MLN*, 32, 363-4, and *Spec*, 33, 195-7; Donaldson, *EIE*, 51, 116-40, and *MLN*, 54, 310-3; Farnham, *SP*, 23, 70-82; Frost, *Spec*, 33, 526-8, and *RES*, 49, 289-304 (ST); Galway, *N&Q*, 50, 486-8; Harder, *MLQ*, 56, 193-8; Henshaw, *SFQ*, 50, 158-9; Kreuzer, *MLN*, 58, 81; Linthicum, *JEGP*, 35, 39-41; Moore, *CL*, 51, 32-46; O'Connor, *Spec*, 56, 120-5; Owen, *MLN*, 52, 336-8, and *ES*, 54, 49-56; Parker, *Spec*, 50, 237-44; *Pratt*, *MLN*, 44, 47-9; Pyle, *N&Q*, 36, 128; Root, *ESt*, 11, 1-7; Siegel, *BUSE*, 60, 114-20; Smith, *CEA Critic*, Apr., 61, 6; Spitzer, *Lang*, 50, 389-93; Stillwell, *JEGP*, 55, 693-9; Stokoe, *UTQ*, 52, 120-7; Thompson, *SA*, 106-23; Tupper, *JEGP*, 15, 256-70; Wordsworth, *MAE*, 58, 21; Yoffie, *SFQ*, 51, 203-10.

GENRE: Fabliau.

SOURCE: Probably a lost French fabliau combining three motifs: (1) man who is made to fear second flood (for purposes of cuckolding him), (2) the misdirected kiss, and (3) branding of lover's rump; a 14th-century Flemish fabliau (possibly adapted from a French one) contains all three motifs, as do several later versions.

DATE: Probably early 1390's.

GENERAL CRITICISM: Tupper: tale successful as "fabliau of futile jealousy of age" in which carpenter John resembles Reeve. Root 176: *MillT* and *RvT* are "by their very nature not true art," though in *MillT* attention is diverted from nasty features of story. Tup 139: fabliau vulgarizes love, whereas romance conventionalizes and lyric idealizes. Cur 76: tale is direct thrust at Reeve's weak spot—advanced age. Cow 155: with brilliant plot, description, and dialogue, tale is most skillful of *CT*, "as convincing as it is naughty." ManCT 559: portraits of student, wife, and clerk are "brilliant examples of Ch's latest and best methods of portraiture." Low 180-1: for sheer virtuosity in combining setting, action, and atmosphere, tale is perhaps Ch's masterpiece; several echoes of miracle plays. Shel 246: though a minor character, John is finely individualized; he deserves cuckoldry but engages sympathy for his "honest-going stupidity and gullibility," humane concern for Nicholas, praise of ignorance, simple but sincere love of wife. Tillyard 85-92: tale, more than brilliant bawdry, is "a consummate piece of obliquity," most perfectly plotted of *CT*, with "delicate mixing of the sacred and the obscene"; though Ch enjoyed the coarseness, he made it functional, distracting reader from main plot by "very outrageousness of the farce" so as to achieve overwhelming surprise when he returns to it with Nicholas's scream for water in a climax which "gets beyond the social bounds of comedy and impels the reader's mind to exult and expand as it does in enjoying the very greatest art" with "feelings akin to those of religious wonder." Ches 156: "coarse, not to say foul narrative," as though Miller had thrown "a pail of slops" over Monk whom Host chose to tell next tale. Cog 131-2: descending from high style of *KnT* to "churl-style" of fabliaux, Ch the courtier shows new and unexpected power "to create an outrageous and unquenchable cottage laughter" with tales fantastic in plot, but sharply realistic in detail, dialogue, and character. Frost, *RES*: tale makes *KnT* dramatic through burlesque—closing of *KnT* burlesqued in crude justice at end, manners of chivalry in Absolon, cosmic background of *KnT* contrasted with smalltown bourgeois milieu. Tat 98: paradox that tale fits Miller's coarse personality, but brilliance of it shows Ch at his best, no sacrifice of poetic excellence to quality of speaker; "out of the mouths of churls come wisdom and beauty." Sp 127: characterization far above fabliaux; plot shows "masterly dramatic imagination." Donaldson, *EIE*: throughout characterization and dialogue Ch sprinkled clichés from debased vernacular versions of courtly love romances; best example is *hende* Nicholas, connoting "nice" in popular idiom, never used in serious courtly context, here ironically suggesting other meanings (clever, close "at hand"); use of popular idiom fits Miller, but also makes tale ironic parody of popular romance (like *Thop*), reinforces connection with *KnT*, and, above all, is richly humorous in itself. Beichner, *MS*, 52: Ch uses epithet *hende* 11 times to characterize Nicholas through its several meanings: (1) as boarder in Alison's house he is near, "at hand"; (2) in approaching her he is "skillful with the hand" in 3282-7; (3) when she threatens to scream he becomes *hende* in sense of "pleasant, courteous"; (4) he is also "clever" in planning flood episode; (5) he is doubtless "nice looking"; and in climax scene he is both "at hand" and "clever" (*hende* once too often), thus bringing about poetic justice. Stokoe: conflict between Knight's and Miller's views of life and love (*gentils* vs. *cherles*) provides central unifying theme for all of Fragment I. Owen, *ES*: tale, with portrait of Alison, stress on bodily functions, mockery of delicacy, fits sensual Miller; Alison contrasts with unreal Emily in *KnT*, shows incompleteness of Knight's experience; as in *KnT*, lovers are differentiated, but here blatantly–Nicholas seems studious and devout, but only on surface, whereas Absolon, though flamboyant, is basically innocent. Stillwell: sublime-ridiculous theme of Fragment I shows here in contrast between elegant diction and gross situation which Ch found in fabliau tradition but surpassed. Harder: tale is burlesque of probably one particular cycle of miracle plays, with Miller resembling ranting Pilate and Herod, Absolon perhaps an actual clerk who played Herod (buffoon), carpenter episode parodying Noah play. Mus 223-30: mass of solid detail along with characterization gives tale overwhelming force; ironic use of courtly convention (not in fabliau tradition) makes tale a "mordantly pointed comment, from below, on the futility of love *paramours*." Don 905-9: tale is "highest artistic expression of the fabliau" which flourished in France, hardly at all in England; it is earthy Miller's comment on "marvelously impractical" love triangle in *KnT*, and on courtly love convention, with "thoroughly vital country wench" as heroine. Siegel: deliberate, repeated misapplication of religious ideas adds to comic irony of tale; *privee, prively, pryvetee* are constantly used to characterize sly, secretive Nicholas who pretends to reveal God's secret to John while concealing his own.

THE MILLER'S PROLOGUE

I, 3109-3186

All pilgrims praise Knight's tale and Host next calls on Monk. Drunken Miller interrupts, says he knows tale to match Knight's. Host asks him to wait but Miller ("Robin") insists: he will tell of carpenter who was cuckolded. Reeve tells Miller to shut up. Miller soothes Reeve ("Oswald") and proceeds. Readers, don't blame me (Ch) for coarseness of Miller's tale; he is a churl but I must report truthfully. If you disapprove, choose another tale.

15	*male* bag	40	*wyte it* blame it on
19	*quite* equal	43	*wrightes* carpenter's. *set* . . .
20	*dronken* drunkenness		*cappe* made a fool of
21	*unnethe* with difficulty	44	*clappe* noise
22	*avalen* doff	47	*apeyren* injure
24	*Pilates voys* (like ranting	56	*madde* go mad
	Pilate in miracle plays)	65	*foyson* plenty
26	*for the nones* for this occa-	70	*m'athynketh* I regret
	sion (equalling *KnT*)		

24 Parker: Pilate in miracle plays always shown as oppressive, vainglorious, ruthless official (often used to burlesque unpopular contemporary courtiers and churchmen).

34-5 Root 174: Host realizes "discretion is the better part of courtesy."

41-2 Coffman, *MLN*, 35: promise to tell *a legende and a lyf* shows Miller, having just challenged Knight, is now challenging Monk who might be expected to tell saint's legend.

41-66 Tupper: Miller-Reeve antagonism based on trade hostility and cuckoldry motif (more significant basis for quarrel). Man 95-7: Reeve's violent reaction (London Carpenter makes no protest), Miller's knowledge of his name, fact that they ride at opposite ends of pilgrimage—all suggest prior acquaintance as well as trade rivalry. Pratt: wrath of Reeve suggests Miller may have been his servant boy in past (same boy who appears in tale) and may have witnessed cuckolding, since both are named Robin, each is described as *a stout carl for the nones* (*Gen Prol* 545, *MillT* 3469), and each is adept at breaking down doors by brute strength. Lum 51 agrees with Pratt—Reeve fears exposure; also, Miller knows Reeve is married. Owen, *MLN,* disagrees—John too simple, gullible to be Reeve; carpenter's boy unlikely to become miller in later life; aggressive Miller would be sure to let us know if he had part in tale. Galway goes farther than Pratt, connects both Robins with Simkin of *RvT* and, conjecturally, with actual Robert Grymbald of Oxford.

51-66 Shel 208: Miller shrewdly manages both to silence Reeve and to pontificate on husbands, wives, cuckolds.

67-86 Root 175: apology half serious, half playful. Tillyard 86: apology is Ch's specious and ironical (he did not have to bring in churls at all) way of telling reader he would be a fool to skip tale out of prudishness. Law 80-2: Ch apologizes to genteel audience not for immorality of tale but for vulgar speech; sly humor in ironic pretense that "his heart bleeds, but he *must* tell the tale as he heard it."

86 Mal 229: this is Ch's real defense; preceding passage of apology is comedy.

THE MILLER'S TALE

3187-3270

A rich carpenter (John) lives at Oxford and has in house as boarder a young scholar ("hende Nicholas"). Nicholas is expert in astrology, in singing, and in love-making. Carpenter has young wife of 18 (Alison) whom he watches jealously. Alison is good-looking, skittish, and sexy.

88	*gnof* churl	36	*barmclooth* apron
99	*hende* gentle, handy	37	*lendes* loins
00	*deerne* secret	41	*voluper* cap
07	*cetewale* ginger	43	*filet* head-band
09	*longynge* fitting	48	*pere-jonette* early-ripe pear
10	*augrym* algorism (counting)	56	*noble* coin
12	*presse* cupboard	57	*yerne* eager
13	*sautrie* psaltery	63	*wynsynge* skittish
20	*fyndyng* charity	68	*prymerole* rose. *piggesnye* flower
34	*gent* slender		
35	*ceynt* girdle	69	*leggen* lay

90-20 Coffman, *MLN,* 52: in Nicholas, with his music, astrology, and pleasures, Ch has created burlesque picture which acts as foil to portrait in *Gen Prol* of genuine ideal scholar (Clerk). Don 907: Ch shows Nicholas as 14th-century college student with extracurricular interests, also as burlesque romance hero (hende).

00 Donaldson, EIE: *deerne love* had unsavory connotations, a debased term from vernacular romances, here used to parody ideal of secrecy in courtly love code.

04 Ev 164: repetition of *KnT* 2779 provides verbal link for burlesque effect.

16 Tillyard 87: since Nicholas looks something like an angel (see 3202), "we suspect a further meaning in his song's title" (mixture of sacred and obscene throughout tale). Siegel: song is Annunciation hymn ("Angel to Virgin"), and has "its own sly implications."

19-20 Tillyard 87: "the purest honey of Ch's irony."

21-32 Tillyard 87-8: Ch shows comic victim, "self-doomed and star-crossed"; exquisite absurdity of grave suggestion (3227-8) that reading Cato might have saved him—here Ch makes fun of book-learning and "theoretical wisdom" in himself and others; John shown not as tragic victim but as comic sinner "against the wisdom of the race."

33-70 Low 176-8: Alison portrait a masterpiece, true to stock conventions for showing lady's beauty by cataloguing features—forehead, eyes, nose, etc.; but Ch pours new life into hackneyed pattern by drawing similes not from books but from countryside. Pat 181: "Ch saw her as a delicious morsel," who moved him to zestful imagery as Constance and Griselda did not. Albrecht: Alison seems only slightly more self-conscious than animal, and so escapes punishments given to others at end; her only affectation is slight trace of modesty (in moment's resistance to Nicholas), symbolized by brooch made like shield, but this contrasts comically with quick compliance to Nicholas and with episode of misdirected kiss; wives in analogues have *no* modesty—this humanizing touch is Ch's addition to dramatic irony. Donaldson, *EIE:* in Alison Ch brilliantly reduces wornout ideal (heroine of vernacular romance) to "its lowest common denominator of sexuality." Sp 127-9: Alison as wonderfully vital as Wife of Bath; images from animals, fruits, farmyard show her as natural, wild, young, untamed. Brew 143: Ch makes her as alluring as she is vulgar—a comic figure to courtly audience and to us because Ch adjusts our eyes to his vision. Mus 229-30: description more than convention vivified (Low's view); by domesticating catalogue of features, using Oxford instead of Continental similes, Ch retains some of idealizing power, and shows sympathy with Alison (as with Wife of Bath), "the one precious illusion in the poem"; she is ideal as seen from below by Miller, comic as seen from above by Ch's audience. Don 907: description burlesques catalogue of charms of romance heroine; difference between Alison and Emily symbolized in gap between Emily's red and white flowers (*KnT* 1035-8) and Alison's barnyard *piggesnye*.

34 Donaldson, *EIE: wezele* is fresh, effective image; use of *gent* ("stale adjective" from vernacular idiom) instead of *gentil* (courtly term) shows "realistic and pragmatic" view of Alison's body rather than "ideal and esthetic."

37 Donaldson, *EIE: gore* here, in combination with *lendes,* probably has sexual connotation from vernacular literature, as it has in *Thop* 788-9.

54 Donaldson, *EIE: wenche* is "crashing anti-climax" in Ch's mockery of conventional ideals of beauty.

57-8 Kreuzer: in curious swallow image Ch may be alluding to trait of swallows described in *Book of Beasts* (12th-century Latin bestiary): "it [swallow] has a sort of second-sight, because it leaves the nest when this will not stick to the roof-ridge and is going to tumble down"—ironic foreshadowing of tale's plot.

68 Donaldson, *EIE:* crude associations of *piggesnye* (pig's eye) provide reversal of usual ideal flower-comparison.

3271-3306
During John's absence, Nicholas tries to seduce Alison. She finally promises her love whenever they have a good opportunity. Nicholas says he will make one.

75 *queynte* sly   77 *but* unless
76 *queynte* pudendum

82	*trave* frame for holding un-ruly horses	99	*litherly* ill
83	*wryed* twisted	04	*thakked* stroked

71-87 Shel 245: Nicholas's direct attack is technique of country, not of court. Don 907: Nicholas's directness makes fun of idealized love of Palamon and Arcite, and "provides a derisive commentary on his romantic niceness." Beichner, *MS*, 52: Alison's resistance hardly that of courtly romance; colt in trave image (3282) "one of the most brilliant action similes Ch ever wrote," connecting with earlier description (3263).

99-00 Mus 226: Nicholas's error is "faith in intellect and the sufficiency of wit."

3307-3396

The parish clerk, Absolon, is a fancy dresser, very fastidious and amorous. He sees Alison in church and is smitten. He woos her long but in vain; Alison prefers Nicholas.

15	*strouted* spread out	41	*sensynge* incensing
16	*shode* parting of the hair	58	*shot* casement
21	*waget* blue	75	*meenes* agents. *brocage* mediation
22	*poyntes* laces		
24	*rys* twig, spray	77	*brokkynge* quavering
31	*rubible* lute	78	*pyment* sweetened wine
32	*quynyble* high voice	80	*meede* bribes
36	*gaylard* gay	92	*"Alwey . . ."* = "out of sight, out of mind."
37	*squaymous* squeamish		
38	*daungerous* fastidious		

07-11 Siegel: irony of picture of Alison as *goode wyf,* out to do Christ's work; neither she nor Absolon is interested in Christian morality.

12-51 Low 178-9: in Absolon Ch renders brilliant portrait of "small-town dandy;" a perennial type skillfully individualized. Tillyard 89: portrait highly colored; Absolon courts in the open, while Nicholas is swift and secret. Sp 129-30: Absolon's foppishness suggested by fan simile and by "fantastic comedy" of *Poules wyndow corven on his shoos.* Don 908: effeminate Absolon has voice, delicacy, manners of court lady, but yet is realistic picture of dandified clerk who "seems more concerned with the ritual of hopelessly loving a girl than with winning her."

14-6 Low 178: "with uncanny accuracy" Ch hits pride in hair, in-invariable mark of rustic dandy (Absolon was barber). Beichner, *MS,* 50: luxuriant hair and name connect Absolon most fittingly with Biblical Absalom, son of David, most beautiful man in Israel, but usually viewed as proud and effeminate by medieval writers.

17 Donaldson, *EIE:* "words that a minstrel would normally apply to a pretty girl" (grey eyes common in medieval heroines; Ch's only other use of *rode* in *Thop* 727).

24 Donaldson *EIE:* cliché usually describing woman's flesh.

35 Collins, *MLN: Solas* means not pleasure or solace (Sk), but refers in this musical context to Absolon's singing of "sol-las," notes of musical scale. Brown disagrees, favors obsolete meaning of *solas* as that which gives pleasure (Absolon's playing, singing, etc.).

48 Donaldson, *EIE: joly* normally applied to pretty girl; note also lovely look (3342) and *love-longynge* (3349), both clichés of popular poetry.

61-2 Moore: 2 lines of love song probably known in full by Ch's audience.

84 Sk 5, 104: parish clerks often acted in miracle plays; Herod was important role.

3397-3489

Nicholas lays in food for two days and hides in his room. John, worried, sends servant (Robin) to see whether Nicholas is ill. Nicholas pretends to be in trance. John orders Robin to break down door. They shake Nicholas: he finally wakes.

04	*sely* foolish	70	*haaf* heaved
25	*adrad* afraid	79	*crouche* mark with sign of
28	*tikel* precarious		cross
44	*capyng* staring	80	*nyght-spel* charm to ward
45	*kiked* gazed		off evil
65	*underspore* pry up	85	*verye* evil spirits
69	*for the nones* for this pur- pose (breaking door open)		

31-78 Tillyard: "brilliant pictures of domestic life," with servant peeping through cat-hole, gaping swoon of Nicholas, breaking open of door.

40-1 Tat 98: realistic touch "which no medieval but Ch would have thought of."

49 Cline: John's swearing by St. Frideswide is fitting because priory of St. Frideswide was at Oxford and her shrine was believed to have healing powers (John thinks Nicholas is ill).

54-61 Owen, *ES:* irony of John's belief in safety of ignorance, impracticality of scholars; in the end it is John who does not see what is right under his nose. Mus 226: illiterate, superstitious carpenter who believes in spells, whose religion is "self-satisfied, unthinking."

66 Pratt: servant boy Robin has same name as Miller; perhaps same person in youth.

80-6 Yoffie: White Paternoster, or night-spell to ward off evil spirits at retiring, perhaps derived from ancient Hebrew night-prayer; white signifies purity and goodness as guardians against evils of night.

83-6 Pyle: lines should be read as 4-stress verse, rhythm of night-spell (compare *WBT* 655-8). Low 181: superb mocking irony as "duped and doltish carpenter, making the sign of the cross, utters the night-spell to ward off . . . elves and wights."

3490-3600

Nicholas secretly tells John there will be great flood, worse than Noah's. He can save only himself, John, and Alison. He orders John to hang 3 tubs in rafters by ropes, store them with food. When water rises they will cut ropes, float out through hole in gable.

03	*wreye* reveal		47	*in* house
09	*labbe* tell-tale		48	*kymelyn* shallow tub
21	*drenche* drown		89	*atwynne* apart
27	*reed* advice			

13-21 O'Connor: whole scheme based on folk tradition of Noah as expert astrologer, predicting Flood by stars as well as by divine revelation; this is only way Nicholas can overcome John's anti-intellectual suspicion of astrology (3455-6); he also appeals to John's pride in making him believe he is chosen confidant of God (2nd Noah). Farnham: Ch has Nicholas use crude popular astrology (which John knew about and understood) instead of learned terms; moon was popularly known as ruler of tides and floods.

22-3 Shel 247: John thinks first of wife he dotes on, "one of the most human touches in all Ch."

3601-3656

John tells secret to Alison, sends servants away, prepares tubs, etc. At night all 3 climb into tubs and lie still (Nicholas's orders). John falls asleep; Nicholas and Alison sneak down and go to bed in John's bed.

05	*queynte cast* strange scheme	37	*furlong way* short time
24	*his owene* with his own	38	*clom* mum (be quiet)
25	*stalkes* uprights	46	*goost* spirit
26	*balkes* rafters	47	*routeth* snores

14-42 Dem 38: humorous contrast of John's preparations for flood with previous efforts to keep wife *narwe in cage.*

52-4 Donaldson, *EIE:* obscene Miller uses worn-out romance terms for feast (revelry and melody, mirth and solace) to describe adulterous love-feast, with husband's snores providing *melodye,* lovers enjoying *solas,* "that seemingly innocent word for delight" used earlier (3200).

53-6 Pres 194: "coolly brilliant" transition.

3657-3743

Meanwhile Absolon, thinking John absent, dresses sprucely and arrives outside bedroom window to woo Alison. Alison tells him to leave. Absolon begs for kiss; Alison agrees to one. She opens window and shoves out bare buttock; Absolon, in dark, kisses it.

61	*upon cas* by chance	97	*semy* gentle
84	*mette* dreamed	09	*com pa me* come kiss me
89	*at poynt-devys* to perfection	13	*a twenty devel wey* in devil's
92	*trewe-love* leaf of herb paris		name

22 *hust* hush   38 *yherd* haired
26 *oore* favor

85-08 Mus 227-8: elaborate caricature of conventional courting, but in idiom of Oxford rather than of French romance—"crushingly conventional."

04 Donaldson, *EIE:* "Miller's own audacious contribution to the language of love"; fine example of Ch using conventional image in new way, "wholly devastating."

26 Donaldson, *EIE:* further brilliant exploitation of love clichés for comic effect.

40 Cog 132: "perhaps the funniest line in the funniest story in the world."

3744-3854
Furious at this insult, Absolon wakes nearby blacksmith (Gervais) and borrows colter with red hot blade. He returns to window, begs another kiss. This time Nicholas presents his behind and Absolon strikes with colter. Nicholas screams for water. His cry wakes John who thinks flood is coming, cuts rope, comes crashing down from rafters and breaks arm. Neighbors gather. Nicholas and Alison convince them that John has lost his mind.

47 *froteth* chafes   21 *foond* found time
52 *awroken* avenged   22 *celle* floor-boards (sill)
53 *ybleynt* turned aside   27 *gauren* gaze
54 *yqueynt* quenched   30 *stonde* put up with
68 *rathe* early   39 *par compaignye* for com-
70 *upon the viritoot* on the   pany
        move   41 *cape* stare
08 *yblent* blinded   50 *swyved* seduced

47-9 Wordsworth: only rhetorical question in Ch's fabliaux, echoes *KnT* 1454-6, 1870-1, 2652-3, is further evidence of burlesquing of *KnT;* 3748 is parody of catalogue and repetition techniques of high style.

76 Owen, *ES:* *coulter* (hot and used in plowing) conveys both Ab-

solon's intense anger and revulsion and, symbolically, his sexual inadequacy.

98-15 Smith: Ch handles potentially obscene material with delicacy and skill, playing down nastier aspects, stressing comic incongruities and surprises, such as contrast between vulgar image of Nicholas's posture at window (his "backside decorating the night air like a great white flower, like the inviting target it is so shortly to become") and the tender tones of Absolon's *sweete bryd* speech.

11-23 Tillyard 90: "the surprise, the sudden union of the two themes is sublime."

18 Sk 5, 111: *Nowelis flood* is error for *Noes;* illiterate carpenter knows *Nowel* of Christmas carol better than Bible.

50-4 Tillyard 90-1: characters get what they deserve; Alison already has her punishment in being married to jealous old husband.

The Reeve's Tale

COMMENTARIES: Gr 195-7; Ham 275-6;/ Don 909-10; ManCT
560-1; Rob 686-8; Sk 5, 116-28;/ Brew 145-7; Cur 71-9; Dem
271-9; Ev 144; Fr 217-9; Low 175-81; Lum 53-7; Mal 166, 180,
197-8, 229-30; Man 84-94; Mus 198-204; Root 173-9; Sp 131-2;
Tat 99-100;/ Baum, *PMLA*, 56, 225-46, and 58, 167-70; Block, *Spec*,
54, 239-43; Cline, *MLN*, 45, 480-2; Coffman, *Spec*, 34, 249-77;
Dempster, *JEGP*, 30, 473-88; Dieckmann, *MP*, 29, 279-82; Eliason,
MLN, 56, 162-4; Emerson, *N&Q*, 57, 277-8; Forehand, *PMLA*, 54,
984-9; Hart, *PMLA*, 08, 1-44, and *SA*, 124-47; Jones, *MLQ*, 55,
3-15; Kaske, *ELH*, 59, 295-310; Montgomery, *PQ*, 31, 404-5;
Myers, *PQ*, 34, 222-6; Owen, *ES*, 54, 49-56; Pratt, *MLN*, 55, 324-5,
and *JEGP*, 60, 208-11; Stillwell, *JEGP*, 55, 693-9; Turner, *N&Q*,
54, 232; Whiting, *Med. Stud. in Honor of J.D.M. Ford*, 1948, 319-31.

GENRE: Fabliau.

SOURCE: Probably a lost French fabliau; several analogues in-
volving the cradle-trick have been found.

DATE: Early 1390's.

GENERAL CRITICISM: Hart, *PMLA:* tale is improvement of fabliau techniques, anticipates modern short story except for lack of
unified point of view (action chiefly seen through eyes of students,
but sometimes through Simkin and sometimes his wife). Root 173-9:
"extreme indecency" shows lack of artistic discrimination but not
immoral character in Ch; effectiveness depends on poetic justice in
Simkin's fate. Low 175-81: one of best of *CT*, with setting from
personal knowledge. Dem 271-9: Ch surpassed fabliau tradition by
enriching ironical dramatic contrasts and by developing better characterization. Mal 230: tale is told for own sake, not to reveal character of teller which is only incidental. Brew 145-7: sex enters tale because Simkin's pride is tenderest there (illegitimacy of wife). Owen:
in tale Reeve presents "world of spiritual corruption and economic
maneuver in which he himself lives"; he makes villain Simkin re-

semble Pilgrim Miller but ranks himself with churls by vulgarity of tale; also, he unconsciously chooses tale in which young win out over shrewd, avaricious elders—a pattern which gives point to his own Prologue on old age. Mus 198-204: tale is enrichment of fabliau; humor more bitter than in *MillT*, shows "particularly bilious view of life"; biting satire deflates intellectual and social conceit of Simkin and is aimed at class-conscious Pilgrim Miller. Don 909-10: greatest fabliau in literature after *MillT*, but revenge theme and Reeve's "dark-mindedness" cast shadow on otherwise wonderfully funny and skillful tale; like clerks in tale, Reeve takes sly revenge on burlier antagonist.

THE REEVE'S PROLOGUE

I, 3855-3920

Most of pilgrims laugh heartily at Miller's tale; but Oswald, the Reeve, does not like it because he is carpenter. He adds that he is getting old and is subject to ills of old age—desire without physical vigor, avarice, gossiping dotage, etc. Host orders him to get on with his tale. Reeve says he will pay back Miller.

63	*lite* little	88	*coltes tooth* = sexual desire
64	*theek* (thee ik) may I thrive	94	*tonne* wine cask
70	*mowled* decayed	95	*chymbe* rim (of cask)
71	*open-ers* medlar (fruit)	04	*soutere* cobbler. *leche* doctor
73	*mullok* rubbish heap	11	*sett his howve* (hood) =
76	*hoppen* dance		make fool of him
77	*nayl* hindrance	12	*of-showve* repel
80	*evere in oon* continually	19	*stalke* bit of straw
82	*yreke* raked	20	*balke* beam
83	*gleedes* coals		

55-20 Coffman: Ch, fascinated by theme of senility, forgot Reeve, who is not old but is shown in *Gen Prol* as in prime of life ("mature middle age"). Sp 131-2: Reeve, offended by attack on carpenters, also feels self-pity because of old age; senility theme perhaps deeply felt by aging Ch himself; imagery is agricultural. Mal 180: monologue turns into "characterization of old people generally." Forehand disagrees with Coffman—Reeve is old (carries rusty sword, rides last because he tires easily, etc.). Lum 53ff: Reeve's view of himself not inconsistent with *Gen Prol*—he is old. Don 909: Reeve "casts the shadow of his own meanness over the story."

59-63 Cur 77:   mild anger due to timidity of choleric type; Reeve "a coward at heart," fears Miller, rides last. ManCT 560: Miller-Reeve enmity probably of long standing, since Carpenter in group of guildsmen does not take offense. Lum 53ff: Reeve's anger subdued because he is relieved Miller did not connect him directly with cuckolded carpenter; he tells tale to draw attention to trade rivalry and away from possible cuckolding reference.

78 Cur 71-9:   boasting of *grene tayl* aimed at offsetting ridicule of Reeve's (John's) old age in *MillT*.

88 Whiting: *coltes tooth* usually refers to "youthful amorousness in an old body."

89-98 Baum lists possible puns on *tonge* (of a bell) and *bore* (brought forth and made a hole in). AHM: wine-cask image astonishingly complex and suggestive figure for course of human life from spirited youth to enfeebled old age.

12 Montgomery: a widely known legal maxim. Myers disagrees; English law never fully adopted idea, was opposed to self help.

THE REEVE'S TALE

3921-3986

Simkin, miller of Trumpington near Cambridge, is proud, aggressive, armed to the teeth, and a sly stealer of meal. His wife, daughter of local priest, is well educated, well dressed, and very snooty. Simkin is proud and jealous of her. Their daughter, 20 years old, is handsome but still unmarried because she is heiress of her choosy grandfather, the priest.

27	*beete* mend	35	*piled* bald
28	*turn coppes* turn cups on lathe	36	*market-betere* swaggerer at markets
29	*panade* cutlass	38	*abegge* pay for it
31	*poppere* dagger	41	*hoote* was called (also possible pun on hot-blooded).
33	*thwitel* knife		
34	*camus* flat		*deynous* disdainful

53	*typet* cape	65	*hoker* disdain. *bisemare*
54	*gyte* gown		scorn
62	*algate* anyhow	72	*propre page* fine boy
63	*smoterlich* besmirched	79	*mesuage* house
64	*digne* haughty	80	*straunge* difficult

25-86 Low 175-81: brilliant conciseness of sketches of Simkin, wife and daughter.

25-55 Cur 71-9: Simkin has physical traits of Pilgrim Miller; Reeve attacks person of Miller because his own sexual pride has been wounded. ManCT 561: Reeve makes Simkin twin brother of Pilgrim Miller. Jones: Simkin is popular view of miller type; he craves social status, wears red hose and sword (both illegal for lower classes), is heavy drinker, dishonest, married to priest's daughter (dishonorable), has flat, broad (*camus*) nose indicating low class origin. Pratt, *JEGP:* both Simkin and Pilgrim Miller wrestle, carry similar weapons, are thieves, wear gay clothes, play bagpipes, become pale from drinking.

27 Block: bagpipe used symbolically (erotic symbol for belly and male organs) and realistically to suggest both gluttony and lechery typical of millers; it also connects Simkin with Pilgrim Miller.

28 ManCT 561 (also Rob 687): *turne coppes* means woodworking. Pratt, *JEGP:* phrase may come from line in song for old drinking game ("Drink up yur liquor and turn yur cup over"); Rob's woodworking explanation is too tame.

42-68 Don 910: illegitimacy of Simkin's wife troubles neither of them (cp. Brew in GEN. CRIT).

42-86 Mus 198-204: biting irony in revelation of church "connections" of Simkin.

44-5 Eliason: puns on *panne of bras* (brass penny) and *allye* (ally and alloy).

70 Don 910: daughter at 20 is old maid by medieval standards, waiting for eligible man.

83-6 Eliason: possible pun on *hooly* (holy or wholly)

3987-4045

Simkin has been stealing regularly from Cambridge college (Soler Hall), even more during illness of manciple. Two Northumbrian students, John and Alan, get leave to take grain to miller and promise not to be cheated. They arrive, planning to watch Simkin carefully.

87	*sokene* toll	27	*boes* it behoves. *swayn* servant
99	*fare* to-do		
01	*craketh boost* talks loudly	30	*wanges* molars
04	*testif* headstrong	33	*heythen* hence
11	*reve* rob	36	*hopur* hopper
		37	*gas* goes (Northern form)

22ff Tat 99-100 (also Ev 144) : northern dialect of students provides dramatic and individualizing expression. Don 910: dialect would have seemed "excruciatingly funny" to southern Englishmen of Ch's audience.

4046-4113

Simkin, determined to trick them, secretly unties their horse, then grinds their grain under watchful eyes. When job is done John finds horse gone. He and Alan chase horse for hours. Meanwhile, miller steals half bushel of their flour which his wife makes into large cake. Weary students return to mill at dusk with horse.

51	*crekes* tricks	86	*wight* swift. *raa* roe
53	*bren* bran	88	*capul* nag. *lathe* barn
61	*levesel* bush	89	*fonne* fool
64	*laus* loose	96	*make a clerkes berd* cheat a student
68	*note* task		
74	*atanes* at once (No.)	01	*jossa* down here! *warderere* look out behind!
78	*geen* gone (No.)		
85	*alswa* also (No.)	10	*hethyng* contempt

4114-4167

Simkin agrees to feed and house students overnight for a price. In evening he gets drunk; then all retire to one bedroom. Simkin and wife sleep in one bed with cradle at foot; students in another; daughter in a third.

19	*herberwe* shelter. *peny* money	49	*vernysshed* oiled (got drunk)
22	*streit* small	51	*yexeth* hiccoughs
29	*taa* take	52	*quakke* hoarseness. *pose* head cold
30	*slyk* such		
34	*tulle* lure	58	*crowke* crook
40	*chalons* blankets	61	*dwale* sleeping potion
45	*roumer* roomier	63	*fnorteth* snores

23-6 Owen: Simkin's sneer at students' impractical learning back-fires later, since it is very *streitness* of room which gives students chance for revenge.

27 Cline: John's oath by St. Cuthbert is appropriate here because St. Cuthbert was (like John) a Northumberland man and there was popular story of how he was rewarded for his hospitality (irony).

49-53 Pratt, *JEGP:* Simkin's drunkenness "facilitates the nocturnal adventures" of students.

65 Dieckmann: *burdoun* means droning hum which was unique song form in North England, is appropriately noticed by one of northern students.

4168-4198

While others sleep, students talk. They know miller has tricked them. Alan boldly plans to get revenge by sleeping with daughter; he sneaks into her bed and is well received.

71	*swilk* such. *complyn* evening song. *ymel* among	78	*swyve* seduce
		87	*sale* soul
73	*ferly* weird	94	*uprighte* on her back
76	*nafors* no matter	97	*aton* united

74 Baum: pun on *flour* (flower and stolen flour).

79 Baum notes pun on *esement* (legal compensation and simple enjoyment).

93-7 Turner: daughter's *camus* nose was sign of unusual amorous-ness, gave Alan confidence for easy seduction. Emerson: Alan was fairly sure of easy conquest because he knew her already (see 4022-3), and her loose character is shown by her own use of word *lemman*, connoting promiscuity (4240, 4247), and by Alan's and Reeve's references to her as *wench* (3973, 4167, 4178, 4193, 4194).

4199-4233

Meanwhile, John quietly moves cradle from miller's bed to his own. Later, miller's wife gets up to urinate; in returning through dark room she feels cradle at foot of wrong bed and climbs in with John, thinking he is miller. John promptly takes sexual advantage of her.

05	*auntred* ventured	10	*unhardy is unseely* a coward	
06	*draf-sak* sack of chaff		has no luck	
08	*daf* fool. *cokenay* milksop	30	*ful yoore* for a long time	

4234-4324

Near dawn Alan leaves daughter (Malyne) who tells location of stolen flour. Because of switched cradle he makes same error as wife, crawls in with miller. Thinking miller is John, Alan whispers of his success. Miller is furious and wild fight ensues. Miller falls across other bed, waking his wife and John. In dark wife tries to help miller by hitting students with club, but in dark she knocks out miller instead. Students escape, picking up stolen flour on way out. Thus I have repaid the Miller for his tale.

35	*swonken* labored	80	*sporned* stumbled
39	*seel* soul	85	*breyde* started
40	*lemman* sweetheart, lover	95	*estres* interior
53	*toty* dizzy	03	*volupeer* nightcap
57	*a twenty devel way* = with devilish bad luck	06	*pyled* bald
		09	*greythen* dress
59	*cropen* crept in	20	*thar* it needs. *wene* expect
73	*throte-bolle* Adam's apple	21	*gylour* trickster

34-48 Brew 145-7: "somewhat rapidly-sprung affection" between daughter and Alan is genuine—comic pathos in farewell. Stillwell: ironic contrast of romantic sentiment and bawdy situation; Ch

found this device in French fabliau, but heightened it artistically.
Kaske: farewell speeches are burlesque of continental *aube* or dawn
song (conventional farewell of chivalric lovers after night together),
hence are intended as pure comedy—no pathos.

86 Pratt, *MLN:* wife's invoking cross of Bromholm (75 miles from
Trumpington) is fitting since it was credited with health-giving
miracles.

The Cook's Tale

COMMENTARIES: Gr 197-8; Ham 276-7;/ Don 911; ManCT 562-3; Rob 688-9; Sk 5, 128-31;/ Brew 147-8; Cog 133-4; Cur 51-2; Kit 172; Law 13; Lum 59-61; Lyon, *Ch's CkT and Its Background* (Univ. of Cal. dissertation, 1938); Mus 242-6; Pres 197; Shel 251; Sp 132-3; Tat 101; Tup 100-3;/ Call, *MLQ*, 43, 167-76; Lisca, *MLN*, 55, 321-4; Lumiansky, *MS*, 55, 208-9; Lyon, *SA*, 148-54; Rickert, *TLS*, Oct. 20, 32, 761; Tupper, *PMLA*, 14, 93-128, and *JEGP*, 15, 256-70.

GENRE: Fabliau.

SOURCE: None has been found; tale probably original with Ch.

DATE: Early 1390's.

GENERAL CRITICISM: Tupper, *PMLA*: tale has earmarks of story on sin of Gluttony, told by glutton. Kit 172: tale, "fortunately a fragment," was to satirize innkeepers as reply to Host's attack upon sharp practice of cooks. Lyon 145: Ch probably left tale incomplete because he planned wholly original story and found such composition unsatisfactory. Shel 251: tale would have been another brilliant fabliau, giving "an incomparably full and rich picture of London life." Cog 133-4: tale clearly planned as "piece of town-scurrility" well suited to Cook. Law 13-6: Ch planned indecorous tale, "unhappily not finished." Tat 101: Ch probably attempted original story of London underworld; this tale, like almost all of Ch's other fragments, has no known source—a suggestive fact. Brew 147-8: a promising start for tale of City that Ch knew intimately; shows how Court and City interests mingled in his audience. Lisca: tale makes some points descriptive of both Cook and historical Roger of Ware—Perkin is of victualing craft and is dissolute (Roger was convicted of being "common nightwalker"). Mus 246: tale probably would have been "rawest" of Ch's works. Don 911: "promising anecdote" which Ch probably broke off because 3 fabliaux in a row would be excessive.

THE COOK'S PROLOGUE

I, 4325-4364

The Cook (Roger or "Hodge" of Ware) praises Reeve's tale and offers to tell another comic story. Host agrees, jokes about Cook's unsanitary shop and sharp practices. Cook says he will later tell tale of an innkeeper.

26	*him thoughte* it seemed to him	50	*percely* parsley
39	*stynte* stop	51	*stubbel goos* old goose fed on stubble
46	*laten blood* drained of its gravy	57	*sooth pley, quaad pley* a true jest is a bad jest
47	*Jakke of Dovere* warmed-up pie	60	*hostileer* innkeeper

25-64 Cur 51-2: Roger's drunkenness, loose morals, fondness for dirty stories all fit sketch of diseased Cook in *Gen Prol* with *mormal* perhaps caused by eating tainted meats in his shop and by dissolute living. Lyon 24: Ch probably drew Cook from real individual, Roger of Ware, whom he knew, though details are also typical of cooks in general. Lum 59-61: passage suggests Host-Cook antagonism resulting from trade rivalry.

38-9 Mus 242: philosophy of Cook is that of "a fool who sees life as a continuous jape."

45-64 Tupper, *JEGP*: trade rivalry embittered by fact that Host had inn in Southwark, outside of London, and thus could serve food to travelers; this was forbidden to innkeepers in City where victualers had monopoly. Lumiansky: by jeering at Cook, Host puts himself in danger of exposure of his own shady practices; he recalls this later in *MancT* 69-75 when he warns Manciple against talking too much and antagonizing Cook.

46-52 Sp 132-3: description of shop shows Ch's unerring selection of telling details; "it is great art which can thus achieve its object with the minimum of means."

50-2 Sk 5, 128: insinuation that flies were mixed in parsley served in stuffing of Cook's geese.

THE COOK'S TALE

4365-4422

Perkin Reveler, apprentice to a London victualer, was a ladies' man, skilled at dancing, singing, gambling, and drinking. Finally, he asks for and receives certificate of apprenticeship and is released by master. He goes to live with a friend of similar tastes whose wife is a prostitute.

67	*gaillard* gay. *shawe* wood	10	*shende* corrupt	
83	*setten stevene* made a date	14	*leve* desist	
89	*chaffare* business	15	*lowke* accomplice	
93	*abye* pay for	17	*brybe* steal	
95	*convertible* interchangeable	21	*for contenance* for appear-	
01	*snybbed* chided		ances	
04	*papir* certificate of com-pleted apprenticeship			

65-22 Lyon 98-9: Perkin is traditional type of bad apprentice, whose idleness leads to riot, gambling, lechery, and finally theft (compare Geo. Barnwell in Geo. Lillo's play *The London Merchant,* 1731). Shel 251: Perkin seems headed for criminality, but has appealing vigor of young animal, full of life and high spirits. Sp 133: despite brevity of fragment, Ch creates amazingly vivid character in Perkin.

77 ManCT 562: *ridyng* was usual term for any procession, *Chepe* (Cheapside) being main street in heart of City and favorite scene for processions.

04-11 Call: *papir* means certificate of completed apprenticeship and release from indenture, not "account books"; *he* (4404) refers to Perkin, not master; thus passage means that Perkin asked for his certificate which master, to get rid of him, granted.

21-2 Pres 197: "Ch goes as far as the door of the brothel, and then turns," since he is temporarily tired of low-life tales.

The Man of Law's Tale

COMMENTARIES: Gr 198-201; Ham 277-83;/ Don 911-3; ManCT 563-74; Rob 689-97; Sk 5, 132-68;/ Baum 115-8; Brew 147-50; Bron 115; Cow 16, 70, 156-7; Cur 164-94; Dem 93; Ev 139-40, 151; Fr 220-33; Kit 168-9; Law 100-5; Lum 61-71; Pres 203-4; Root 181-8, 288; Schlauch, *Ch's Constance and Accused Queens* (N.Y., 1927); Shel 266-9; TatDC 187; Tup 104;/ Baum, *MLN*, 49, 12-14, and *PMLA*, 56, 225-46; Beichner, *Spec*, 48, 70-5; Block, *PMLA*, 48, 572-616; Bowen, *MLN*, 56, 165; Brown, *SP*, 37, 8-35; Browne, *MLN*, 08, 53; Cowling, *RES*, 26, 311-7; Curry, *JEGP*, 23, 347-68; Curtiss, *JEGP*, 27, 24-32; Duffey, *ELH*, 47, 181-93; Edwards, *PQ*, 40, 306-9 (W); Jones, *JEGP*, 25, 512-47; Kimpel, *ELH*, 53, 77-86; Knowlton, *JEGP*, 24, 83-93; Manly, *PBA*, 26, 95-113 (ST); McNeal, *MLN*, 38, 257-8; Root, *TLS*, 43, 43; Rose, *Cweal*, 40, 225-7; Schlauch, *SA*, 155-206, and *PQ*, 50, 402-12; Skeat, *MLR*, 10, 430-4; Smith, *JEGP*, 48, 343-51; Sullivan, *MLN*, 53, 1-8; Tupper, *Nation*, 14, 41, and *JEGP*, 34, 352-72; Yunk, *ELH*, 60, 249-61.

GENRE: Sentimental tale, with some elements of saint's legend, based on folk tale motif of the Calumniated Wife.

SOURCE: Nicholas Trivet's Anglo-Norman *Chronicle* (ca. 1335), with possibly some influence of John Gower's version of the story (also based on Trivet) in *Confessio Amantis*. The Prologue to line 121 and a few scattered lines in the Tale are paraphrased from Pope Innocent III's *De Contemptu Mundi*.

DATE: About 1390.

VERSE FORM: Prologue and Tale are in Rime Royal (7-line stanza of iambic pentameter, rimed a b a b b c c).

GENERAL CRITICISM: TatDC 187: unworldly and poetic tale, certainly not written for shrewd, prosaic Lawyer. Browne: tale quite in style of lawyer pleading in court. Knowlton agrees; lawyer not necessarily somber character—like Clerk he is shown as dignified in *Gen*

Prol, but shows humor and humanity in tale. Root 185-7: improbable tale with all defects of typical romance or saint's life, but beautiful personality of Constance raises it to true art; she sums up Christian virtues of humility, faith, hope, charity, makes the miraculous seem natural; to make us love and sympathize with such a perfect character is greater artistic triumph than creation of Criseyde. Tup 104: tale of false witness given to Lawyer whose profession was notorious in 14th century for falseness and deceit. Manly: tale sprinkled with narrator's rhetoric, not used dramatically, but apart from tale. Cow 16, 157: tale perhaps written as compliment to Constance of Castile, Ch's wife's mistress; heroine an "uncanonized saint," ideal of womanhood; pathetic comments and dialogue are Ch's own—"he dearly loved a pathetic story." Dem 93: Ch suppressed any dramatic irony in source (Trivet). Shel 266-7: tale has loose structure, gross improbabilities. Duffey: Ch omitted one third of Trivet, basically changed one third, retained one third, with additions and changes aimed at sharpening emotionalism, increasing probability, improving narrative technique; Ch adapted pious story, aiming mainly at sentimental tale with middle class appeal, repetitious, pedestrian, lacking psychological realism, suited to bourgeois Lawyer; Trivet's aristocratic, educated Constance changed to "young, suffering, helpless heroine," passive, static, pathetic throughout, appealing to sentiment rather than piety (as in saints' lives). Smith: Ch's changes in Trivet tend to discourage identification of heroine with Constance of Castile, since his loyalties were divided between king, John of Gaunt, Constance (Gaunt's wife), and Katherine Swynford (Gaunt's mistress, and Ch's sister-in-law). Block: skillful condensation of Trivet, with humanizing, imaginative touches, "superb craftsmanship," rhetorical embellishment, resulting in "poem as emotional and solemn as it is dignified and exalted," saturated with piety; only 18% of tale is close following of Trivet, Ch omitting all irrelevant matter, centering tale on Constance with economy and directness, though (despite vivid details) she remains "too perfect to be a credible human being." Beichner: Ch's art shown in stress on canonical aspects of Sultan's marriage with Constance, fitting Lawyer. Baum, *MLN:* Ch tried to minimize absurdities of story by adding scriptural and astrological matter to account for improbabilities, adding rhetorical outbursts like mock heroic ones in

NPT, adding humorous touches. Schlauch, *PQ:* Trivet heightened pathos of traditional tale; but Ch, aware of defects, added humorous and burlesque touches. Brew 147-50: tale not a failure, cautiously and carefully written pious legend, enriched with Ch's understanding of impossibilities. Lum 68-71: sentimental tale, fitting middle class Lawyer, rather than romance; Lawyer tells it as though pleading before jury, with emotional appeals, scriptural quotations, apostrophes, etc. Baum 115-8: Ch's artistry improved Trivet's "preposterously improbable" story, but did not go far enough to make it first rate. Cur 191: tale has unity of character and careful workmanship unusual for Middle Ages. Yunk: Ch changed Trivet's aggressive, preaching Constance to more passive, feminine, "almost childlike receptacle and instrument of divine guidance"; tale has strong homiletic purpose (possibly first meant for Pr) with providential theme (477-83), stress on need for God's protection in 470-6, 484-90, 639-40, 932-45 (all akin to early Christian prayer used in legends of martyrs), with God as real protagonist.

INTRODUCTION TO THE MAN OF LAW'S TALE
II, 1-38
Host calculates that quarter of day has passed, warns against wasting time, and calls on Man of Law for a tale.

2	*artificial day* daylight hours	30	*Malkynes* generic name for	
5	*eightetethe* 18th		wanton woman	
10	*wit* knowledge	32	*mowlen* decay	
15	*plighte* pulled (plicchen)	34	*forward* promise	
		38	*devoir* duty	

20-32 Fr 220:   Host's "little sermon" on wasting time.
25-8 Sk 5, 134-5:   Host probably wrong in attributing this saying to Seneca.
33-8 Lum 63:   Host, not realizing Lawyer has high rank of Sergeant, calls him simply Man of Law, but sprinkles speech with legal terms (*forward, submytted, free assent, cas, acquiteth, devoir,* etc.)—"Harry intends to leave no doubt that he can address a professional man in the proper professional terms."

39-98

Lawyer agrees, but says Chaucer has already told all the best stories in halting rimes, including love tales in *Book of the Duchess* and *Legend of Good Women*, though he rightly avoided tales of horror and incest. Lawyer will tell a plain tale in prose.

46	*thrifty* profitable		88	*unkynde* unnatural
73	*hals* neck		95	*hawebake* plain fare

45-96 Knowlton: Lawyer knows Ch and is indulging in friendly banter, with no real contradiction in shift from adverse to favorable comment on Ch; also, his statement that he will speak prose fits situation since in comparison to adept Ch his verse will seem like prose. Sullivan: Lawyer is fictitious character whose remarks on Ch and Gower are not to be taken at face value; rather, the errors in them are satire on Lawyer's pretended wisdom which would be clear and comic to Ch's audience. Kimpel: no evidence that Lawyer recognized Ch; tone of criticism implies he did not.

45-55 Root 181: depreciation of Ch's skill is poet's "half-humorous modesty," not dramatic presentation of Lawyer's opinion. Sullivan: disparaging remarks show Lawyer as pretentious and condescending, are not to be taken as Ch's own opinion of himself. Lum 64-5: possibly Lawyer alone recognizes Ch and pokes fun at him; germ of dramatic antagonism which is not developed.

61-76 Sullivan: lawyer lists 7 or 8 women *not* treated by Ch in *LGW*, omits 2 who are; Ch is here satirizing Lawyer's pretended knowledge.

77-96 Lum 65-6: complimentary passage is complete reversal from earlier jokes about Ch's lack of skill (45-55).

77-85 Sk 5, 140: both tales of incest were included by John Gower in *Confessio Amantis;* passage thus seems to be a fling at Gower. Bowen: reference to incest may not apply to Gower, but to folk tale of Incestuous Father (of which *MLT* is a variant), very popular in 14th century; Ch did not want to mix this theme with religious tale. 85 Sullivan: this detail not in Gower; humor in pompous Lawyer's confusion and "blunder in accusing Ch's 'moral Gower' of immorality"; Gower may not have appreciated joke and therefore removed compliment to Ch in revising *Confessio Amantis*.

96-8 Tupper, *JEGP:* suggests Lawyer was originally supposed to tell prose *Mel* (use of epithet *thrifty* in 46 and 1165 supports this); "one of Ch's chief oversights in revision." Lum 66-7: passage leads us to expect start of tale, but instead we get Prologue first—failure to revise.

THE PROLOGUE OF THE MAN OF LAW'S TALE

99-133

Poverty causes many miseries and encourages many sins. Rich merchants are very fortunate. Also, they carry news from afar; here is a tale one of them told me.

04 *maugree thyn heed* in spite of your head (all that you can do)
05 *despence* expenses
08 *wytest* blame
11 *gleede* live coal
15 *selve* own
24 *ambes as* 2 aces, a losing throw at dice
25 *sys cynk* 5 and 6 (11), a winning throw

99-33 Tupper, *Nation:* Prologue on theme of Impatient Poverty (as much a vice as a virtue) is linked with sin of Envy which was related in popular mind with occupations of both merchants and lawyers. Brew 147: Prologue has nothing to do with tale of Constance, "a lack of unity reminiscent of Ch's earlier work." Lum 67: Prologue on poverty (as unmitigated evil) does not fit tale since Constance's "hardships do not result primarily from poverty."
31-3 Lum 67: "for the second time, the way is cleared for the tale."

THE MAN OF LAW'S TALE, PART I

134-203

Rich Syrian merchants, trading in Rome, hear reports of wondrous beauty and virtue of Constance, the emperor's daughter. They see her, and on their return to Syria they tell Sultan about her. Sultan falls in love with their description of her, perhaps fated by stars from birth.

35	*sadde* sober	47	*herbergage* lodging
36	*wyde-where* far and wide	68	*fredam* generosity
38	*chaffare* merchandise	71	*han doon fraught* have
39	*deyntee* pleasure. *chaffare*		caused to be loaded
	trade	81	*regnes* kingdoms
44	*message* messenger	85	*ceriously* minutely

45 Baum 118: though Ch's style is generally smooth and competent, there are several unhappy "lighthearted insets" which clash, such as *this is the ende* here, and again in 255, 965.

85 Baum, *PMLA:* pun on *ceriously* (seriously and minutely, in detail).

94-7 Duffey: here and in 309-15 Ch adds astrological lore which "eases the reader's acceptance of the whole improbable plot by glossing it in the equivalent of popular scientific terms."

204-245

Sultan puts problem to his council. They see only one answer: marriage. Sultan decides to marry Constance, even though this means that he and his vassals (Mohammedans) must become Christian. Arrangements are made with emperor and pope at Rome.

09	*hye* haste	36	*mawmettrie* Mohammedan-
14	*abusioun* deceit		ism
32	*dilatacioun* diffuseness	43	*founden* provided

04-31 ManCT 567: medieval Christians viewed all heathens as idolaters whose chief god or prophet was *Mahoun;* Ch was not bothered by fact that Mahomet was only a child at time of historical events in tale. Block: anachronistic references to Mahomet and Koran (332), not in Trivet, are Ch's attempts to add local color and realism easily understood by audience. Beichner: Lawyer views proposed marriage of Christian and Mohammedan as problem in canon law. Lum 68-9: Ch added privy council debate of legal problem (not in Trivet), showing that he consciously suited tale to teller.

246-322
Constance and her entourage prepare to sail for Syria, with great grief at parting. The positions of stars are unfavorable for voyage; why did the emperor not realize this? Constance leaves.

47	*purveiance* providing	02	*tortuous* oblique
59	*gree* favor. *viage* voyage	08	*weyved* forced
71	*condicioun* character	12	*eleccioun* chosen time
77	*out-taken* except	13	*namely* especially
85	*no fors* no matter. *spille* die	14	*roote* "epoch," time (of
96	*sweigh* motion		birth)

60-87 Shel 268-9: shows "true artist's patience and loving care for detail."

72-3 Lum 70: accepted antifeminist view from conservative Lawyer.

81-7 Lum 69-70: Constance's unquestioning obedience to authority of parents, husbands (see 842-3) is possibly preparation for discussion of *maistrye* in marriage which comes later in *CT*.

95-17 Curry: Constance's horoscope (position of stars at birth), added by Ch to Trivet, is exact and integral to whole tale, showing Constance doomed to unfortunate marriages, troubles, and death, unless protected by divine intervention; she is repeatedly saved from star-fated death by God; Ch shows laws of astrology as valid, but ultimately subject to God's will; here he makes astrology serve artistic purpose in re-creating tale which was already fixed in outline. Curtiss disagrees with Curry, argues horoscope refers to position of stars at time of voyage, not at birth, reveals inconsistencies in details; artistic purposes required only suggestion of evil influences (Mars, etc.) at work against Constance.

323-385
Evil mother of Sultan calls her loyal private council and states she will never give up her religion. She will pretend to accept baptism, but plans to murder Christians. (Women, following Eve, are often instruments of Satan.) She visits Sultan, says she will receive baptism,

and invites Constance and whole entourage to a feast. Sultan is pleased.

28	*in-feere* together	54	*quite* pay back
31	*lete* give up	65	*thilke* that very
34	*heete* promise	69	*fordoon* destroy
40	*reneyed* denied. *creance*	72	*warye* curse (warien)
	faith	76	*lay* law
47	*fonde* provide	77	*fonge* seize
52	*coold water* baptism		

58-64 Duffey: apostrophe added by Ch to sharpen highly emotional climax; here Ch "launches forth in his own person."

PART II

386-437

Constance arrives in Syria and is greeted by Sultan. Sultan's mother gives feast at which the Sultan and all Christians except Constance are treacherously stabbed to death.

88	*sonde* message	22	*spreynd* sprinkled
91	*agayn* to meet	24	*fyn* end
94	*yfeere* together	30	*tohewe* hewed in pieces.
04	*goost* spirit		*stiked* stabbed
06	*caste* plans		

438-504

Constance is cast adrift in a small boat. For over 3 years she drifts in the Mediterranean, through the straits into the Atlantic, preserved from death by miracle.

38	*foot-hoot* hastily	66	*bayte* bite
48	*steere* steersman	79	*triacle* remedy
51	*cleere* shining. *auter* altar	01	*sanz* without (Fr: sans)
57	*oonly* alone	04	*foyson* plenty
60	*flemere* banisher		

49-62 Pres 204: prayer (added by Ch) shows "clarity of the medieval religious vision."

60 Sk 5, 155: allusion to supposed power of cross over evil spirits. Ev 139-40: Ch probably used alliteration here since it was so common a device in ME religious poetry that he felt it would help to create fitting mood for Constance's prayer.

70 Duffey: here Ch uses "greatness of God's power to explain certain unlikelihoods," as again in account of voyage to England and in 932-8 (not in Trivet).

505-580

Constance finally lands near castle in Northumberland where she is received kindly by constable and wife. She converts wife (Hermengyld) to Christianity, then the constable himself. Constable commands castle in absence of King Alla.

05	*oure occian* Atlantic	34	*payens* pagans
06	*oure see* North Sea	40	*route* assemble
07	*nempnen* name	43	*plages* regions
17	*twynne* separate	57	*furlong wey* 2½ minutes
20	*algates* anyhow	72	*lay* law
23	*sonde* sending		

19 McNeal: unique parallel to Constance's speaking Latin in Boccaccio's *Decameron,* V, 2, suggests (along with other general similarities) that Ch used Boccaccio's story of Gostanza or its source. Duffey: *a maner Latyn corrupt* actually would have been Constance's native tongue, whereas Trivet has her miraculously speaking Saxon; stanzas on fate of Christian Britons (540-53) also show Ch's desire to give tale historical support.

35 Block: stress on Hermengyld's intense love for Constance makes her later conversion more convincing.

581-679

Young knight, foiled in attempt to seduce Constance, murders Hermengyld and plants knife on Constance. King Alla returns and Constance is tried, accused by young knight. While swearing on Bible, knight is miraculously struck down and a voice (God) states Constance's innocence.

84 *quite hir while* repay her
    time (or trouble)
91 *despit* spitefulness
96 *forwaked* exhausted with
    watching
14 *agryse* tremble
20 *berth on hond* accuses false-
    ly

28 *motyf* idea
33 *starf* died
36 *kithe* show
37 *swithe* quickly
46 *prees* crowd
49 *bistad* beset, endangered
67 *fet* fetched
79 *wreche* vengeance

31-68 Sk 5, 157: a beautiful addition by Ch.

45-51 Duffey: almost only sharp, realistic passage in tale, "one of
the few touches obtained by asking the reader to react to other than
literary stimuli." Pres 203: "a remarkable expression of terror" in
repetition of *face* which "conveys the appearance and reappearance
of the pallor of the man as he is led to execution." Ev 151: best thing
in tale. Lum 69: vivid picture of courtroom scene comes naturally
from Lawyer.

59-61 Block: here Ch effectively humanizes the king.

680-714

Guilty knight is executed. Alla is converted and weds Constance
against wishes of his evil mother Donegild.

00 *make* mate, wife
01 *stree* straw

08 *skile* reasonable

08-14 Baum, *MLN:* "gratuitous reference to connubiality of even
the holiest of women" is in very bad taste if Ch meant poem to be
read seriously. Lum 70: typically antifeminist comment by Lawyer.

715-756

Alla begets a son christened Mauricius who is born when Alla is
away fighting Scots. Constable sends message of birth to Alla, but
messenger stops at Donegild's. She gets him drunk and substitutes
forged letter saying child is a monster.

15 *knave* boy
24 *dooth forth come* has come
    forward

33 *sithe* times
43 *sadly* heavily

757-805
Alla grieves at false message but sends letter ordering that Constance
and child await his homecoming. Messenger on return trip stops
again at Donegild's; she substitutes letter ordering constable to set
Constance and child adrift again in boat.

73	*biwreyest* reveal, betray		95	*Up peyne* upon pain. *juyse*	
82	*mannysh* unwomanly			justice	
89	*underpighte* stuffed		05	*cast* planned	
90	*fnorteth* snores				

60-3 Yunk: Alla's passive acceptance matches Constance's.
62-3 ManCT 569: lines do not seem to belong in letter.
86 Edwards: *kynges moodres court* is Knaresborough Castle in
Trivet and Gower, a place ill-famed for treasonous acts, having sheltered Becket's murderers in 1170; Ch omitted name because castle
was now owned by his patron John of Gaunt, whose wife was Constance, and who had been accused of treason in early 1380's.

806-875
Constable receives falsified order and regretfully carries it out amid
general grief of the people. After prayers, Constance sets sail.

07	*nexte* nearest	42	*eggement* instigation	
19	*shames deeth* death of shame	52	*refut* refuge	
33	*steere* rudder	68	*blisseth hire* crossed herself	
37	*breyde* snatched	72	*heryed* praised	

20-68 Root 183: "sublimely beautiful lines" showing resignation
and trust in God—added by Ch. Brew 149: "nothing more exquisite"
in all Ch. Baum 117: Ch takes pains to make us sympathize with
Constance's sufferings.

PART III

876-899
Alla returns and discovers treachery. Messenger is tortured, reveals
all. Alla kills Donegild and mourns Constance.

79 *colde* grow cold   86 *biknowe* confess. *plat*
                                        bluntly

900-952

After drifting for over 5 years, Constance lands near pagan castle. Steward of castle attempts to rape her, but in struggle falls overboard and is drowned. Through miraculous strength, Constance escapes and sails through Strait of Gibraltar.

10 *in point to spille* in danger   24 *unwemmed* unspotted
     of perishing   25 *luxurie* lechery
12 *gauren* stare   35 *maat* dead
15 *reneyed* denied   47 *Septe* Ceuta
17 *lemman* lover

04-45 Root 185: episode unconnected with what precedes and follows—structural defect.

953-987

Meanwhile, Roman emperor has avenged massacre of Christians by sending senator with army to ravage Syria. Sailing home, senator picks up Constance and child, brings them to Rome. Constance says nothing of her origin, lives as servant to senator's wife.

53 *throwe* short time   86 *lete* leave

988-1050

Some time later Alla comes to Rome to do penance for killing Donegild and is received by same senator. He sees boy (Maurice) who resembles Constance, and asks to see mother.

97 *herbergeours* providers of   21 *stounde* moment
     lodgings, harbingers   29 *prikke* point
99 *rood hym agayns* rode to   35 *sighte* sighed
     meet him   50 *unnethe* scarcely
14 *metes space* mealtime

37-1071 ManCT 570: passage added by Ch "in his characteristic psychologizing manner."

1051-1127

Alla and Constance are reunited. Alla explains forged letters; they are happy. At Constance's request, Alla arranges for her to meet her father, the emperor. General joy results. (In later years Maurice succeeded as emperor.)

60	*halwes* saints	91	*sente* as to send
88	*nyce* foolish	17	*lette* delay

70-1 Baum, *MLN:* a typically Chaucerian bit of levity, inappropriate here (see also 1127).

1128-1162

Alla, Constance, and Maurice return to England to live happily until Alla dies a year later. Constance returns with boy to Rome where she lives out her life in quietness and virtue.

28	*say* saw	37	*talent* desire
32	*heete* promise		

THE EPILOGUE OF THE MAN OF LAW'S TALE
1163-1190

Host praises tale, calls on Parson for next one. Parson deplores Host's swearing, and Host sneers at him as a Lollard. Shipman breaks in rudely to say he will not allow Parson to spoil fun, will tell a tale himself.

69	*can* know	89	*phislyas* (meaning uncertain,
75	*digne* worthy		perhaps "physik"—medicine,
76	*predicacioun* sermon		or "filas"—legal files or
80	*glosen* interpret		cases). *queinte* elaborate
83	*cokkel* weeds		

63-90 Root 188: rich humor and irony of showing worldly Host and Shipman as bitterest opponents of heresy. Don 913: passage designed to introduce tale of different kind than *MLT,* and to develop conflict between next teller and Parson.

65 Sk 5, 165: *thrifty* is unifying expression, referring back to line 46.

66-77 Lum 242: Parson refuses to be provoked, wins first round of Parson-Host controversy continued in Parson's Prologue.

66-9 Kit 168: Host violates good taste; in calling for serious tale "he swears like a pirate."

68-9 Lum 87: Host shows condescension of practical man toward supposedly impractical bookish man.

70-7 Kit 168: in reply to Parson's rebuke over swearing, Host jokingly accuses priest of being Lollard.

72-7 Root 288: Ch's humor in having Host suggest that "the one thoroughly worthy ecclesiastic in the company is a heretic."

78-90 Skeat: passage more fitted to Shipman than Squire, but became useless since Ch had no *ShipT* ready to follow. Jones: passage meant to precede *ShipT* as originally assigned to Wife of Bath (phrase *My joly body,* more suited to woman than man, is repeated in *ShipT* 423); Ch first planned to have Wife object here to preachment by Parson, then to launch into lines 1-193 of present Wife's Prologue (her vindication of sensual pleasures of marriage) as prelude to *ShipT,* developing debate on marriage and chastity with Parson, with Wife winning out. ManCT 573: speech is impossibly ill-suited to Squire (named here in some MSS). Tupper, *JEGP,* rejects both Squire and Summoner (as in some MSS) as speaker here; link written to connect *Mel* (originally assigned to Lawyer) with low-class *ShipT* (whether by Shipman or Wife); thus *philosophie, phislyas, termes queinte of lawe* in 1188-9 refer to legal and philosophical jargon in *Mel* rather than in *MLT.* Root: most probably written for Summoner, not Shipman. Fr 232-3: probably confusion in Ch's own papers over assignment of next tale. Law 103-5: speech well suited to Shipman whose tale should follow, thus rectifying sequence of localities in *CT.* Don 913 favors Wife as speaker, thus giving "coherence to the chosen order" of tales.

78-87 Kit 169: Shipman objects not to Lollardry, but to a sermon; he is "desperately afraid of being bored."

80-3 Lum 73: Shipman dislikes religious hairsplitting, prefers "comfortable acceptance of the fundamentals." ManCT 573: humor of lines in mouth of rascal (Shipman or Summoner) is "too exquisite to be lost."

88-9 ManCT 572: lines describe *Mel* well, but are wholly unsuited to *MLT.*

The Wife of Bath's Tale

COMMENTARIES: Gr 202-6; Ham 296-300;/ Don 913-6; ManCT 574-86; Rob 697-704; Sk 5, 291-322;/ Bald 109; Baum 133-4, 196; Brew 128-30, 160-4; Bron 62-3; Cog 141-50; Cow 167-9; Cur 91-118; Dem 59-61; Eisner, *Tale of Wonder: Source Study of WBT* (Wexford, Ireland, 1957)); Ev 145-7; Fr 272-84; Ger 72-80; Kit 185-92; Low 186-90; Lum 117-29; Mal 215-8; Maynadier, *WBT: Its Sources and Analogues* (London, 1901); Mus 204-13; Pat 221-2, 244-53; Pres 241-8; Root 231-44; Sedg 257-63, 290-3; Shel 215-24; Sp 136-49; Tho 89-94;/ Baum, *PMLA*, 56, 225-46; Bradley, *JEGP*, 56, 624-30; Coffman, *Spec*, 45, 43-50; Coomaraswamy, *Spec*, 45, 391-404; Curry, *PMLA*, 22, 30-51; Dempster, *MLN*, 42, 173-6; Francis, *PMLA*, 53, 1126-41; Hinckley, *PMLA* 17, 292-305 (W); Howard, *MP*, 60, 223-32; Huppé, *MLN*, 48, 378-81; Jones, *JEGP*, 25, 512-47; Kenyon, *JEGP*, 16, 282-8, and *MLN*, 39, 133-7; Kittredge, *MP*, 12, 435-67 (W, ST); Loomis, L., *SP*, 41, 14-33; Loomis, R., *Brown*, 129-48; Lowes, *MP*, 10-1, 305-34, and *PMLA*, 15, 342-58; Moore, *N&Q*, 46, 245-8, and *MLQ*, 49, 49-57; Owen, *JEGP*, 53, 294-311 (W, O); Pratt, *MLN*, 50, 243-6, and *Baugh*, 45-79; Rockwell, *N&Q*, 57, 84; Roppolo, *CE*, 51, 263-9; Schlauch, *PMLA*, 46, 416-30; Shumaker, *ELH*, 51, 77-89; Slaughter, *MLN*, 34, 83-5, and 50, 530-4; Tatlock, *Flügel*, 228-32, and *MLN*, 35, 294; Townsend, *MLR*, 54, 1-4; Train, *MLN*, 35, 85-7; Tupper, *Nation*, 13, 354-6, and *JEGP*, 14, 553-65; Whiting, *SA*, 207-68.

GENRE: Prologue is combination of confession (a traditional genre) and brilliant argument in favor of female sovereignty; tale is an exemplum of argument in Prologue, and is based on folk tale.

SOURCES AND ANALOGUES: Prologue is largely original in conception, but shows literary influences of ancient antifeminist tradition, including Theophrastus, *Golden Book of Marriages* (ca. 300 B.C.); Juvenal, *Sixth Satire* (ca. 50 A.D.); St. Jerome, *Against Jovinian* (*Adversus Jovinianum*, ca. 400); Walter Map, *Letter to Rufinus*

(*Epistola Valerii ad Rufinum,* ca. 1200); portraits of La Vieille (Old Woman) and Le Jaloux (jealous husband) in *RR* by Jean de Meun (ca. 1280); and Eustache Deschamps, *Miroir de Mariage* (1380's). For tale no direct source is known, but it is ultimately based on widespread folk theme of the Loathly Lady or Transformed Hag, and analogues survive in John Gower's *Confessio Amantis,* in the romance *The Wedding of Sir Gawain and Dame Ragnell,* and in fragmentary ballad *The Marriage of Sir Gawain.*

DATE: Probably about 1393-4.

GENERAL CRITICISM: Hin 262: W's "voluble confidences" in Prologue were doubtless stimulated by ale. Kit 171, 191-2: Ch created W to precipitate marriage debate, gave her 5 husbands and "monstrously heretical tenet as to the Subjection of Men." Lowes, *PMLA:* W is "magnificent abstract" of 7 Deadly Sins ("the Deadly but Delightful Seven—all their strength and all their sweetness rolled up into one ball"). Hinckley: most unifying theme in Prol and tale is "W's practical search for a 6th husband." Curry: W embodies, in physique and character, a "conflict in astral influence" (Venus and Mars) of which she is aware and makes capital (see 609-16). Root 232-4: Ch probably saw fallacy of celibacy as medieval ideal (see *MkT* 1924-64; *NPT* 3447-60), and through W he demolishes it with "almost revolutionary daring" (Renaissance spirit), allowing W to quote and refute St. Jerome; W glories in traits attacked in antifeminist monastic literature, and Ch "by his art forces us to take her point of view, and all but sympathize with her." Cow 167-9: Prol is superb, self-revealing characterization with especially excellent dialogue; W seems to express Ch's own view that virginity is impractical "for those who carry on the secular duties of the world." Leg 52: Prol is Ch's most original work. ManCT 574: Prol belongs to medieval literary and satiric convention of the "confession" (like Elizabethan dramatic soliloquy), in which character reveals intimate truths he would ordinarily never dream of expressing publicly. Low 182, 187: Ch took sheer delight in W, greatest of his characters, with her verve, raciness, inimitable speaking style; tale is old story "told with a felicity and clothed with a beauty it had never attained before." Sedg 263, 290: Prol too long, out of proportion; fine tale, but perhaps out of character for W. Pat 123, 146, 245-52: W is Ch's "most

whiche yifte what a gift   56   *kan* know
a *Goddes half* in G's name   60   *defended* forbade
brynne burn

193 Kenyon, *JEGP:* W's discussion of multiple marriage and
virginity is digression in main theme of woe in marriage which she
resumes at line 193. Jones: first argumentative part of Prol (to 193)
was originally preceded by Shipman's Prol plus transitional lines
(later omitted), the whole intended to introduce *ShipT* of woe in
marriage (first intended for W) which W promises Pard (172-4);
second, expository part of Prol (after 193) is very different in tone,
themes, sources. Shel 192: W's rejection of established marriage
doctrine, though perhaps hers and not Ch's, clearly anticipates
Renaissance individualism, faith in reason.

1-3 Kenyon, *JEGP:* this is W's direct response to *NPT,* especially
to *NPT* 3263-6 where Priest refers to *auctours,* and to fact that he
tells not of his own but of Chauntecleer's experience. Lum 121: W's
topic, *wo* in marriage, shows negative attitude—how to avoid misery.

9-25 Mus 209-10: by hearsay device in 9 Ch deftly overcomes problem of making W's Biblical learning seem plausible; further remarks
in 14, 19-25 enhance realistic effect—"naked textualism is swallowed
up by the dramatics of the delivery."

20-5 Pat 245-6: W is really puzzled by problem of why 5th man
wasn't a husband; there is "kind of humility as well as daring in the
tone of what she says."

45 Cog 148: no response from pilgrims—"not one was ready to
swim where 5 had drowned before."

46 Mus 206: W's "flatfootedness of assertion" here (also in 111-2,
147-51, 154, 423-5), which "can be heard in rhythm itself," is fine
individualizing device.

47-8 Howard: W is presently a widow. AHM: lines definitely show
5th husband is still alive, yet other passages suggest he is dead (see
7, 505, 525, 822-7)—a seeming inconsistency.

62-114
Virginity may be a higher spiritual state than marriage, but is imprac-

magnificent creation"; she is "militant suffragist rampant for her
rights" who ruins her case by exaggeration; she enjoys coarse language and euphemisms which "conceal nothing but, on the contrary,
frame the unmentionable with rococo delight"; Prol is not cynical
display of folly, but stresses W's robust vitality, "characteristic belief
in life." Shel 205, 215-24: Prol, dramatic monologue 500 years before
Browning, is "beyond all praise," unsurpassed for sheer artistry, rich
humor; W's opinions, based on experience, are her own even when
she cites authorities; brilliantly naturalistic, gradual unfolding of W's
character in rambling, disjointed, but dynamic, distinctive speech,
with huge gusto and fluency. Coffman: tale shows Ch's ironic sense
of incongruities in life and in courtly love convention. Moore notes
unique parallels to Prol in *Lamentations* of Matheolus which Ch
may have known in French version. Ches 157: huge Prol develops
W's "glorious and garrulous egotism," immense vitality. Cog 141-9:
as comic figure, Falstaff is W's only equal; she is "violently coarse
and derisive, thoughtfully theological and in a sense religious, very
restless, very overbearing, amazing in her self-knowledge, yet blind
as to whether it is love or power that she is really seeking"; Prol
shows Ch's narrative skill at best, full of racy, colloquial vigor, masterly shifts in tone, delayed climaxes. Mal 216-7: W not at home in
romance world of tale, which Ch gave her not because it suits her
character but because ending fits her views on marriage; with Ch,
tale, not teller, always came first, despite Kit; tale is only partially
adapted to W's style, not wholly integrated with Prol. Roppolo: W
distorts tale to prove female sovereignty, submerging knight's story
which points another moral (*gentilesse*); irony in fact that W "cannot qualify under her own definition of gentilesse." Sp 136-49: in
Prol W wins sympathy because opposed to "age-old theologically
sanctioned and authorized male prejudice and tyranny"—nature and
sense are largely on her side; W deftly uses scholastic method of
clerks to satirize their attitudes and exalt her own, coolly misapplying
Bible texts; continuous flow of subtly stylized gossip leads to superb
dramatic climax of fight with Jankyn ("grand buffoonery"). Ger
76-80: perfect dramatic adaptation of tale to W's character and speech
habits—"there never was a clearer case to illustrate the suspension of
disbelief"; irony in Prol of making arch-wife reveal marriage perils

so devastatingly; W is beautifully integrated, believable despite contradictions; she gives eloquent argument, but is really "controlled by instinct and feeling rather than by reason," proves nothing "except that women can subjugate their menfolk if they will make the effort." Pres 241-8: less evil, more complex than Pard, W is no heretic, but "content to remain an imperfect Christian"; in tale she "comfortably identifies herself" with hag whom Ch makes as human as possible for W's sake. Brew 161-4: in Prol W's assertion of rights is itself superb satire on women, "glorious comedy of wifely oppression"; we "quail before her insatiable appetite, her incessant talk, her joyously predatory vitality"; in tale, one of Ch's best, W's coarseness contrasts delightfully with graceful charm of story, religious-legal doctrine of male supremacy with courtly love doctrine of obedience to lady. Owen: tale allows W to burlesque unrealistic romance conventions, indulge in wish-fulfillment (old woman-young husband, magic transformation); it also unconsciously reflects contrast between her marriage theory and practice in Prol. Townsend: only ½ of tale is narrative, rest echoes tone and substance of Prol; knight is original characterization, "kind of young fellow who could commit rape and still be the darling of the ladies"—he is W's dream-man, just as hag is W herself. Ev 145-7: W's rambling, illogical, idiosyncratic speech in Prol is amazingly lifelike, as though "echoes of some living voice to which Ch had listened with delight and critical intentness." Lum 119-29: W's chief traits, aggressiveness and amorousness, lead to perfectly unified argument on female sovereignty in Prol ("a masterful piece of dialectic"); but she is unaware that "audience can very easily equate her present situation with that of her first 3 husbands, whom she held up to such ridicule." Bradley: throughout Prol Ch uses ironic contrast between ideal wisdom of medieval "mirror" literature (W repeatedly refers to wisdom) and W's shameless worldly lore, so that Prol becomes ironic "mirror for marriage," with orthodox Christian values "just discernible within her garbled discourse"; W's admired "wit" is only a "refinement of deceit," her wisdom ironically shown through imagery of nonrational creatures—cat (348-56), horse (386-7), lioness (637), magpie and nightingale (456-9), spaniel and goose (267-70), etc. Mus 204-13:

following pattern of La Vieille in *RR*, Ch presents W
"philosophic naturalism") naturalistically, improving
Meun's technique of dramatic monologue; W's folksy,
makes for illusion of solid reality, while Ch manages to
a vast amount of learned matter "under a realistic disgu
this by using much that was already familiar or proverbia
W bring in learned matter as *told* to her, by bold use o
monologues (by old husbands, Jankyn)—result is "stylistic
Baum 133-4: Ch successfully maintains fairyland atmospher
out, without any jarring realism to break spell; rationally, a
setting, tale is thoroughly immoral (rapist wins lady by a
trick question). Don 914-6: W's portrait in Prol satirizes ti
antifeminist view of women because W (epitome of that
"monstrous perversion of what experience shows" to be true;
also weaves in traits that show W as "precisely what exp
teaches," so that women too are satirized, and Ch has it both
yet W's positive zest for life adds another dimension—she is mor
"enormously funny parody of a woman invented by woman-h
and becomes "a high and gallant symbol of a humanity in w...
weakness and fortitude are inextricably mingled"; tale's analogues
aim to show courtesy of hero, but W's hero is "convicted rapist,"
reluctant bridegroom, whose reformation proves W's point of woman's potential if allowed to dominate.

THE WIFE OF BATH'S PROLOGUE

III, 1-61

Having had 5 husbands, I am qualified to speak of woe in marriage. Scriptures do not forbid successive marriages; we are told to multiply. Solomon, Abraham, Jacob, etc., had more than one wife.

1	*auctoritee* authoritative text	27	*expres* clearly (adv.)
5	*on lyve* alive (petrified dative)	33	*bigamye* marrying 2 husbands in succession. *octogamye* marrying 8 husbands
16	*repreeve* reproof		
26	*devyne* guess. *glosen* interpret	35	*heere* hear. *daun* Lord
		37	*leveful* permissible

tical for most people. Virginity is for those few who aspire to perfection—certainly it is not for me!

70	*with the dede* in so doing	89	*tow* tinder
75	*dart* prize	92	*freletee* frailty
84	*repreve* sin	96	*preferre* be preferable to
85	*make* mate, husband	01	*tree* wood
86	*withouten excepcion* not excepting	10	*foore* footsteps

62-162 Kit 186: W's first heresy is contempt for celibate ideal of Church (though she pays lip service to it), but her expression is so jovial that pilgrims do not take offense. Root 234-5: despite playful tone, W's argument is sound—Ch is at least half in earnest. Tho 94: harangue on virginity is so pointed it may represent Ch's own rejection of celibate ideal.

05-10 Pat 246: W's logic is delightful and unassailable.

115-162

If all were meant to be virgins, why were we given sexual organs? I will certainly use mine freely; I have no envy of virginity.

27	*ese* pleasure	48	*precius* finicky
32	*sely* blessed	51	*daungerous* standoffish
36	*harneys* equipment	54	*lette* deny
44	*hoten* be called		

163-192

(Pardoner interrupts W to say he was planning to wed, but now has doubts. W replies that he hasn't yet heard half of the woe in marriage. Pardoner urges her to continue.)

67	*what* why	77	*abroche* broach, tap
68	*to-yeere* never	80	*war* warned
70	*tonne* cask	87	*praktike* technique

63-92 Moore: Pard's interruption gives W idea for second part of Prol (terrifying picture of woe in marriage) which is both direct answer to Pard's question and brilliant burlesque of antifeminist literature and official Church view of marriage—a "penetrating critique."

63-8 Pat 164-5: eunuch Pard's interruption is "hardened bluff" showing his great insecurity, "piercingly sad." Lum 207-8: Pard interrupts W's heresy to test depth of worldliness affected by listening pilgrims; since no one joins in his objections he will feel safe in revealing his own vices; eunuch Pard poses as prospective bridegroom —"an amazingly shrewd way of pointing to her [W] as a breaker of established rules for behavior in marriage." Baum 48: Pard makes a fool of himself with this joke. Cur 70: eunuch Pard's last, empty boast which knowing pilgrims allow to pass unchallenged.

70-1 Hin 159: W suggests Pard has already been drinking, through use of *tonne* metaphor.

75 Kit 188: here W introduces second "heretical doctrine of a startling kind" which is real subject of Prol—female sovereignty.

84-7 Lum 208-9: here Pard shows W as experienced person misleading youths with unorthodox views; he invites pilgrims to object (*spareth for no man*) in further test of their tolerance.

92 Kittredge: jovial W says she speaks in jest, but whole Prol is rude attack on meek Clerk who bides his time.

193-234

Of my husbands 3 were good and 2 were bad. The first 3 were old and rich; I wore them out with love-making, and thus got them to give me their property. I nagged them into submission as follows:

95	*tho* those	20	*fawe* eager
98	*unnethe* scarcely	26	*bere hem wrong on honde*
03	*tolde of it no stoor* gave them no credit		put them in the wrong
		29	*by* for
08	*tolde no deyntee* set no value	32	*cow* chough (gossipy bird)
17	*fet* fetched		

235-302

"You old fool, why don't you buy me decent clothes? Why do you chase other women? You get drunk and preach to me of the wickedness of wives. You say we nag our husbands and show our vices once we are wed—there should be trial marriages."

35	*kaynard* fool	68	*hire to chepe* do business with her
41	*rowne* whisper		
47	*with yvel preef* bad luck to you!	72	*his thankes* willingly
		73	*lorel* wretch
49	*costage* expenses	77	*welked* withered
50	*parage* parentage	87	*bacyns* basins. *lavours* lavers (wash bowls)
54	*holour* lecher		

35-378 Moore: this "curious dramatic monologue" becomes mock-sermon against matrimony.

35-41 Mus 210-1: Ch here uses "sample" monologue to extend scope of W's remarks "without violating her personality."

42-378 Mus 234-5: Ch carries "sample" monologue device a step farther by this bold dramatic passage given as W's *invention* of what husbands said, allowing him to work in a mass of learned anti-feminist literature in natural-seeming way, blending with W's "boisterous feminism."

85-91 Mus 208: Ch chose this Theophrastus passage because its "magnificent immediacy" blends well with "list of common things which we have already seen in the web of the W's ordinary speech."

303-378

"You suspect me falsely of an affair with our apprentice; you hide your money from me. You should be generous and trust me. A man who spies on his wife or tries to keep her at home is a fool. You say that a shrewish wife is the worst evil man must endure."

15	*maugree thyne yen* in spite of your (spying) eyes	40	*enforce thee* support your argument
19	*leve* believe	44	*perree* jewelry
21	*kep* notice	46	*rubriche* interpretation
27	*who hath . . . in honde* who rules	56	*borel* coarse wool cloth
		59	*warde-cors* bodyguard
29	*what thar thee* why is it necessary to thee to	61	*make his berd* deceive him. *thee* prosper
33	*werne* forbid	76	*shende* destroy

33-5 Bradley: lighted candle, traditionally a symbol of wisdom and virtue in "mirror" literature, is here perverted into argument for marital infidelity.

379-452

I assured my old husbands that they spoke thus when drunk; all was false, but served to put them in the wrong. I would also get money from them by withholding my favors in bed. I won every argument by refusing to give in, or by pretending to love them.

80	*baar on honde* convinced	07	*namely* especially
88	*spilt* ruined	18	*bacon* old meat
89	*grynt* grinds	22	*quitte* paid
91	*blyve* quickly	33	*ba* kiss
96	*wende* imagined. *chiertee* affection	35	*spiced conscience* tender disposition
98	*dighte* lay with	49	*tooth* sexual desire
02	*kyndely* naturally		

98 Baum: pun on *dighte* (lay with, and dressed—in view of W's complaint over her shabby clothes in 356).

33 AHM: probable pun on *ba* (kiss, and sound made by sheep mentioned in previous line).

35 Rockwell: *sweete spiced conscience* means bland, gentle disposition; contrasts with *spiced conscience* of *Gen Prol* 526, meaning peppery, easily aroused indignation.

453-502

My 4th husband was a young rascal, had a sweetheart on the side. In those days I danced and drank, which aroused my desires. I had a wonderful time in youth; now that is gone, but I will still be merry. I got back at 4th husband, torturing him with jealousy. He died and I buried him cheaply.

56	*joly as a pye* gay as a magpie	67	*vinolent* drunk. *defence* resistance

72	*boote* good	92	*wrong* pinched
74	*envenyme* poison	96	*ygrave* buried. *roode beem*
75	*pith* strength		beam which supports a cross
79	*fonde* manage		(in church)

55-68 Lum 127: W's charms are fading; she needs wine to support sexual powers.

69-80 Sp 141: "we are suddenly made conscious of the profound and rich humanity of the W of Bath as a complete Chaucerian character"; pun on *flour* in 477 (flour, and flower).

69-73 Kit 188-9: "one of the great dramatic utterances of human nature"—almost sublime. Low 189: these lines are "Ch himself to the core."

74-9 Root 237: W's fear of old age, her forced gaiety and bravado (especially in 479), shows profound sadness which underlies whole Prol, also reveals Ch's moral balance, his realization that "unstinted gratification of sense is not the road to happiness."

76-8 Shel 222: "her old pagan heart is as stout as ever"; she will "find zest even in selling the bran."

81-2 Dem 81: ironical reversal that 4th husband is "exactly what she had accused his predecessors of being."

84 Baum: pun on *croce* (stick to beat him, and cross for him to bear).

503-626

My 5th husband was a wonderful lover, but standoffish to me. He was a clerk, boarding at my friend Alisoun's house, and I married him for love. Once when my 4th husband was in London I walked with clerk Jankyn, told him that I would wed him if my husband died. When this happened, Jankyn was one of the pall-bearers. He was young and handsome and, since I am a sensual and aggressive type (born under Venus & Mars), I had to have him.

17	*wayte what* whatever	56	*vigilies* festivals on eves or
29	*gossib* friend		vigils of saints' days
51	*leyser* leisure	59	*wered upon* wore (put on).
53	*grace* destiny		*gytes* clothes

61 *frete* ate
66 *of my purveiance* with fore-
    sight
69 *bobance* boast
77 *mette* dreamed
78 *upright* on my back

87 *beere* bier
02 *coltes tooth* strong sex de-
    sire
04 *seel* birthmark
06 *bigon* made

03-14 Cog 146: "only Ch and Shakespeare can compound a poetry in which comedy takes its strength from tragedy"; W has come close to disaster, though she wins in end.

14 Baum: pun on *daungerous* (standoffish, and dangerous—in view of later fight over manuscript).

16 Baum: obscene pun on *queynte* (strange, and pudendum).

51-8 Tupper, *Nation:* Venus (W's star) was ruling star of pilgrimages.

59-62 Sp 143: W's fresh clothes challenge Biblical warning that "on earth moth and rust corrupt."

65 Baum: pun on *daliance* (talk, and sport or amorous toying).

72-3 AHM: pun on *leek* (leek, and leak), with additional suggestion of sexual image (compare *RvT* 3878-9).

85-6 Mus 206: W's gossiping "finally strangles the narrative and makes her lose the thread of her argument completely"—fine realistic touch.

87-05 Sp 143: W at husband's funeral based on popular comic tradition of "profane figure piously disguised."

03-20 Cur 91-118: W is conscious of astrological influences (horoscope in Taurus with Venus and Mars in conjunction) which molded her character; Taurus makes her thickset, amorous, inconstant, gossipy; if Venus alone is in Taurus she will be beautiful, voluptuous but chaste, delicate, imaginative, gay, fond of travel; but Mars casts evil influences (especially in Taurus), making her ugly, lascivious, semi-fat, adulterous, aggressive; all of these influences are reflected by birthmarks; W is thus a split personality through conflicting powers of Venus and Mars, her coarseness partly a mask to hide bitterness; in tale she gives expression to Venerean love of beauty and imagination wholly consistent with character, with pathos in her yearning for *gentilesse;* astrological background, instantly clear to medieval audience, is only part of complex creation, but W is perhaps Ch's "most tragic figure because . . . she is the most nearly completely human."

14 Root 235-8: line masterfully points up W's unconscious conviction that her way of life is not the right one; despite gaiety, she is unhappy, restless. Low 189: "a cry which sums up half the passion and pain of the world." Slaughter, *MLN,* 34: W realizes Church disapproved multiple marriage and excessive intercourse within marriage. Shel 222: an "immortal line" coming suddenly as "a sigh from the depths." Sp 144: conflict between Church's moral law and W's natural law (explained by astrology) "gives rise to that cry from the natural heart." Bald 109: W's "puzzled acknowledgement that something is amiss."

627-710

A month after funeral Jankyn wedded me and I gave him my property; we quarreled bitterly. He told me Roman and Biblical stories of punishment of wicked wives. He had a book in which he constantly read to me accounts of evil women. Clerks never speak well of women.

28	*hende* pleasant		55	*salwes* willow twigs
33	*suffre* allow. *list* desire		59	*sett noght an hawe* cared
34	*lyst* ear			not a bit (haw)
40	*sworn* forbidden		65	*forbere* put up with
42	*geestes* histories		92	*peyntede the leon* told fable
45	*open-heveded* bare headed.			of lion
	say saw		96	*mark* likeness. *redress* make
52	*faste* firmly			good

27-10 Slaughter, *MLN,* 50: marriage to widow prevented a man from taking clerical orders—added motive for Jankyn to torment W and for pilgrim Clerk to resent her (see Envoy of *ClT*).

27-31 Dem 81: ironic reversal of situation in W's first 3 marriages, a fact of which she seems only dimly aware.

34-6 Cog 147: deafness is "the legacy of her only love."

41-785 Tup 112-3: Jankyn's anthology really reflects common medieval view of women as inferior and basically evil, fleshly thorns in lives of men.

69-785 Mus 212-3:   here again Ch uses hearsay device to make learned antifeminist literature seem to come naturally from unlearned W. 88-91 Law 138 thinks this is attack not on Clerk but on Nun's Priest who has satirized women in tale (sees *NPT* as preceding *WBT* in order of tales).

711-828

One night he read me a long series of tales of bad women: Eve, Delilah, Xanthippe, Pasiphae, Clytemnestra, etc. Finally, I tore 3 pages out of his book and knocked him into the fireplace. He then hit me on the head, and I fell to the floor as if dying. When he kneeled down to kiss me at my request, I hit him on the cheek. At last we came to an agreement: I was to have control of the property and he burned his book. Since then, we have never disagreed.

13	*sire* husband		88	*fyne* cease
19	*expres* clearly		90	*plyght* plucked
21	*tho* then		99	*breyde* waked
43	*ouche* clasp		06	*wyte* blame
46	*sory grace* death		09	*wreke* avenged
61	*herte despitus* broken hearts	15	*hond* acts
81	*that* what			

27-32 Mus 208-9: Ch alters this story from St. Jerome to make it more domestic, concrete, to harmonize with W's folksy speech.

65-71 Pratt, *MLN:* Ch adapts these incidents from John of Salisbury's *Policraticus,* reshaping them as gruesome crimes of wicked wives.

88-93 Mus 212-3: symbolic meaning of domestic squabble—W is "embodiment of experience ripping out the pages of the book of authority, and of militant feminism fetching traditional masculine domination a healthy blow on the cheek."

04-5 Pat 244-5: fight scene is "the more gorgeous" because "these two brutal fighters love each other desperately."

08-22 Cog 147: W is wholly feminine, wins by "intuitive stratagem" impossible in a man.

WORDS BETWEEN THE SUMMONER AND THE FRIAR
829-856

Friar laughs at length of W's prologue. Summoner rudely tells him to shut up—friars are always interfering. Friar promises to tell a tale of a corrupt summoner; Summoner swears he will reply with a tale of friars. Host silences them and asks W to continue with her tale. W agrees.

32	*gale* exclaim	38	*pees* peace! (shut up!)
34	*entremette* meddle	39	*lettest* hinder

29-56 Kit 190-1: no real quarrel between Friar and W: Sum's intrusion aims to snub Friar, is uncalled-for; thus W involuntarily becomes "moving cause" of Friar-Sum quarrel. Mal 228: quarrel has slight motivation, is merely device for comic effects, not intended as "serious characterization" of pilgrims involved. Bron 62-3: Pard, Friar, Sum, all of whom interrupt or comment on W's discourse, are "professional rivals . . . for her purse"; they hover about her as a "natural prey," and their common aim of exploiting her increases mutual hatred of Friar and Sum.
37-8 Tatlock, *Flügel* (also Baum): pun on *preambulacioun* (walking), referring back to Friar's comment on *preamble* (preface) in 831.

THE WIFE OF BATH'S TALE
857-881

In old days of King Arthur, fairies and elves were everywhere; these have now been chased out and replaced by friars. (Irony).

71	*thropes* villages. *shipnes* stables	80	*incubus* evil spirit who lies with women, always causes conception
75	*undermeles* afternoons		

57-81 Root 241: W opens tale, pays back Friar at same time; "combination of delicate imagination with coarse insinuation" makes fine transition from Prol to tale. Leg 196: "There is nothing more maliciously roguish in La Fontaine himself." Sp 147-8: passage of "brilliant comic fantasy," apt reply to Friar, also suggests W's basic attitude—her sympathy with ancient nature cults as opposed to "new ecclesiastical order." Mal 217: opening attack on Friar gives "full flavor of the W's personality." Bron 63: W's ironic remark on friars as victimizers of women ("modern incubi") shows she is aware of predatory views of Pard, Friar, Sum.

64-81 Cog 149: "deft revenge" on Friar, linking Arthurian world and world of pilgrimage, leading straight into tale. Ger 74-5: lines have "Rabelaisian particularity."

75 Tatlock, *MLN: undermeles* means late mornings, not afternoons.

882-918

Young knight rapes maiden and is condemned to death by King Arthur; the queen successfully begs for his life. She gives knight one year and one day to find satisfactory answer to question: What do women desire above all? Failure means death.

84	*fro ryver* from hawking by the river		98	*spille* destroy, kill
87	*maugree hir heed* in spite of her head (all she could do)		06	*iren* iron, the ax
			09	*leere* learn
91	*dampned* condemned		13	*siketh* sighs
			17	*purveye* provide

82-8 Dem 59-60: irony of knight's change from "sheer violence" (rape) to "perfect meekness" in attitude toward women; Ch probably added rape for comic effect. Pat 221-2: rape not in Gower, adds irony. L. Loomis: Ch probably borrowed rape from *Sir Degaré* (Breton lay). Huppé: rape of peasant girl was excusable, but not encouraged in courtly love convention; thus knight is given chance to show he understands doctrine—lady is sovereign. Roppolo: Ch nowhere says girl was peasant; knight is shown here as lustful, selfish, deserving of death; Ch focusses on knight, drops girl (who in some analogues becomes hag and heroine). Ger 74-5: rape grotesquely out of key with Arthurian romance, but fits "sex-obsessed" W.

04-5 Roppolo: test question is exactly calculated "to remove some of the conceit from a male who perhaps believed himself to be the answer to that question"; quest serves for suspense, for further characterization of knight. AHM: this sort of test or trial in which hero is required to find answer to a hard question or riddle is a commonplace in romance literature.

919-951

Knight seeks in vain for answer; women he interviews all give different replies.

24	*in-feere* together	49	*stele* handle
34	*ylymed* limed, caught	50	*hele* conceal
38	*nyce* foolish	51	*Myda* Midas
40	*clawe on galle* scratch on sore spot		

19-51 Root 242: changes from 3rd person (925) to *we* (929 ff.), from past to present (935 ff.) subtly suggest W returns here from fiction to reality. Mal 217: though most of tale does not fit W well, this passage does. Townsend: somewhere here W forgets story, speaks for herself.

952-982

Digression: story from Ovid of Midas' wife who could not keep his secret (ass's ears under hair), but finally told it to the water.

65	*dyde* would die	72	*bitore* heron. *bombleth* sputters
70	*mareys* marsh (cp. Fr: marais)		

52-82 Townsend: even in this digression W is not thinking of Midas but of her own trouble in keeping mouth shut.

983-1022

Returning in despair, knight sees vision of 24 ladies who vanish, leaving only a hideous hag. Knight asks hag question; she will give him answer, but if answer is accepted, he must grant her one wish.

93	*yerne* eagerly		18	*calle* headdress
08	*wisse* instruct		21	*pistel* message (epistle)
09	*plight* pledge			

89-99 Train: passage of fairy lore, 24 ladies (perhaps taken from Walter Map's *De Nugis Curialium*), was added by Ch to prepare reader's mind for supernatural power of hag.

09-22 Root 242-3: hag does not specify request or reveal answer as in Gower's version—added suspense.

1023-1057

Prompted by the hag, the knight gives the right answer to queen and court: women most desire power over husbands. The hag then requests that knight marry her.

| 24 | *hight* promised | | 62 | *shrewe* curse |
| 34 | *best* beast | | | |

33 Baum: pun on *worldly wommen* (women of *this* world as distinguished from those of fairy world of tale, and women of mundane interests like W as distinguished from those of spiritual interests).

34-41 Dem 60: irony of knight gladly stating a truth about women "that will soon be illustrated at his own expense."

Cog 148-9: this is W's own solution "upon which she had attempted to build her life."

1058-1105

Knight vainly tries to persuade hag to make a different request. Reluctantly he marries her in secret. On wedding night, the knight turns away from hag; she asks why; he replies that she is poor and old and ugly.

| 64 | *oore* ore | | 90 | *dangerous* fastidious |
| 85 | *walweth* rolls | | | |

62-6 Owen: this is "crucial passage," ending quest plot, starting husband's dilemma, as hag "must first secure her man before she can offer him her alternatives"; her "quest for love" is tale's second theme, an instinctive one underlying W's theories, requiring miracle at end.

73-8 Francis: Ch uses device of "self-conscious abbreviation" for humorous effect.

00-1 Coffman: hag is of low class, wholly outside courtly love convention; like peasant girl, she is viewed only as animal by knight. Roppolo: knight ignores and brutally chides hag because his vanity is deeply wounded.

1106-1218

Hag delivers sermon on "gentillesse"; it is a gift from God and is not dependent on material wealth; the honorable man is spiritually rich, though poor. Illustrations from Dante, Boethius, etc. Old people should be honored; ugliness is a guarantee of chastity.

08	*so* if	69	*drede* doubt
13	*looke who* whoever	76	*weyve* put aside
20	*parage* birth, rank	85	*halt hym payd* is satisfied with
28	*his branches smale* his own little efforts	96	*bryngere out* encourager
36	*fyne* cease	99	*alenge* wretched
42	*lye* blaze	03	*spectacle* eye-glass
49	*in his kynde* from natural causes	15	*filthe* ugliness
52	*han pris* have esteem	16	*wardeyns* guardians

06-18 Tupper, *JEGP:* irony of harangue on Pride in tale of W, proudest of pilgrims. Root 243-4: W's democratic view fits her as member of rising middle class; high poetry of sermon prepares reader for magic transformation (Ch wisely refrains from any detailed description of lady's ugliness or beauty). R. Loomis: passage on true nobility is not rhetorical commonplace, is really revolutionary (comparable to Burns's *A Man's A Man for A' That*); Ch is more radical than Langland on this point. Coffman: sermon sums up Christian, Senecan, Boethian, Dantean idea of *gentilesse* as given in RR, emphasizes baseness of knight's conduct and "incongruity of the whole concept of feudal society and of courtly love." Tho 89-90: sermon lacks dramatic probability, certainly expresses Ch's own view. Mal 216: sermon's "sweet reasonableness" and "gentle persuasiveness" are foreign to W's character who here is merely Ch's mouthpiece. Roppolo: sermon is turning point of tale. Brew 88: here Ch sacrifices narrative flow to bring out theme. Lum 126: contrast between W's unethical conduct and admirable rules of hag; W identifies herself with hag (hag-knight situation resembles that of W-Jankyn). Rob 704: argument of sermon was Christian commonplace, "in no sense an evidence of radical or advanced opinion on the part of Ch." Baum 134: like story of Midas, sermon is "padding" for tale.

09 Baum 196: knight has said nothing of *gentilesse*—unrealistic point of departure for sermon.

60 Kenyon, *JEGP: thyne* is "telling personal application to the knight." Dempster: *thyne* probably means anyone's but is ambiguous.

96 Baum: pun on *bryngere out of bisynesse* (reliever of anxiety over thieves, and encourager of industry).

1219-1238

Hag gives knight choice: Would you rather have me old and ugly but ever true to you, or have me young and fair and take your chance of cuckoldry? The knight leaves choice to her.

34 *I do no fors* I don't care

19-26 Schlauch: marital dilemma Ch uses comes from Latin satirists rather than folklore. Ger 76: both irony and suitability in having knight's initial rape lead to this dilemma.

29-31 Roppolo notes that knight uses these complimentary terms *before* magic transformation (he has been converted by sermon); also, lady does not reveal transformation till she is sure of sovereignty (1249).

1239-1264

Since knight gives her sovereignty, hag will be both true and fair. Magic transformation. They live happily ever after. All husbands should likewise give in to wives.

42 *sterven wood* die mad   60 *overbyde* outlast
54 *a-rewe* in a row

39-41 Lum 128: knight wins happiness not because he gave wife sovereignty, as W thinks she is showing, but because, as converted sinner, he has earned it.

50-1 Coomaraswamy: transformation is a universal mythical pattern. Lum 128: transformation is wishful thinking by W.

55-6 Brew 161: W here contradicts herself on wifely sovereignty. Lum 129: statement that knight's wife obeys him goes beyond W's intention as storyteller.

57-64 Kit 191-2: "medieval feminism has had its say." Mal 216: passage "in the wife's best vein." Don 916: "coarse vigor" of benediction restores full robustness of W's personality.

The Friar's Tale

COMMENTARIES: Gr 206-8; Ham 300-1;/ Don 916-7; ManCT 586-9; Rob 704-6; Sk 5, 323-30;/ Baum 134-5; Brew 164; Cog 158-65; Cow 169-70; Dem 42-5; Fr 284-7; Law 64-5, 68-9; Lum 134-6; Man 102-22; Mus 269; Pat 160, 222; Pres 248-50; Root 244-9; Sp 149; Tup 56-62;/ Aiken, *SP*, 38, 1-9; Baum, *PMLA*, 56, 225-46; Birney, *MS*, 59, 17-35; Hieatt, *N&Q*, 60, 5-6; Immaculate, *PQ*, 42, 240-4; Kellogg, *N&Q*, 59, 190-2; Kuhl, *MLN*, 25, 321-38; Lowes, *RR*, 14, 368-85, and *PMLA*, 15, 237-371; Robertson, *MLN*, 54, 470-2; Sutherland, *PQ*, 52, 436-9; Tatlock, *MLN*, 35, 294-5; Taylor, *PMLA*, 21, 35-59, and *SA*, 269-74; Tupper, *JEGP*, 15, 256-70.

GENRE: Fabliau, with some qualities of moral exemplum.

ANALOGUES: No definite source is known, though several analogues have been found for the slight anecdote which Ch vastly enriched with original characterization and description.

DATE: About 1393-4.

GENERAL CRITICISM: Tupper: tale illustrates Cursing phase of sin of Wrath, fitting scheme (common in *CT*) whereby character is guilty of very sin which his tale condemns ("curses react upon the head of a cursing Summoner"). Lowes, *PMLA*, refutes this view—summoner in tale does not curse; archdeacon, carter, and widow do the cursing in 3 different senses (excommunication, angry curse not from heart, curse from heart); tale illustrates Avarice rather than Wrath. Root 245: Friar-Summoner quarrel due to professional enmity between regular clergy (Fr) with papal authority and secular clergy (Sum) under national church. Cow 169: one of best of *CT*, "a jolly excursion into the never-never land of diablerie," giving impression "with masterly ease" that devil is naive compared to hardened Sum. Dem 42-5: tale has "very striking unity," much dramatic irony, effectively grim humor. Pat 160: a "masterly story" with great charm and vitality. Cog 162-3; tale in "Ch's maturest vein," is masterly expansion of commonplace exemplum, artful blend of cursing motif with condemnation of summoners, full of "lively and intelligent conversation," suaveness fitting Friar of *Gen Prol,* with "naturalness, economy, and scorch seldom found outside De Maupassant." Law 64-5, 69: only one of 7 fabliaux that is "entirely unobjectionable"; tale is riotous fun, "the cream of Ch's art." Sp 149: dialogue is "masterpiece of sinister familiar tone" like conversations between Faustus and Mephistopheles in Marlowe's *Dr. Faustus.* Brew 164: tale amusingly attacks "coarse oppressiveness and stupid arrogance" of Sum. Lum 136: tale shows superb economy, motivation, dialogue, with ironic characterization, climactic structure, but is "free of bitter and ugly vituperation" of *SumT.* Birney: one of most careful, unified, dramatic of *CT* in development of "ironies latent in a Faustian situation"; also one of Ch's most original, with subtle moral implications and withheld climax. Don 917: "brilliantly told," Ch's greatest moral exemplum after *PardT.* Baum 134-5: tale is fine blend of supernatural and actual, has better structure and more "criticism-of-life" than other similar poems of Ch; "Ch was never more successful" in tale which perfectly fits Fr's portrait in *Gen Prol.*

THE FRIAR'S PROLOGUE

III, 1265-1300

Friar frowns at Summoner, praises W's tale, says he will now tell one of an evil summoner. After Host's plea for courtesy, Summoner repeats his threat to tell of a vicious friar. Host asks Friar to begin his tale.

66	*maner lourying chiere* kind of frowning look	84	*mandementz* summonses
77	*scole* schoolwork	85	*ybet* beaten
82	*yvele apayd* offended	93	*which* what

65-79 Lum 134-5: here Fr repays Wife of Bath for digs at friars by suggesting that her performance was boring, that she usurped clerical function by preaching, that he will now tell joke about summoner to relieve dullness of *WBT.*

65-7 Tupper: here Ch clearly turns from theme of Pride in *WBT* to illustration of Wrath.

70-7 Pres 248: planning attack on Sum, Fr has paid attention to
WBT only toward end.

76 Sk 5, 322: direct reference to *WBT* 1208, clearly linking the 2
tales.

90-00 Lum 135: Sum is violent, but Fr remains calm; Host's courtesy
to Fr suggests he realizes this difference.

THE FRIAR'S TALE

1301-1374

Once there was a very strict archdeacon in charge of a church court.
His summoner was a thorough rascal. (Here the Summoner breaks
in with angry comment, but is silenced by Host). This vicious summoner was in league with bawds and whores whom he used for
blackmail purposes.

06	*avowtrye* adultery	49	*atte nale* at an ale-house
07	*reves* robberies	52	*duetee* income
12	*yshent* punished	62	*pile* rob, pillage
14	*asterte* escape	65	*thee thar* it is necessary for
23	*espiaille* group of spies		you
32	*styves* stews, brothels	69	*dogge for the bowe* dog to
36	*gale* cry out		follow up deer
43	*approwours* agents		

01-24 Kuhl: concreteness of passage is Ch at his best, with "delicious reference to the archdeacon who punishes simony."

02 Man 111-22 conjecturally identifies archdeacon *of heigh degree*
(ironical) with Richard de Ravenser, greedy archdeacon of Lincoln
(1368-86) who was certainly known to Ch and would be known by Fr
of nearby Holderness district of Yorkshire (see *SumT* 1709-10).

14 Kellogg: "He [the sinner] could escape no pecuniary punishment"—subject of sentence is composite sinner (*lecchours* and *smale
tytheres*), not the "fine" (Rob's interpretation).

17 Tatlock: sarcasm in *hook,* meaning bishop's crozier intended to be
used as shepherd's crook is—to draw back sheep from peril.

22-72 Birney: build-up of summoner as self-confident master trickster is necessary to irony; "and it is precisely this self-confidence which will betray him."

27-8 Baum: play on words *hare* and *harlotrye;* also, *his* (1328) may refer to Pilgrim Sum or to summoner in tale or to both.

29-32 Sk 5, 324: friars were exempt from jurisdiction of local church courts, as were also the licensed prostitutes.

32-7 Lum 136: "As usual, the Sum's rebuttal is vulgar"; Host shows disgust at him, respect for Fr.

38-40, 69, 1375 Birney: use of hunting images—summoner's relation to sinners is that of hunter to hunted; ironical that summoner (hunter) becomes himself hunted by greater devil (also shown in hunter's garb in 1380-3).

53-4 Baum 135: tale's language is both fittingly colloquial and striking (as here and in 1408).

56 Sk 5, 324: title of "Sir" was commonly given to secular priests.

1375-1446

This summoner, on way to extort bribe from poor widow, meets a yeoman. Summoner, ashamed of his trade, pretends to be a bailiff. Yeoman says that he too is a bailiff from the north country, that he has a hard master and gains his living by extortion. Summoner swears blood brotherhood with yeoman, and reveals that he also lives by extortion.

77	*ribibe* "fiddle" (slang for old woman)	08	*waryangles* shrikes (birds)
78	*brybe* get a bribe	15	*wisse* inform
84	*atake* met	27	*daungerous* overbearing
86	*shawe* forest, wood	31	*algate* at any rate
94	*for the name* because of the bad name	37	*conseil* dealings
		42	*shrifte-fadres* confessors

75-46 Root 248: delicious humor of hints by which devil gradually shows identity.

79-83 Robertson: green is dress of hunters, also of Celtic underworld, thus fitting to that old hunter, the Devil.

93-4 Pat 222: "wonderful thrust."

00-2 Birney: gold and silver are devil's lure; his *shire* is hell.

03-33 Birney: irony of repeated expressions of faith and trust by both summoner and devil in 03, 04, 20, 24-5, 33.

05 Dem 42:   "touch of grim irony."

12-6 Dem 43:   devil's conscious irony makes his threat "more calmly, more terribly threatening."

13 Sk 5, 326:   in Teutonic mythology hell was believed to be in north.

35-6 Birney: points forward to end when summoner gets his last gift—curse which proves so heavy and hot it sinks him to hell.

1447-1534

Under questioning, yeoman reveals that he is a devil from hell, that he can take any shape to suit his purpose, and that he sometimes acts as God's instrument in punishing or in tempting men. He cuts Summoner's questions short, telling him that he will soon have direct knowledge of hell. Summoner agrees to stay with him and share spoils.

49	*purchasyng* holdings		00	*hente* seize
51	*purchas* pickings. *effect* substance		09	*renably* reasonably
55	*preye* victim		12	*do no fors* care nothing
65	*go* walk		14	*algates* entirely
78	*entende* attend		18	*konne in chayer rede* learn to read from pulpit or chair (professorial)
86	*art* methods. *figures* shapes			

59-72 Aiken: passage on variable shapes of demons agrees with medieval theological opinion, especially as expressed by Vincent of Beauvais.

59-60 Cow 170:   summoner is "ever curious to learn new wiles."

73 Birney: "it never crosses the summoner's mind that the devil might be interested in anything so immaterial as a soul."

82-16 Aiken: 3 methods of demonic temptations and affliction of men, and admission that devils are sometimes forced to serve godly men— all these ideas agree with views of Vincent of Beauvais. Cog 163: most notable passage in tale; "seldom can the subtleties of theological speculation have sounded so gay and easy." Pres 248-9: fine comic treatment of problem of evil and interaction of evil and good; fiend resembles Pardoner—compare especially 1483-1500 with *PardT* 429-32.

01-3 Aiken: allusion is probably to miraculous playing of St. Dunstan's cithara, as told in Vincent of Beauvais' *Speculum Historiale*. Immaculate: *servant* here implies subjection of demons as instruments of God's will; St. Dunstan allusion is to story of several visits from devils whose power Dunstan was able to counteract and control, told in *Vitae Dunstani* (Rolls Series, 1874).

13-6 Dem 43: an "open threat" epitomizing dramatic irony of whole scene, yet summoner seems "incredibly deaf" to obvious danger.

17-20 Birney: summoner does not protest or even pay attention; "it is his silence, his heedlessness, his terrible preoccupation with what he can get out of the devil, not what the devil may get out of him, that carries the poem into the realm of the ironies of fate."

1535-1570

Summoner and devil come upon hay cart stuck in mud. The driver swears: "Devil take horses, cart, and hay!" Summoner urges devil to do just that; devil replies that driver doesn't really mean it. Horses pull out of mud and driver blesses them.

41 *deep* deep in mud
46 *tholed* endured
47 *hors* horses (plural)
49 *as noght ne were* as if nothing were happening
54 *caples* nags
59 *thakketh* whacks. *croupe* rump
63 *twight* pulled. *lyard* gray

70 *upon cariage* in return for giving up my claims to his cart and horses (a legal phrase—feudal lord had right to free use of tenant's carts and horses; tenant could deny lord's claim to carrying equipment only by paying fee called *cariage*)

43 Man 106: names *Brok, Scot* are Northern dialect, also *hayt, tholed* (1546), *caples* (1554), showing Ch consciously set tale in North England, as he did in *RvT* and *SumT*. Mus 269: Manly's case is poor, since *Brok, Scot, hayt* are also found in East Anglia, and *tholed, caples,* etc., in Midland and Southern texts.

59-65 Lowes, *RR:* incident in life of St. Eloy connected him in popular mind with horses; thus carter's oath is fitting.

67-8 Birney: summoner misses point of this, thinks devil has simply "muffed a chance" and he (summoner) is now in position to score over him.

1571-1664

Summoner will show devil his skill by getting money from stingy widow. He knocks at widow's door with fake summons. Widow is sick and cannot go to court. Summoner offers to forget whole thing for 12 pence, which widow does not have. Summoner then threatens to take her new pan. Widow swears: "I give you and my pan to the devil!" Since this is a sincere oath, the devil, who is standing by, carries off both Summoner and pan. Now, fellow pilgrims, may you all be saved from the devil, and may these summoners repent.

73	*rebekke* old woman	09	*kithe* show
82	*virytrate* hag	17	*hoom* court. *correccioun* fine
87	*up peyne of cursyng* on pain of excommunication		
94	*priketh* pains	30	*stot* hag (slang)
95	*libel* copy of charge	44	*leve* allow
		49	*agryse* shudder

79-80 **Dem** 44: summoner goes further than usual in cruelty to widow to stress contrast between his practical tactics and "foolish niceties" of devil (with carter).

81-3 Cog 248: Fr is so confident of his superiority over Sum in game of devastating satire, he feels he can afford to concede that a friar may be with widow—a point which won't matter by end of tale on summoner.

83-97 Birney: summoner assumes widow is guilty of something, and widow's first reactions (request for delay, failure to assert innocence, etc.) confirm this belief, encourage summoner to press harder.

01 Birney: ironically, summoner's *maister* is no longer archdeacon, but devil who will take *profit* of both pan and summoner himself.

10 Tupper: irony in summoner's cursing himself without, of course, expecting literal fulfillment of curse.

13 Hieatt: summoner swears by St. Anne, patron saint of mothers and elderly women—added irony.

28-32 Root 249: summoner is "fatally blind" to danger he risks in proudly rejecting repentance. Birney: summoner's last chance to save himself.

42 Birney: though *after his ymage* is insincere hope from Fr, it serves to remind us that summoner's sin was insensitivity to idea he was molded by God, determination to take on image of devil.

45-62 Sutherland: passage seems to be outline of sermon based on divine office of Compline (which uniquely stresses warning given here) in *Breviarium Romanum,* a favorite of friars.

53-60 Lum 136: Fr "manages to equate the Sum with Satan."

The Summoner's Tale

COMMENTARIES: Gr 208; Ham 301-2;/ Don 917; ManCT 589-90; Rob 706-8; Sk 5, 330-41;/ Cog 163-5; Cow 170; Ev 145; Fr 288-90; Kit 192; Leg 189; Low 100, 182, 186; Man 102-22; Pat 213-36; Root 249-52;/ Baum, *PMLA*, 56, 225-46; Beichner, *MS*, 50, 135-44; Chapman, *PMLA*, 29, 178-85; Curry, *MLN*, 23- 253, and *ESt*, 24, 24-60; Greenfield, *MLR*, 53, 51-2; Hamilton, *MLN*, 42, 655-7; Hart, *SA*, 275-87; Kuhl, *MLN*, 25, 321-38; Lowes, *PMLA*, 15, 237-371; Owen, *CE*, 55, 226-32; Shain, *MLN*, 55, 235-45; Southworth, *Expl*, 53, item 29; Stanford, *JEGP*, 20, 377-81; Tatlock, *MLN*, 14, 143, and *Flügel*, 228-32; Tupper, *PMLA*, 14, 93-128, and *JEGP*, 15, 256-70, and 16, 56-106; Whitesell, *MLN*, 56, 160-1; Williams, *Spec*, 53, 499-513 (ST), and *MP*, 56, 117-20, and *SP*, 60, 463-78.

GENRE: Fabliau.

SOURCE: For Prologue, a widespread vulgar jest. For Tale, a current anecdote of which another version survives in French fabliau "Le Dis de la Vescie a Prestre" (Story of the Priest's Bladder) by Jacques de Baisieux.

DATE: About 1393-4, shortly after *WBT*.

GENERAL CRITICISM: Kit 192: "an incomparable satire on begging friars, worked up on the basis of a trivial and sordid fabliau." Root 251: tale coarse, but not at all vicious. Tupper, *JEGP*, 15: sin of Wrath is subject of Friar-Summoner controversy; double irony of angry Summoner telling tale against anger, his most obvious vice, and of furious friar within tale acting contrary to his own advice against anger. Lowes refutes Tupper's view of tale as centered on Wrath, arguing tale illustrates Gluttony as much as Wrath, noting sermon against Gluttony (1873-1941), irony of friar's own gluttony (1838-45), and inclusion of passage on drunkenness (2043-78) in friar's sermon against Wrath. Cow 170: Ch's weakest tale in structure ("expanded anecdote"), drawn out too long to offset excessive coarseness of climax. Leg 189: what matters is not coarse joke of plot, but superb, detailed character study of wheedling friar. Low 186: sketch of friar is greatest of Ch's portraits within a tale in *CT*. Pat 217: satire "not truly mordant," more in style of Horace than Juvenal, of Fielding than Swift. Cog 163-5: superb picture of country life, both in cottage and in great hall of feudal lord. Williams, *Spec:* Ch's friars probably not fair representatives of friars as a whole, since he naturally took the side of secular clergy in their struggle against mendicant orders. Owen: Summoner's fierce anger takes control of and unifies his tale, causes anticlimactic ending, exposes his scurrilous mind. Don 917: Friar-Summoner controversy centers on satire against intellectual achievement; issue, raised in *FrT,* is seized on by Summoner who tells of hypocritical friar (resembling Hubert) whose special pride in intellectual superiority is flattered by peasant Thomas and flippant squire; Ch allows low and scurrilous Summoner to degrade Friar with last word in quarrel.

THE SUMMONER'S PROLOGUE

III, 1665-1708

The Summoner, furiously angry, speaks: "Give me chance to answer this false friar. Friars are well acquainted with hell. Once a friar visited hell in dream and noticed no friars there. His guide, an angel, led him to Satan and ordered Satan to lift his tail, whereupon 20,000 friars swarmed out of Satan's anus."

88	*carryk* ship	06	*of verray kynde* by his very
92	*furlong wey* time to walk furlong (about 2½ minutes)		nature

65-08 Kit 192: Wife of Bath has been innocent cause of white-heat quarrel (see *WBT* 829-56); "nowhere in the pilgrimage is the dramatic interplay of character more remarkable." Root 249-50: Summoner gives unsavory anecdote as *hors d'oeuvre;* he is so furiously angry that he cannot wait for slower revenge which comes in tale. Curry, *MLN:* anecdote derives from Dante's description of Lucifer in 9th circle of Hell (Inferno, xxxiv).

07 Baum notes pun on *save* (except and save).

THE SUMMONER'S TALE

1709-1764

In Holderness, Yorkshire, was a friar who, when he preached, persuaded folk to pay for masses for souls in purgatory. Then he would
beg from door to door with another friar and servant to carry gifts.
He would write the names of those who gave, promising to pray for
them; once outside, he erased names. (Friar breaks in to say Summoner lies; Host silences him.)

17	*trentals* 30 masses for souls in purgatory	45	*ascaunces* as if
22	*possessioners* monks and priests allowed to have private property	46	*reye* rye
		47	*kechyl* little cake. *trype* small piece
30	*oules* awls	50	*brawn* flesh of boar
37	*scrippe* satchel. *ytukked* robes tucked	51	*dagon* piece
		55	*hostes man* servant to the guests
41	*tables* writing tablets	58	*planed* erased
42	*poyntel* stylus	60	*nyfles* silly stories

46-53 Ev 145: wheedling tone skillfully suggested by grammatical
construction—*Yif us* followed by string of nouns and noun clauses,
broken by parentheses.

51 Southworth: *blanket* means a lesser cut of meat rather than piece
of cloth.

1765-1850

Friar arrives at house of generous peasant Thomas who is sick. He
enters alone, greets Thomas, and sits down. Friar kisses and flatters
Thomas's wife, scolds Thomas for being angry with her, and orders
his meal.

69	*bedrede* bedridden	03	*narwe* tightly
70	*Deus hic* God be here	10	*amende defautes* mend my defects
76	*potente* staff		
92	*glose* interpretation	11	*algates* anyhow
94	*lettre* literal text	15	*throwe* while

20 *fisshe* fish for
25 *pissemyre* pismire (ant)
27 *wrye* wrap
32 *je vous dy* I tell you (Fr.)
33 *maketh* brings

38 *sanz doute* without doubt
   (Fr.)
46-7 *penyble to wake* painfully
   on guard

75 A splendid realistic touch (noted by virtually all critics).

04 Sk 5, 334: kissing was customary mode of salutation in 14th century.

16-8 Williams, *Spec:* friars were notorious for stealing confessional business of parish clergy.

42 Sk 5, 334: friar gives strong hint that he always expects especially good food prepared for him.

1851-1947

Thomas' wife reports their child has died. Friar replies he saw child rise to heaven in vision, and his whole convent prayed for him; the prayers of clean living friars are most effectual. "We fast like Moses; we are wedded to poverty, unlike secular priests. We pray for your health constantly."

55 *dortour* dormitory
58 *wisse* guide
59 *fermerer* friar in charge of infirmary
62 *walke allone* (instead of in pairs)
72 *burel folk* laymen
88 *wombe* belly
92 *leche* physician, redeemer

06 *mendynantz* mendicants, begging friars
28 *diffye* distrust
31 *spence* pantry
34 *cor meum eructavit* my heart threw up (belched)
35 *foore* footsteps
38 *sours* upward flight

51-14 Curry *ESt:* passage shows Ch's interest in dreams; he uses occult mysteries here to develop character of friar.

65-6 Tatlock, *MLN: Te Deum* always sung after a miracle or after death of member of order (Thomas was lay member); friar says no bells were rung perhaps because Thomas lived within earshot and would know this.

69 ff. Shain: defense of friars is loaded with rhetorical devices—

balance (1872-4, 1877-8), word play (1916-7), Latin pun (1934), rhetorical question (1935-8), etc.; whole sermon shows Ch's skilled use of pulpit rhetoric, though it does not conform to strict rules of sermon structure. Cog 163-5: sermon rambles from abstinence, to alms, to patience, anger, drunkenness, back to alms; it may be purposely disjointed to satirize preaching of friars.

16-7 Tatlock, *Flügel:*   pun on *chast;* "chased out, and chaste in, what a beautiful thought!"

29-31 Low 100: friar surpasses in robustness his source, *Jerome Against Jovinian* ("lovely monk, fat, shiny, bepowdered, stepping like a bridegroom").

34 Hamilton: point lies not so much in pun on *eructavit* as in inappropriateness of joyful Psalm xliv (Vulgate) as prayer for dead. Beichner disagrees; real point of line is that it acts as vivid climax of satire on friar's hypocritical scorn for appetites and gluttony in 1870-5, 1911-4, 1923-34.

1948-1980

Thomas says that prayers have not helped him, though he has given to several kinds of friars. Friar replies that he should concentrate his alms, give all to him or to his convent: "What good is a farthing divided in twelve?"

52 *biset* bestowed   61   *jape* trick

67 Whitesell: friar is same as lisping Friar Hubert of pilgrimage, who suggests to Thomas his own reward by mispronouncing *ferthyng* ("What is a ferthyng worth parted in twelve?").

1981-2088

Friar preaches long sermon to Thomas on the sin of ire, warning him not to be angry with his patient wife (she may turn on him!). Examples of havoc wrought by angry lords—Cambises, Cyrus, etc. It is prudent to flatter lords, though one should point out a poor man's vices.

98	*lemmans* lovers	30	*reed* plan
02	*tret* treads	17	*potestat* potentate
08	*viker* vicar	24	*deme* condemn
		29	*wenden* supposed

37   *algate* by all means
43   *dronkelewe* addicted to
     drink

75   *Placebo* I will please (be a
     yes-man)
81   *dreynt* drowned

81 ff. Chapman: friar begins sermon on Ire not in approved manner
with Scriptural text, but with definition; he ends with paraphrase of
Proverbs xxii, 24-5.
93-5 Baum notes obscene pun on *serpent*.
78 Owen: shows friar has contempt for poor, excessive respect for
wealth and power.

2089-2159
Friar asks to hear Thomas's confession. Thomas refuses; he has just
been shriven by priest. Friar then begs for money to help convent.
Thomas, angered by friar's hypocrisy, promises a gift on condition
that it be shared equally by convent. He tells friar to reach down into
bed and presents him with gift of a fart. Thomas's servants then chase
furious friar out.

90   *squyre* carpenter's square
95   *curat* curate, priest
03   *fundement* foundation
05   *wones* dwellings
07   *harwed* harrowed
09   *predicacioun* preaching
11   *bireve* take away
16   *Elye* Elijah. *Elise* Elisha
28   *oure dame* i. e. Thomas's
     wife

36   *cavillacioun* cavilling
45   *clifte* cleft
48   *tuwel* hole
50   *capul* nag
54   *for the nones* for this occa-
     sion
55   *abye* pay for
56   *meynee* household

03 Baum notes pun on *fundament* (foundation and buttocks).
16 Sk 5, 339: friar is Carmelite, since Carmelites claimed to have
been founded by Elijah when he retired to Mt. Carmel (see I Kings.
xviii, 19-20; also Williams, *MP*). Man 104-5: friar is Franciscan (since
Pilgrim Friar Hubert is one), must have belonged to Franciscan
house in Beverly (S. E. Yorkshire), only one in Holderness district.

41 Baum: play on verb *grope* (groping in bed and feeling out of Thomas's conscience as in 1817).

2160-2215

Friar, in a rage, goes to lord of village to complain and denounce Thomas. Lord's wife is sympathetic, concludes that Thomas is mentally sick.

62	*paas* distance	09	*frenesye* frenzy
76	*despit* insult	11	*wreke* avenged
87	*Raby* rabbi	15	*with meschaunce* bad luck
89	*no fors* no matter		to him!
92	*per consequens* consequent-ly		

65 Man 119 identifies lord of manor conjecturally with Michael de la Pole, great feudal lord in Holderness and benefactor of Franciscan friars.
85-8 Root 252: even in rage friar pauses to protest inappropriate title of "master," thus showing his habitual skill in shamming.

2216-2294

The lord is fascinated by problem of dividing such a gift among 13 friars of the convent. His squire suggests a solution: get a wheel with 12 spokes; place a friar at end of each spoke, with soliciting friar at hub; have peasant deliver gift at hub. Lord is delighted with ingenious solution.

22	*ars-metrike* arithmetic (L. ars metrica; pun obviously intended)	32	*thee* prosper (theen)
		61	*parfourne up* complete
		64	*sadly* firmly
28	*with harde grace* bad luck to him!	67	*toght* taut
		68	*tabour* drum

16-94 Cow 170: cartwheel suggestion is "unsavoury and unnecessary." Root 251: friar's callous hypocrisy deserves this coarse insult, which comes as relief after his miserable pretenses; ingeniousness of squire's suggestion makes coarseness forgivable.

61 Sk 5, 341: *his covent* implies that friar was prior of his convent or cell (prior and 12 members).

81 ff. Sk 5, 341: lines suggest that squire and rest of household had been bored by friar's sermon that morning.

94 Greenfield: *towne* does not refer to Sittingbourne (mentioned in *WBT* 847) as critics have assumed, is merely tag-word to rime with *gowne;* hence no discrepancy in Ellesmere order of tales here.

The Clerk's Tale

COMMENTARIES: Gr 209-13; Ham 302-9;/ Don 917-20; ManCT 590-6; Rob 708-12; Sk 5, 342-53;/ Baum 120-2, 140-2, 191-2; Brew 164-6; Bron 103-14; Cog 139-41; Cow 171-2; Fr 290-313; Griffith, *Origin of the Griselda Story* (Univ. of Wash., 1931); Hin 184-209; Kit 189-200; Law 139-42; Lum 141-151; Mal 207-9, 222-5; Mus 190-7; Pat 136, 156, 188-9; Pres 202, 250-7; Root 253-62; Severs, *Literary Relationships of Ch's ClT* (Yale, 1942); Sisam ed. *ClT* (Oxford, 1923); Shel 103, 108, 272-80, 306; Sp 151-5;/ Baldwin, *PMLA*, 27, 106-12; Cate, *SP*, 32, 389-405; Dempster, *MP*, 43, 6-16; Farnham, *MLN*, 18, 193-203; Heninger, *JEGP*, 57, 382-95; Landrum, *DA*, 54, 1725; Lyons, *ELH*, 35, 252-62; Moore, *MLQ*, 49, 49-57; Morse, *MLQ*, 58, 3-20; Pearsall, *MLN*, 52, 529-31; Prins, *ES*, 56, 111-6; Rose Marie, *Cweal*, 40, 225-7; Severs, *PMLA*, 32, 431-52, and *SA*, 288-331; Sledd, *MP*, 53, 73-82 (ST, W); White, *Neophil*, 53, 113.

GENRE: Folk tale, with some elements of religious allegory.

SOURCE: Petrarch's Latin *De Obedientia ac Fide Uxoria Mythologia,* which is itself a translation of Boccaccio's *Decameron,* x, 10; Ch certainly used, in addition, a French translation of Petrarch's Latin version; though Boccaccio's is earliest known literary version, the story ultimately derives from fairy-tale combining themes of story of Cupid and Psyche and ballad of *Fair Annie.*

DATE: Uncertain, but probably in *CT* period.

VERSE FORM: Rime Royal (7-line stanza of iambic pentameter, rimed a b a b b c c); Envoy in 6-line stanza (a b a b c b).

GENERAL CRITICISM: Hin 186-7: probably earlier work adapted for *CT* by adding Prologue and Epilogue; Gris views Walter mainly as feudal lord, herself as serf; tale illustrates intense, unbalanced ideals of medieval Christianity, but, even so, Gris combines sweetness and strength common to nearly all great virtues. Kit 189-96: tale is dramatically motivated by Wife of Bath's heretical views on marriage and attacks on antifeminist clerks (including 5th husband, an Oxford clerk); pilgrim Clerk, orthodox and virtuous, bides his time, makes brilliant, subtle reply to Wife in tale of "wifely fidelity and woman's fortitude under affliction"; Gris is obviously "complete antithesis" to Wife. Root 259-62: Gris, as both wife and vassal, has double obligation to obey, thus merely practices "what all her contemporaries held in theory," but Ch probably viewed her as impossible ideal; basic inconsistency in Walter who is first popular and kindly, then seems selfish, immature, spoiled, though he does not mean to be cruel. Cow 171-2: pathetic tale like *MLT,* but better; despite true pathos, there are serious flaws for modern readers—what did Gris see in Walter? Leg 140: "a thorough panegyric of feminine devotion and sustained sentimentality." Pat 136, 156, 188-9: to pathos, Ch added touches of rebelliousness in Gris and humorous framework for tale which "uncovers depths of slyness we might not have suspected in the scholar"; tale also shows peasant's patience under aristocratic injustice, suggests remarkably democratic sympathies in Ch. Shel 108, 272-80: "a new and perfect telling" by Ch—no real question of indebtedness; despite folk tale or fairy origins, tale is true to life (in Boccaccio, Petrarch, Ch); like Constance, Gris is medieval woman—long-suffering, faithful, understanding Walter's obsession, only occasionally protesting his cruelty, sensitive and wise throughout, not weak but heroic, a type not unknown in modern times (cp. Hardy's *Tess of the D'Urbervilles*); Walter, notwithstanding his obsession, is no monster, clearly loves Gris and children, is "at bottom an ideal husband and father." Cog 139-40: "too cruel, too incredible" a tale which "even Ch could not stand" and had to disclaim in ironical epilogue; magic of oriental folk tale has become monstrous through heavy moralizing, so that not even Ch's superb expression and moving pathos could redeem it. Law 140: tale begins innocently, but becomes deadly retort to Wife of Bath. Mal 222: tale fits teller perfectly, but deals chiefly with ideals of Christian behavior, not with marriage; Ch added epilogue relating to Wife of Bath for sheer amusement. Sp 151-5: tale contrasts sharply with both *WBT* and *MerchT* in marriage debate; its very grotesqueness is probably part of its timeless fascination; Gris is mainly personification of wifely patience, but at times shows humanity and "peculiar tenderness" like that of Constance and child in *MLT;* Ch's changes in Petrarch all tend to humanize folk tale, with some touches of religious allegory, several Biblical associations. Pres 202, 250: tale is about "spiritual principle, and about the struggles of a soul to abide by it"—Gris is Patience personified; tale has been undervalued because misunderstood. Brew 164-5: Ch's additions—making Gris more charming, sensitive, motherly, pathetic, Walter more real—all tend toward excessive naturalism which obscures tale's quality as religious myth (faith in goodness despite all) and makes it seem more intolerably painful. Sledd: tale should not be seen as improbable view of real marriage, but as fiction, frankly marvelous, teaching moral lesson; in Parts I and II, Walter and Gris are so idealized as to make incredible tests and submissiveness acceptable to reader; cruelty is softened by repeated hints of happy ending; tale is fair success, with "comfortable pathos," even sentimentality, rather than gross improbability; in Envoy Ch risks clashing fiction against reality, gets his laugh. Landrum: marriage ideal here harmonizes with Church's view, making tale a powerful answer to Wife of Bath who turns marriage upside down. Lum 144-5: major theme is obedience to constituted authority, not surprising in orthodox Clerk (see 24, 230, 319-22, 528-32, 570-2, etc.); but alongside this idea are repeated objections to cruelty (455-62, 621-3, 697-707, 722-35), whereby Clerk keeps audience in doubt as to tale's chief lesson, placates Wife till he is ready to attack her directly in Envoy. Heninger: tale is more than "just another point of view in the Marriage Group"; Ch's additions stress scholastic idea of "divinely-ordained universal order," requiring obedience and subordination in social hierarchy, as opposed to human mutability; Gris is immutable, maintains God's order, and is justly rewarded; tale uses marriage only as example of broader principle. Mus 190-7: "a triumph of Ch's conventional style," finely controlled, stripped bare of all that would distract from austere Christian theme (fitting Clerk) of obedience to God's will, with minimal characterization, clear, simple plot, every detail stressing idea of paternal, political, marital sovereignties (Janicula, Walter) as copies and symbols of "divine fatherhood, lordship, spousal"; to blame Gris as a mother in this symbolic context is as absurd as to criticize "Abraham's carelessness of Isaac"; extravagant Envoy fits tale into marriage debate, also protects this fine "latter-day parable" from "vulgar questioning."

Baum 120-2: interesting as study of Ch's skill in close translation, in handling improbable plot successfully except for final reconciliation scene. Don 918-20: Ch tried to humanize tale (from Petrarch's version) by stressing Walter's "dreadful obsession" and abnormality, by increasing Gris's vitality; her devotion is not so much to monstrous husband as to ideal of constancy and truth to her own sworn promise; tale connects with Marriage Group as answer to *WBT,* but really deals with values very different from Wife's interests; Envoy brings idealism down to earth. Bron 103-9: Ch presents Gris not as personification but as real human being, as shown by repeated judgments of Walter's cruelty by ordinary moral standards; hence Ch is forced to try (in vain) to make Gris's suffering acceptable by raising Walter to symbolic level of Deity (like God in Abraham-Isaac story), but this effort "splits on the rock of Walter's too too solid flesh" and explicit motive (no inscrutable mystery); as a result, tale involves "perversion of values" (Gris's sacrifice of children, etc.) of which ironic Envoy "serves as a genuine, though unconscious, repudiation."

THE CLERK'S PROLOGUE

IV, 1-56

Host notes shyness of Clerk, urges him to be merry and tell plain tale that all can enjoy (no "high style"). Clerk agrees to tell story learned at Padua from Petrarch, but omitting long preface describing North Italy.

3	*bord*	table	22	*yerde*	authority
5	*sophyme*	subtlety	43	*prohemye*	preface
16	*termes*	technical words.			
	colours	ornaments			

1-8 Low 165: Host speaks with "that benignant affability with which the man of the world indulges the scholar." Mal 207-8: Host is mildly baiting Clerk, exaggerating for fun; comparison with modest bride not to be taken seriously.

5-14 Lum 143: Host takes pains to show he can use professional vocabulary of Clerk.

5 Heninger: Clerk has been planning antidote for Wife's heresy.

22-5 Mus 191: Clerk's "own talent for obedience." Heninger: Clerk supports moral and social order (theme of tale) by submitting to authority.

26-38 Root 254: delightful "flash of enthusiasm" for Petrarch fits scholar.

41-51 Hin 187: inartistic repetition of Petrarch's preface here and in 57-63 strongly suggests Prologue was written at later date than first stanza of tale.

44 ManCT 592: here and throughout Ch gives French forms of names (except Vesulus), suggesting use of French version of Petrarch.

THE CLERK'S TALE, PART I

57-140

Walter, young marquis of Saluzzo, is popular with his people and lives happily though unmarried. Walter's subjects, worried since he has no heir, petition him to marry soon so that no stranger will succeed him.

67	*liges* lieges, subjects	86	*flokmeele* in a flock
68	*yoore* for a long time	12	*sovereyn hertes reste* supreme peace of mind
69	*drad* feared		
75	*gye* govern	22	*smyt* smites
85	*bar so soore* took so hard	37	*slake* cease

64-70 Mus 195: "imagery of lordship and domination," reiterated throughout tale, part of texture of style.

70 Hin 192: lords and commons is English touch, not in Petrarch.

76 Baum 121: hint of faults in Walter which show up later.

16-26 Heninger: a forthright statement of the facts of mutability.

36-9 Heninger: lack of heir to "royal-sacred authority" would violate natural order.

141-196

Walter replies he enjoys single life, but agrees to wed provided that he may pick own wife and that people promise to honor whomever he chooses. People gladly agree, ask Walter to set day for wedding.

44	*streyne* constrain	66	*dure* last
57	*bountee* goodness. *streen*	74	*but* unless
	stock	86	*buxomly* obediently
61	*bitake* entrust	91	*purveye* provide

PART II

197-245

In nearby village lives a poor old man, Janicula, with fair and virtuous daughter, Griselda. Walter has often noticed Griselda, decides to wed her.

98	*shoop* planned	20	*sad* steady
99	*throop* village	27	*seeth* boiled
03	*after that* according as	29	*kepte on-lofte* cared for, sus-
15	*tonne* wine cask		tained

06-7 Hin 193: allusion to Christ's birth. Rose Marie: lines suggest comparison of Gris with Virgin Mary (also 291), chosen by Lord unexpectedly to be mother of Jesus who was later taken away to be killed; whole tale a parable of our duty to accept God's will. Sp 154: Biblical echoes here and in 290 (water pot recalls Biblical virgin at the well), 871-2, suggest religious allegory.

21-8 Sp 153-4: Gris, "precariously poised between the human and the non-human," derives some reality as local peasant girl, but is even here idealized by Christian idea of blessed poverty.

29-31 Heninger: Gris as dutiful supporter of natural order.

246-287

On wedding day Walter has prepared clothes and feast for Griselda, but told no one. Griselda innocently hopes to finish work in time to see Walter ride by with new wife.

60	*undren* mid morning	66	*last Ytaille* farthest Italy, or
64	*houses of office* store-rooms		Italy extends (contraction of
65	*deyntevous* choicest		*lasteth*)
		83	*fonde* try

288-392

Walter comes to village in morning, meets Griselda, asks to speak with her father. Janicula, astonished, agrees to proposal. Walter then calls in Griselda, asks her to swear never to disobey or argue with him. Griselda swears oath; Walter announces his choice to people. Griselda is dressed in new clothes, weds Walter, is carried in triumph to palace.

00	*lette* delay	39	*woned* used
01	*fette* fetched	50	*yow avyse* think it over
16	*cas* happening	60	*beede* offer
17	*abayst* abashed	72	*geere* clothing
25	*collacioun* conference	79	*untressed* unplaited
31	*tretys* marriage treaty	82	*nowches* jeweled clasps
34	*tentifly* attentively		

88-94 Sp 153-4: Walter calling Gris seems like "God calling the soul."

51-64 Heninger: Walter openly demands Gris's total obedience to authority, which she solemnly promises.

62-4 Don 919: humanizing touch (deliberately mistranslated from Petrarch) showing Gris's love of life; she has made constancy to Walter supreme, but is not blind to other values.

393-448

As time passes, Griselda is beloved of people and of Walter for her virtue, wisdom, and simple grace. She bears Walter a daughter.

99	*norissed* brought up	37	*aton* in agreement (at one)
09	*thewes* moral qualities	44	*knave* boy
29	*feet* feats		

PART III

449-511

Walter needlessly decides to test his wife's obedience. He tells Griselda people are complaining about low class of her and daughter. To appease them daughter must go. Griselda meekly consents.

50	*throwe* short time	74	*wele* happiness
52	*sadnesse* constance	88	*recchelees* negligent
54	*assaye* test	98	*ameved* changed
55	*affraye* frighten		

56-62 Baum 122: in light of final moral (1156-62), these lines are "structural fault," seem to have "the air of condemning the Most High" for causing us inexplicable suffering.

09-11 Heninger: Gris swears she will never change, and she never does (except in circumstances); her steadfastness and resistance to mutability are repeatedly stressed in 564-5, 599-602, 668, 708-11, 858-61, 925-31, 1044-7, etc.

512-574

Walter sends secret agent, a villainous looking sergeant, to take away baby girl. He acts as though he plans to kill child. Griselda bids child tearful farewell, asks sergeant for decent burial of baby.

16	*furlong wey or two* = in a little while	40	*diffame* ill fame
		51	*barm* bosom
29	*yfeyned* evaded	72	*torace* tear to pieces

19-42 Sp 152-3: "monstrous brutality of man in the huge male shape of the 'sergeant,' whose power like Death's appears irresistible."

56-8 Sp 153: explicit reference to Crucifixion tends to sanctify human feelings here (recalls Mary and Child).

575-609

Sergeant reports Griselda's behavior to Walter who then orders daughter taken safely to Bologna to be raised by his sister secretly. Griselda never murmurs.

85	*cofre* chest. *lappe* piece of cloth	02	*ylike sad* equally constant
86	*swappe* cut	09	*nempned* named

90 Pearsall: *Panik* means castle of Panico, 18-20 miles south of Bologna, from which noble Da Panico family (10th to 14th centuries) took its name.

PART IV

610-672

Four years later Griselda bears a son. When son is two Walter desires to test wife again, tells Griselda people are grumbling as before—son must go. Griselda accepts decision obediently.

16 *herye* praise
19 *lest* desire, urge
25 *sikly berth* dislike

43 *outreye* fall into a passion
63 *al plesance* every wish

50-1 Don 919: humanizing touch which Ch deliberately mistranslated from Petrarch. Baum 120-1: lines come close to being a *complaint* to Walter, illustrate means Ch used to keep from losing reader's sympathy for ultra-patient Gris.

673-735

Same sergeant arrives to take boy away; again Griselda asks for decent burial. Walter is amazed at her patience, but is obsessed with desire to test her. People hate his cruelty.

81 *grave* bury
85 *as hym no thyng ne roghte*
    as if it mattered nothing to
    him

87 *evere lenger the moore* more
    and more as time passed
00 *sturdinesse* harshness
14 *penyble* painstaking
22 *sclaundre* evil report

01-5 Baum 120: Ch here comments on Walter's most irrational trait (which bothers readers)—his *persistence* in tests.

736-784

When daughter is 12 Walter has forged letter sent to him from Pope with leave to divorce Griselda and remarry. Then he sends word to sister's husband (Earl of Panico) to bring 2 children home incognito and announce that daughter is to marry Walter.

38 *message* messengers
45 *lete* leave

68 *outrely* most particularly
76 *gyde* escort

PART V

785-812

Walter makes public announcement to Griselda that he is divorcing her with Pope's leave to satisfy people. He asks her to return cheerfully to father's house with her dowry.

87	*outtreste preeve* ultimate proof	91	*boistously* roughly
		06	*voyde* vacate

813-889

Griselda consents, says she will live as widow, asks to keep one dress to go home in since she came with nothing.

18	*digne* worthy	48	*dowaire* dowry
19	*chamberere* chamber maid	70	*inwith* within
28	*nobleye* noble estate	75	*smoklees* without a smock
31	*foryelde it yow* reward you for it	83	*gerdon of* reward for
40	*make* mate	87	*wrye* cover

52-61 Baum 120-1: Gris verges on complaint, seems more human and deserving of sympathy here; added by Ch. Don 919: here Gris is not really being patient—she embodies constancy rather than patience (see also 650-1). Bron 106: here Gris is allowed "the release of an implied rebuke."

52-4 Hin 203: "pathetic little outburst," not in Petrarch. Sp 154: "humanly pitiful" touch, truly Chaucerian.

890-938

Walter allows her to wear dress she has on. Griselda goes home to father, resumes simple life without complaint.

03	*lyves* living	24	*as by* to judge by
11	*agayns* to meet	38	*but it be falle of newe* unless it has happened recently
17	*fele* many		

04-5 Baum 121: there is "a small note of the rational in Janicula's premonition."

PART VI

939-980

When Earl of Panico arrives with children Walter sends for Griselda, asks her to prepare rooms for new bride. Griselda meekly does it.

42	*kouth* known	65	*yvel biseye* wretched looking
48	*sely* innocent	66	*devoir* duty

66 Hin 204-5 notes similar commands in ballads (*Child Waters, Nut-Brown Maid, Fair Annie*); "such examples of submission agree, in a way, with the ethical ideals of medieval authors, who constantly exalt one virtue at the expense of all others, and who habitually lean toward authority rather than toward freedom."

78 Hin 206: *shake* means shake beds and mattresses, or shake carpets.

981-1043

Fickle people are pleased with Walter's bride. Griselda helps dress her for wedding, begs Walter to treat her kindly—no more testing.

95	*unsad* inconstant	12	*torent* tattered
96	*fane* weather-vane	26	*pris* words of praise
97	*rumbul* rumor	39	*mo* others
99	*clappyng* chatter. *jane* small coin		

95-01 Shel 306: fine lyric protest. Heninger: Clerk here stresses mutability theme—inconstancy of mob brings evil; "only inevitable mutability prescribed by God is acceptable within the framework of order."

37-43 Hin 206: an "extremely delicate" hint. Root 258: Crowning example of Gris's wonderful patience—no word of reproach, only guarded implication. Ger 87: here for first time reader feels "real force of what she has suffered"; her unselfishness (though superhuman) elicits "profoundest pity." Baum 121: pointed warning falls just short of outright complaint, makes Gris seem more human and sympathetic.

1044-1141

Walter, touched, embraces Griselda, reveals all. She is tearfully reunited with her children. Walter reinstates Griselda as his wife, orders feast. They live happily ever after.

49	*sturdy* stern	99	*swapte* fell
52	*yvele apayed* displeased	03	*arace* removed
58	*keep* notice	13	*yfeere* together
92	*no fors of deeth* death does	20	*hire oghte* was her right
	not matter	24	*welkne* sky

79-99 Mus 193: even in this "flood of maternal response" Ch keeps
style conventional and rhetorical.

96-8 Mal 223: "Walter does not deserve such praise, of course, but
Gris in her humility looks to others for virtue, not to herself."

00-3 Bron 105: tenacious clutching of children, even in swoon,
gives "stabbing sense of the cost of years of unacknowledged suffering," is wholly original with Ch; at this moment (carefully prepared
for by repeated indications of time lapse in 442, 450, 610, 617, 736,
780), Gris seems wholly human, "a creature of aching flesh and
blood."

1142-1176

From Griselda's patience we should learn to accept whatever God
sends. There are few Griseldas nowadays. I will end with song dedicated to Wife of Bath.

44	*inportable* intolerable	53	*boghte* has redeemed
51	*in gree* gladly	67	*alayes* alloys
52	*greet skile* very reasonable	69	*plye* bend

42-76 Kit 197: general Christian moral seems to remove tale from
marriage controversy, until (63-76) Clerk surprises whole company
by turning to Wife of Bath with "serene and smiling urbanity" and
offering her his Envoy. Mal 223: moral shows Gris stands for ideal
Christian rather than ideal wife (tale "has nothing to say, at bottom,
on the subject of marriage"); but Ch then adds second ending, attack on Wife, meant to be funny.

42-7 Root 260:   passage suggests Ch viewed Gris's humility as wholly right, but as unattainable ideal.

49-51, 61-2 Heninger: Clerk states man's moral responsibility to oppose mutability, to "acquiesce to God's natural order," live by His will.

63-1212 Root 260-1: roguish humor restores playful tone of *CT*, shows new side of Clerk's character. Pres 254-5: master of logic offering song to Wife is one of "most amusing spectacles" in *CT;* in Envoy, clearly meant for Clerk, "the poetry is not cancelled by the comedy, and the comic *envoy* is no less poetic than the tale." Bron 103-4: Ch uses device of after-thought for Clerk's "sudden shift of tone and attitude," linking tale and pilgrimage with superb art; "the everyday norm of the pilgrimage is re-established by means of the dramatic mock-reversal of the Clerk's values through his own eloquent lips."

71 Lum 149-50:   *secte* can mean sex or heretical cult; Clerk probably intends both meanings.

ENVOY BY CHAUCER

(Subtitle means passage is original with Chaucer, not taken from Petrarch. Clerk continues to speak.)

   1177-1212

Noble wives, don't try to imitate Griselda; instead, assert yourselves, be strong and fierce as tigers, subdue your husbands with nagging, jealousy, extravagance.

88 *Chichevache* = fabled cow who lives on diet of patient wives, is very thin. *swelwe* swallow	96 *camaille* camel
	99 *egre* fierce
	04 *aventaille* strip of chain-mail from helmet to shoulders to protect neck
90 *countretaille* reply	
91 *bidaffed* fooled	11 *lynde* linden tree
95 *archewyves* masterly wives	

77-12 Hin 208: "stanzas of elegant raillery" in which Ch himself criticizes irrational features of tale; successful experiment in intricate

rime. Kit 199-200: Clerk, not Ch, speaks this "masterpiece of sustained and mordant irony" which perfectly suits his character and rhetorical training, also fits dramatic situation as adroit and devastating attack on Wife of Bath and her principles. Cow 172: Ch's own criticism of Petrarch's improbable, sentimental tale, and his "personal recommendation of the theory and practice of the Wife of Bath." ManCT 596: "masterpiece of versification," unequaled for centuries. Lyons rejects Kit's view of Envoy as ironical answer to Wife; "it is just good fun . . . a frivolous postscript to a sober tale." Cog 172, 140-1: "a minor miracle" of irony in Ch's maturest style, probably written 15 years after tale. Moore: "crude retaliation for the Wife's brilliant performance." Mal 222-5: Envoy is "markedly inconsistent" with Clerk's character (*Gen Prol*), has "no real pertinence" to tale's theme, "actually clashes with the effect which the tale as a whole was intended to produce"; Ch, not Clerk, is real speaker; Ch added this brilliant second ending because he could not resist chance for humor, even at sacrifice of unified tone. Pres 254: both Wife and Clerk "have shown the evil of domination in marriage" (from opposite points of view), and Ch ends tale with high comedy of Envoy. Brew 165-6: "astonishing piece of metrical virtuosity" (only 3 rimes in 36 lines) in which Ch, after restraining satiric urge throughout tale, sends "a deadly shaft of laughter among the emotions he has raised." Lum 150: by exaggerating Wife's views Clerk makes them ridiculous, wins "clear victory" in debate, but at same time avoids advocating opposite extreme. Don 920: "uproarious *tour de force*" in which Clerk (and Ch) "restores balance by reasserting those everyday values that the tale has held in subordination." Morse: Clerk is "full of shocked admiration" for Wife's individualism, disapproves of meek Gris. Bron 104: Envoy skillfully bridges gap between tale's idealism and Wife's reality; it also adds to Clerk's portrait—"the Retort Courteous followed by the Quip Modest."

77-8 Cog 139: here Ch, for only time in *CT,* "openly usurps the mouth of a character [Clerk] to confute him."

96 White: possible double meaning in *camaille* (camel and "camail," French word for piece of defensive armor—same as *aventaille* in 1204).

12 ManCT 595: Merchant's repetition of this line in *MerchT* 1213 shows Envoy was integral part of tale, spoken by Clerk, not Ch.

WORDS OF HOST
1212^{a-g}

Host praises tale, wishes his wife had heard it.

12^c *me were levere than* I would rather than have

The Merchant's Tale

COMMENTARIES: Gr 213-6; Ham 309-10;/ Don 920-3; ManCT 596-7, 624; Rob 712-6; Sk 5, 353-69;/ Bald 24-9; Baum 20, 173, 210; Brew 166-71; Bron 63-5; Cog 166-70; Cow 171-4; Dem 46-58; Ev 158-60; Fr 313-6; Kit 201-3; Law 70, 141; Leg 189-90; Low 184-5; Lum 87, 152-75; Mal 225-8; Mus 230-7; Pat 158, 176, 226-8, 254; Pres 206, 262-71; Root 262-6; Sedg 245-6; Shel 100-1, 188-90, 255-9; Sp 155-62; Tho 92-4;/ Baugh, *MP*, 37, 15-26; Baum, *PMLA*, 56, 225-46; Bradley, *JEGP*, 56, 624-30; Bühler, *Spec*, 49, 410-2; Burrow, *Anglia*, 57, 199-208; Cline, *MLN*, 45, 480-2; Dempster, *MP*, 36, 133-54, and 38, 1-8, and *SA*, 333-56; Donovan, *PQ*, 57, 49-60; Griffith, *Expl*, 57, item 13; Holman, *ELH*, 51, 241-52 (W); Immaculate, *MLQ*, 41, 59-66; Kaske, *MLN*, 60, 1-4; Kellogg, *Spec*, 60, 275-9; Kittredge, *MP*, 11-12, 435-67 (W, ST); Lowes, *MP*, 10-11, 305-34; Main, *Expl*, 55, item 13; Malone, *ES*, 50, 209-15; Mathews, *MLR*, 56, 217-20; Miller, *PQ*, 50, 437-46; McGalliard, *PQ*, 46, 193-220, and 343-70; Owen, *JEGP*, 53, 294-311 (W); Pratt, *Spec*, 47, 419-29; Robertson, *Spec*, 51, 24-49; Schlauch, *ELH*, 37, 201-12; Sedgewick, *UTQ*, 48, 337-45; Shain, *MLN*, 55, 235-45; Tatlock, *MLN*, 17, 374, and 35, 295, and *MP*, 36, 367-81.

GENRE: Fabliau, enormously enriched and expanded.

SOURCES AND ANALOGUES: For first part of tale (discussion of advisability of marriage) Ch almost certainly drew on Deschamps' *Miroir de Mariage;* for passages on relations between January and May he was probably indebted to Boccaccio's *Ameto;* for peartree episode at end there are numerous folk-tale analogues. On the whole, tale is remarkably original.

DATE: About 1393-4.

GENERAL CRITICISM: Kittredge: Ch expands fabliau to "savage satire" in which disillusioned Merchant bitterly denounces marriage, expressing disgust at own folly and evil fate by means of sustained irony (suggested by irony of Clerk's Epilogue); Clerk's irony is intellectual, Merchant's passionate, and egotistical; tale gives Merchant's feelings, not Ch's. Kit 201-2: Merchant, usually cautious, is "half mad with rage and shame," is really punishing himself in exposing repulsive dotard January. Root 265-6: Ch stresses poetic justice in Jan's fate, "a sort of crude morality"; we do not approve of May, yet sympathize with her; whole tale in spirit of broad "humor" comedy of Ben Jonson which sweetens unwholesomeness, with Jan ending up in fool's paradise. Cow 171-4: well balanced and unified tale is Merchant's cynical and ironic attack on faithless wives, with Ch characterizing "disgusting imbecility" of Jan. ManCT 624: tale originally meant for member of religious order, perhaps Monk (see 1251, 1322, 1389-90). Leg 189-90: tale is complex drama of pity and laughter in cynical style, but unlike usual fabliau in arousing sympathy (even preference) for Jan; old egotistical husband with deep affection for May, lyrical appeals, pathetic distress, contrasts with selfish cruelty of May. Dem 46-58: tale stresses old man's folly with deliberate dramatic irony. Low 183: "most cynically disillusioned" of CT. Sedg 245-6: Merchant shows narrow mind, lack of wit, in tale meant to reveal infidelity of wife, but in which husband is real butt. Tatlock, MP: tale has brilliant ironic style; Jan not pitiful, is despicable lecher, coercing facts to fit his self-indulgence, egotistical and self-deluded; May is unsympathetic character too, "not worse than Jan but hardly a person at all"; Damian, like May, is stock character, "a parody of Troilus," courtly lover squatting ludicrously under bush. Schlauch: Ch makes devastating fun of courtly love code transformed into fabliau; Ch aware of fundamental falsity in amoral romance convention, gives dazzling proof of humane genius. Baugh: tale originally meant for Friar, lewd cleric of Gen Prol who could give sermon on marriage (unsuited to Merchant); later Ch conceived Friar-Summoner quarrel, shifted tale to Merchant, added motivating Prologue. Dempster, MP, 38, disagrees with ManCT and Baugh: tale fits Merchant as reply to Wife of Bath's attack on merchants (in ShipT), shows keen interest in morals unsuited to Friar. Pat 176, 226-8: harsh cynicism in tale unusual in Ch; duped Merchant attacks aged husband rather than faithless wife, and "every line of it recoils ironically upon himself"; cynicism and immorality do not represent Ch's own view. Shel 188-90, 255-9: tale has setting and spirit of Italian Renaissance, with worship of the body, spendor of palace, garden, wedding feast—elements of beauty in witty, cruel story; despite satire and cynicism, all 3 characters treated somewhat sympathetically with Ch's balanced realism, May and Damian as courtly love types, Jan as *worthy, goode, noble,* with a few redeeming traits, "a figure of pathos as well as folly." McGalliard, *PQ,* 46, 193-220, disagrees with Manly that tale was first meant for regular cleric—Biblical learning, ideas on marriage were common among laymen; marriage debate, distrust of worldly life probably suggested to Ch by Deschamps' *Miroir de Mariage* (many parallels). McGalliard, *PQ,* 46, 343-70: tale unlike *MillT* and *RvT* in unique way Ch develops plot from implications of characterization of Jan with his extravagant self-deception, obsessive ideas on marriage; Jan is "fundamentally comic" central figure, portrayed psychologically and mock heroically with no fierce or direct satire; narrator is detached and serene, with tone of "rich and mellow irony." Sedgewick: tale always meant for Merchant who reveals his own "self-loathing" in picture of Jan, finally becomes identified with Jan for reader, though only partially aware himself. Cog 166-70: best of *CT,* with "more wit, more feeling, more movement, and more surprise"; perfect for Merchant who reveals himself slightly less directly than Wife of Bath in tone of "sympathy-in-mockery" for Jan who appears "helpless, romantic, generous, tragic, and a silly if not nasty old man simultaneously"; tale is romance with love as theme, Damian and May romantic in thoughts but cynical in actions. Law 70, 141: tale is "mordant irony," fitting "savage attack on wedlock" in Prologue. Miller: bitter irony at end exposes Jan's self-deception, also discredits women. Tho 92-4: tale shows Ch's dramatic skill in putting himself in another's place; Merchant's antifeminist view and bitter irony (favoring neither Jan nor May) are not Ch's. Holman: adultery is aim of whole plot, with morality of courtly love (marriage equals boredom); irony of tale shows Ch condemning both characters and courtly love system—"one of the most savagely obscene, angrily embittered, pessimistic, and unsmiling tales in our language." Mal 225-8: bitterness of attack on Jan shows tale not meant to characterize Merchant (who would be expected to focus on faithless May); he is merely Ch's mouthpiece. Pres 262-71: May is product of Merchant's imagination, not

Ch's. Brew 167-70: least pleasant of *CT* "a sordid adulterous intrigue." Lum 156-75: tale is coldly intellectual, with uniquely bitter irony, unsympathetic characters, "dirtily obscene atmosphere," fitting unsympathetic picture of Merchant in *Gen Prol;* to Host (2419-25) May is villain, but to Merchant Jan is worse, shown with disgust and "caustic irony" throughout; extended use of physical blindness as symbol for mental blindness (1598, 2069-71, 2107-10); Merchant lacks wisdom to see "moral application to his own situation." Mathews sees possible source of tale in Deschamps' ballade no. 880, cites parallels. Donovan shows parallels with Claudian's *De Raptu Proserpinae.* Mus 230-7: thinness of courtly love quality fits "bitter negation" of Merchant's attitude; as in *MillT,* Ch here juxtaposes elevated attitudes and coarse naturalism, exposing Jan's blindness and Merchant's "ugly personal idiosyncracy." Burrow: tale tends to generalize and allegorize (names, garden, etc.), thus extending its meaning and modifying its obvious irony, giving double view of Jan; he is "pathetic, absurd, and repulsive," but pathos increases toward end, though without any moral concession on Ch's part; irony is controlled by fact that Jan shows general human frailty and *fantasye;* this use of allegory distinguishes tale from all other fabliaux. Baum 20, 210: basic situation is moral, with poetic justice; but "by the frivolous *dei ex machina* the justice is reversed, cuckoldry is justified, and immorality palliated by a hearty laugh"—artistic failure. Don 920-3: contrast between Merchant's earlier illusions and present bitter experience of marriage accounts for tensions in tale, ironical praise of attitudes he now abhors; he shows May as increasingly degraded, feels superior to Jan because, though he shares Jan's crass attitude to women, he is undeceived; his "cynical condemnation of Jan and May becomes a profoundly sad commentary not only on their failure to understand, but on his own." Bron 63-5: satiric tale, unprepared for in *Gen Prol,* motivated by Merchant's animosity toward Wife of Bath and Clerk (with his tale of wifely patience); bitterness is Merchant's, not Ch's.

THE MERCHANT'S PROLOGUE

IV, 1213-1244

Merchant says his wife, wed 2 months, is overbearing shrew, unlike

Griselda. Host asks for story; Merchant will tell of marriage but not his own.

22   *at al* out-and-out   36   *ryve* pierce

13-44 Kittredge: stately Merchant reacts violently to tale of patient Griselda and to Clerk's closing words of ironic praise of Wife of Bath which are more than he can stand. Tatlock, *MLN:* Merchant's restrained personality erupts into "controlled savagery." Mal 226: comic effect in contrast between picture of dignity in *Gen Prol,* speaking arrogantly of financial gains, and Merchant who here unburdens himself indiscreetly to whole group. Lum 155: angered by Wife of. Bath's treatment of husbands, Merchant forgets usual restraint. Don 921: Merchant exposes own vileness in trying to refute Clerk's view of women and marriage.

13 Sk 5, 353: *Wepyng and waylying* echoes *ClT* 1212, links tales. Ev 159: echo of Clerk also shows Merchant's "overcharged heart," prepares reader for bitterness of tale.

30 Cline: swearing by *Seint Thomas of Ynde* fitting here because this saint was popularly noted for incredulity.

40-2 Lum: Host loves to draw personal revelations from pilgrims.

THE MERCHANT'S TALE

1245-1398

January, old lecherous knight of Pavia, decides to marry at 60. He convinces himself of many advantages of marriage, citing several classical and Biblical authorities on subject. He discounts chance of infidelity, calls friends for advice.

51   *seculeer* secular clergy   13   *commune* common rights
79   *brotel* insecure   14   *moebles* movable goods
82   *arrest* restraint   42   *swynke* work
87   *buxom* submissive   74   *of* by. *enhaunced* promoted
95   *what force* what matter   75   *gree* rank

45-1688 Root 265: delicate irony of whole marriage debate, proclaiming joy of wedlock while making clear that Jan's rosy vision is to be sheer mockery.

45-1398 Dem 46-50: dramatic irony in Jan's praise of marriage in light of what happens. Baugh: no evidence of irony, sermon on marriage is sincere; tale meant for Friar, not Merchant. Dempster, *MP*, 38: praise of marriage is Merchant's paraphrase of Jan's thoughts, with ironic intention obvious, especially in 1252-4, 1266-9; refutes Baugh—passage does not stress Christian aspects of marriage; Bible known to all. Sp 155-6: ironic praise of marriage enriches whole marriage discussion in *CT*, is marked by comic exaggeration and fantasy. McGalliard, *PQ*, 46, 343-70: ironic praise of marriage represents Jan's thoughts, reveals his own unconscious self-deception, his absurdity. Sedgewick: complex passage of multiple meanings; through mind of Jan marriage is both glorified and tainted, and as spoken by Merchant glowing words are "really ironic curses" which fall on Merchant himself as well as Jan. Owen: passage is symbolic, unifying, foreshadowing Jan's increasing folly. Shain: defense of marriage uses common devices of medieval sermons (as in *PardT*), probably first intended for clerical teller. Lum 159: false reasoning "comes forth as musings which pass through Jan's mind." Mus 232: "a sarcastic reversal of meaning" from Merchant's words on marriage in Prologue.

51 Baugh: *seculeer* means laymen, not regular clergy. Dempster, *MP*, 38, disagrees; this would make line express unnecessary rudeness to laymen on trip. McGalliard, *PQ*, 46, 193-220, agrees with Baugh; Jan's loose conduct represents worldly life of laity, which Deschamps in *Miroir* calls "seculiere."

52 Immaculate: 60 should be understood literally here, but generally in 1248 where it means large, indefinite number.

54 Lum 159: double meaning in *corage* (religious piety as in *Gen Prol* 22, and sexual potency as in *NPT* 3452) points up Jan's rationalizing, use of religion to cloak lechery, which makes cuckolding inevitable.

96-04 Lowes: Ch here uses Deschamps' *Miroir* (Chap. 21) for paraphrase of Theophrastus. Dem 49: passage intensifies bitter tone and lets us anticipate Jan's future troubles more definitely. Lum 159: Theophrastus' views ironically foreshadow May's actual conduct.

96 Baum: pun on *housbondrye* (care of household goods and desire to function as husband); same pun in 1380.

18, 92 Lum 173: these comments, inconsistent with Jan's musings, are Merchant's own bitter remarks showing his unwarranted feeling of superiority over Jan.

62-74 Lum 160: irony in fact that husbands of Rebecca, Judith, Abigail, and Esther all suffered.

1399-1468

He tells friends he plans to wed a young wife who can be molded and bear children. He states he is still sexually potent, asks friends to confirm his decision.

99 *sad* serious
03 *despended* used up
10 *fonde* manage
19 *pyk* pike. *pykerel* young pike (pickerel)
22 *bene* bean. *greet forage* coarse fodder

25 *broken harm* petty annoyances? (Sk)
35 *avoutrye* adultery
54 *meschief* trouble
58 *stark* strong

29-30 Dem 51: irony of wax simile in light of fact that Jan is later betrayed by May through wax impression of key to garden; further irony in Jan's specifying innocent young girl so he can control her and feel secure in having her all to himself.

36-40, 57-66 Miller notes Jan's desire for heir and confidence in his virility, both of which ironically facilitate May's adultery in garden. .

1469-1576

His 2 brothers Placebo and Justinus argue. Placebo (yes-man) praises January's decision. But Justinus advises caution in choosing wife; he warns of danger in wedding young woman. January takes Placebo's opinion.

83 *weyven* turn aside
12 *apayd* served
14 *stapen* advanced
16 *pyn* peg
36 *mannyssh wood* man-crazy? or perhaps virago-like (with

masculine manners and mad)
42 *thewes* virtues
53 *wryngeth* pinches
68 *panyer* basket
73 *letteth* hinders

78-65 McGalliard, *PQ,* 46, 193-22: Placebo is typical courtier; Justinus advises caution, does not argue against marriage *per se,* because he knows Jan has already decided. Sp 157: Placebo and Justinus are moral allegorical characters of false and true counselors, corresponding to moral powers vying for Jan's soul; but they are also human types.

78-18 McGalliard, *PQ,* 46, 343-70: Placebo serves to characterize Jan who should be insulted by too obvious desire to please, but Jan is too self-deceived to be resentful.

85-6 Bühler: Biblical proverb which also occurs in *MillT* 3530, *Mel* 1003.

19-65 McGalliard, *PQ,* 46, 343-70: Justinus tactful, does not ridicule Jan or 'Placebo, confines himself to good advice as true friend who finds Jan's folly disturbing (though to readers it may be hilarious); characterization of Justinus shows Ch's sound psychology. Lum 161: Justinus "only clear-thinking individual in the whole story," contrasts sharply with Jan and with Merchant. Don 921: only character Merchant approves is Justinus "whose hard-headed and cheaply cynical counsel makes the good mercantile point that a man ought to examine goods very carefully before he buys them" (see also 1655-88).

66-76 Shel 255-9: Jan wants help, not advice, stubbornly accepts only advice he likes. McGalliard, *PQ,* 46, 343-70: Jan seeks not advice, but agreement with fixed idea which is an obsession, "an aberration in the character."

1577-1688

After considering several, January settles on young girl and calls friends together to approve. He fears he may be so happy on earth that he will be denied Heaven. Justinus scoffs at this fear, says that wife may be purgatory enough, as Wife of Bath has shown.

00	*purtreyed* pictured		52	*on lyve ys* is alive, lives
14	*abregge* shorten, end		54	*assoilleth* answer
18	*boone* favor		•56	*japerye* mockery
25	*smal degree* low rank		70	*paraunter* perhaps
30	*parten* share		71	*meene* instrument
46	*delicat* delicious		77	*lette* hinder

77-87 Sp 159: Jan suffers from fantasy (see also 1598-1610) and moral confusion, so that he worries about whether he can have both earthly and heavenly paradise (1634-54)—keen irony.

82-5 Bradley sees passage as example of technique (common to several of *CT*) of ironic contrast between paragon of "mirror" tradition and corrupt reality.

99-10 Lum 161: "a whiff of the old knight's malodorous mind."

34-54 McGalliard, *PQ*, 46, 343-70: passage is the ultimate absurdity, climax of Jan's preliminary characterization and self-deception.

40-1 Dem 53: tree mentioned here anticipates peartree incident.

69-70 Dem 52: a side attack on Wife of Bath, leading up to direct attack in 1685-7.

85-7 Sk 5, 359: lines obviously belong to narrator, not to Justinus— perhaps an oversight by Ch. Kittredge: direct reference to Wife of Bath has been prepared for in previous allusion to her (1423-8) and quotation of her (1670-3); the "slip" in putting these words into Justinus' mouth is not Ch's but Merchant's and is dramatically fitting.

1689-1794

Marriage treaty is soon drawn up and January weds young girl called May. He gives great wedding feast at which young squire Damian sees May and falls in love with her.

97	*scrit* deed	22	*shynketh* pours out
98	*feffed in* put in legal posses-sion of	76	*swelte* died
07	*croucheth* marks with sign of cross	84	*bedeth* offers
		85	*false hoomly hewe* false do-mestic servant
11	*deys* dais	86	*naddre* adder, viper
19	*tromped* trumpeted. *for to heere* for people to hear	90	*borne man* vassal

97-8 Lum 162: shows May's mercenary aims which Jan affects not to see.

01-8 Tatlock, *MLN*, 17: "Truly the church did all she could for Jan"—withering irony. Immaculate refutes Tatlock's assertion (*MLN*, 35) that *hooly sacrement* means Blessed Eucharist; rather it means marriage ceremony proper, since priest wears stole (1703), right vestment for this ceremony, and since satire requires stress on marriage idea and "holiness" of Jan's motives (see 1261, 1319, 1507, 1628). Pat 254: abuse of marriage ceremony (and Biblical quotes elsewhere) do not show that Ch felt sacrament itself or Bible were at fault; distortion of original meanings gives comic effects that medieval audience would instantly recognize.

09-94 McGalliard, *PQ*, 343-70: description of feast is mock heroic; absurdity is lost on self-deluded Jan.

42-5 McGalliard, *PQ*, 46, 343-70: May, "Jan's nemesis," is picture of "demure acquiescence" (see also 1603-4), her personality and feelings unknown until she announces love for Damian in 1982-5.

50-64 Sp 160-1: fantastic delusion of Jan at feast which has allegorical aspect in names of May and Jan, "spring impulses in midwinter." Dem 54: cruel dramatic irony in Jan's joy and tender feelings toward May.

55-60 Lum 163: "savage irony" in Jan's vow to restrain himself destroys all sympathy for him.

72 Tatlock, *MP*: Damian's name fitting, since there were sexual elements in popular cult of 11th-century Italian St. Peter Damian.

82 Mus 232: frequency of phrase *fresshe May* (also *noble* Jan) shows Merchant's sarcastic, negative attitude.

84 AHM: probable pun on *bedeth* (offers, from OE *beodan,* and puts to bed, from OE *beddian*); that is, Damian is household enemy who not only offers his service (to Jan), but puts his service to bed (with May); clearly sexual context and proximity to *bedstraw* (1783) strongly suggest intentional double-entendre.

1795-1865

January retires with May after taking stimulants. With coarse whiskers and slack skin he is revolting to her.

95	*diurne* daily		09	*letuarie* medicinal syrup
00	*route* crowd		12	*eschu* averse
07	*ypocras* a cordial. *clarree*		17	*travers* curtain
	sweetened wine. *vernage*		25	*houndfyssh* dogfish
	sweet white wine		48	*jargon* chatter. *pye* magpie

07-12 Lum 163: Jan's use of these aphrodisiacs belies his earlier boasts of his virility.

18-57 Tatlock, *MP,* notes many similarities to bedroom scene in Boccaccio's *Ameto.* Shel 255-9: humorous and satiric scene in which Jan is as delighted with himself as he is with May, oblivious of his own absurdity. Lum 163-4: "most nauseatingly unpleasant" scene in tale, a "devastating description of this ridiculous newlywed." Mus 234: scene of "graphic ugliness, the more ugly for the romantic context."

21-41 Sp 161: horror of Jan's delusion, his moral confusion in "persisting conception of marriage as licensed sin."

56 Kaske: compare *RvT* 4237; both lines parody courtly "aube" or dawn-song in which lover is forced reluctantly to leave lady; same ironic parody of aube tradition in 1763.

1866-2020

Meanwhile, Damian, prostrate with lovesickness, writes letter to May. January hears Damian is sick, sends May to cheer him. Damian slips letter to her. She reads it secretly, takes pity, and agrees to give love to Damian at first opportunity. Damian recovers promptly.

73	*biwreye* reveal	76	*deme* judge
79	*penner* pen-case	87	*franchise* generosity
00	*entendeth* attends	88	*narwe* carefully
06	*me forthynketh* grieves me	05	*twiste* squeezed
37	*bille* letter	11	*preyneth* trims. *pyketh*
43	*kyd* revealed		adorns
53	*cloutes* shreds	14	*dogge for the bowe* dog
58	*strepen* strip		trained to hunt with archer

66-2020 McGalliard, *PQ,* 46, 343-70: Ch describes affair in mock heroic style; "May has his dramatic sympathy," but not moral approval.

66-9 Baum 173: deliberate parody of formal rhetoric.

97-28 Dem 55: Jan's interest in and praise of Damian, also his sending of May to cheer him, are Ch's original ironic touches.

20-8 Shel 258: irony in Jan's sending May to Damian; he is "un-

done by his own goodness and generosity" (Ch's balanced realism).
50-4 Tatlock, *MP:* romantic quality of love affair ruined by May's
reading love letter in privy. Lum 164: "the locale in which this love
missive is read by May sets the tone for her subsequent relationship
with Damian."
86 Schlauch: Ch gives line "an inexpressibly sardonic tone" through
treatment of whole situation, though it would be wholly fitting in
conventional romance.

2021-2096

January builds garden with high wall and locked gate where he
sports with May. Suddenly he goes blind, and thereafter jealously
keeps one hand on May at all times.

22	*stant* consists		46	*clyket* key
39	*fayerye* fairy band		55	*dure* last
43	*deyntee* delight		61	*brotil* precarious
45	*wyket* gate		80	*soul* solitary

21-56 Dem 56: Jan ironically plans garden himself for protection
of marriage, only to be duped therein (not in sources). Tatlock, *MP:*
garden in Boccaccio's *Filocolo* which bloomed in winter may have
suggested idea to Ch. Pat 226: garden here anticipates garden in
FranklT, just as *MerchT* is ironic "companion piece" to *FranklT*.
Robertson: garden related to medieval literary gardens symbolizing
charity and cupidity; Jan builds garden to make secret his cupidity,
while Damian and May use it for their cupidity; green laurel (2037)
perhaps symbolizes "the pattern of the Fall . . . perennial in human
experience."
21-96 Owen: garden, blindness, and tree are linked images—in story
of Adam and Eve, wife is man's earthly paradise only if one is blind
to tree of forbidden fruit; Jan is not only literally blind in garden,
but also "blind in the paradise of his wife's arms"; Jan consummates
his folly in garden which is symbol of his marriage. Burrow: garden
"seems to dignify and strengthen Jan's feelings by generalizing them,"
countering the irony; garden represents Jan's earthly paradise, his
heigh fantasye as well as his "sexual fantasy."

31-7 Kellogg: Ch aims at making Jan as disgusting as possible by referring to courtly love of *RR*, then to Priapus (this effect further developed by irony of 2141-8, 2160).

2097-2218

Damian and May plot to deceive old man. May takes wax impression of garden key; Damian makes key. On June morning January takes May into garden. May signals Damian to enter first with key, later to climb into peartree in garden.

06	*fyn* object	35	*eggyng* urging
12	*poure* peer	49	*lewed* wanton
13	*blent* deceived	77	*wyte* blame
15	*ese* pleasure	96	*sterve* die
29	*kept streite* closely watched	01	*drenche* drown
30	*rownynge* whispering	17	*pyrie* peartree

17 Tatlock, *MP:* through wax mold Jan is ironically deceived by wife whom he thought he could mold like wax; his physical blindness represents mental blindness to facts, and May's final triumph is justified.

38-48 Sk 5, 366: whole passage made of fragments from *Song of Solomon*. Robertson: ironic comedy, showing how cupidity "often leads to ridiculous self-deception." Mus 236: "supreme twist of the narrative's bitterness and of the poet's virtuosity." Kellogg: passage also alludes to "grotesque carnality" of story of Susannah in Daniel. xiii, 20 (Apocrypha) in which 2 old judges try to seduce Susannah in fruit garden ("Behold the doors of the orchard are shut, and nobody seeth us, and we are in love with thee; wherefore consent to us, and lie with us").

88-06 Lum 168: May's first speech in tale, shows Merchant's effort to keep focus on Jan.

10-1 Owen: tree represents Jan's virility, bearing fruit which is not his; later he aids wife to forbidden fruit, adultery; Merchant unwittingly shares in blindness of Jan in that he does not realize extent to which he is telling his own experiences and feelings.

2219-2319
Pluto and Proserpina, roaming in garden, see the situation. Pluto comments on deceitful women, says he will restore January's sight. Proserpina defends women, says she will give May tongue to brazen it out.

33	*grisely* grim	84	*geestes* histories
46	*bountee* goodness	96	*forbode* forbidden
56	*cokewold* cuckold	97	*emplastre* whitewash
60	*ayen* again	08	*brouke* enjoy
73	*visage it hardily* boldly face it out		

25-19 Kittredge: Pluto-Proserpina debate is "violation of dramatic propriety," but cynical Merchant wants to reinforce his lesson, echoes arguments between Wife of Bath and her husbands. Root 266: "delicate conceit" of debate relieves coarseness of tale. Tatlock, *MP:* Pluto and Proserpina are "divine counterparts" of Jan and May. McGalliard, *PQ,* 46, 193-220: debate is only comprehensive statement on marriage and women in general in Ch, is similar to debates in *Miroir de Mariage.* Sedgewick: underworld deities are fitting witnesses to "erotic blindness of men." Sp 162: similarity of contrasting ages between Pluto and Proserpina and Jan and May. Donovan notes parallels in Claudian's *De Raptu Proserpinae* in which Pluto, like Jan, is old, lustful, has 2 brothers, desires young wife and heirs, is cleverly duped by wife; in tale Pluto and Proserpina are fiend-like characters, intended to illustrate Merchant's comment in Prologue (1218-20).

32 Pratt: Ch's use of and reference to Claudian not pretentious since his audience were long familiar with Claudian's writings.

57-61 Main: pun on *lechour* (lecher and healer or doctor); the lechery healed Jan's blindness. Griffith adds evidence in fact that Damian is named for St. Damian, patron saint of physicians.

64-10 Low 184: Proserpina wins argument "with a point-blank bluntness worthy of the Wife of Bath."

77 Low 184: "the timeless denizens of Faërye" invoke Biblical authorities "with enchanting anachronism."

2320-2353

May craves pears, asks January to give her boost up peartree. He does so, encircling trunk with arms so none may follow. Damian makes love to May in tree.

22	*papejay* popinjay (bird)	40	*no fors* no matter
25	*agaynes* up to	49	*twiste* branch
35	*plit* condition	51	*glose* gloss over
38	*knave* boy		

38-53 Dem 56-7: Jan's pathetic devotion to May is cruel stroke of dramatic irony; having May suggest Jan's holding tree trunk (unparalleled in other versions) gives Merchant added chance to show women as "repulsively cynical." Miller: May uses supposed pregnancy to get into tree, thus playing on Jan's self-deluding confidence in his virility—the final irony.

2354-2418

Pluto restores sight to January who looks up and roars with anger. May explains she seeks to heal his eyes by struggling with man in tree; she argues he does not yet see clearly. January accepts this story, calls May down, kisses her happily.

67	*stoore* bold	91	*lief* beloved
76	*algate* all the same	00	*adawed* awakened
78	*swyved* copulated with	05	*ysatled* settled
79	*hals* neck	13	*clippeth* embraces

54-14 Lum 170: Jan "rejects what he sees and willfully remains blind."

61 Baum: pun on *dressed* (arrayed and addressed).

96 Lum 171: "May shamelessly and exultingly taunts him."

18 Baum 210: Ch's last word—"if this is not blasphemous flippancy, it is sarcastic self-criticism of a high order."

EPILOGUE

2419-2440

Host comments on deceitfulness of wives, says his wife is true to him but is a nagging shrew. He could reveal more, but fears someone might tell his wife.

23	*sely* poor, innocent	36	*meynee* company
28	*labbyng* babbling	38	*outen* . . . *chaffare* bring
32	*teyd* tied		out . . . merchandise
34	*nyce* foolish		

19-40 Kit 203: Host, too, is "having his little fling at the Wife of Bath." Malone: Host's confidence his wife is faithful is meant to be funny, coming right after May has convinced Jan of her fidelity despite evidence of his own eyes. Mal 227: similarity between Host's and Merchant's words on their wives; each contrasts his wife to virtuous woman in previous tale (*CLT* and *Mel*). Lum 87: Host, perhaps thinking of own wife, misses point of tale, blames May, fails to see that Jan's lust has blinded him.

The Squire's Tale

COMMENTARIES: Gr 216-9; Ham 310-4;/ Don 923; ManCT 597-605; Rob 716-21; Sk 5, 370-87;/ Brew 168-70; Cog 166-7; Cow 174; Fr 316-9; Hin 210-36; Kit 204-6; Law 142-3; Lum 175-80; Mal 230-1; Pat 210; Pres 271-3; Root 266-70; Shan 321;/ Baum, *MLN*, 17, 377, and *PMLA*, 56, 225-46, and 58, 167-70; Bennett, *MLN*, 53, 531-4; Braddy, *MLR*, 38, 41-4, and *JEGP*, 42, 279-90, and *MLN*, 47, 175-9; Chapman, *MLN*, 53, 521-4; Francis, *PMLA*, 53, 1126-41; Getty, *PMLA*, 29, 202-16; Jones, *SA*, 357-76; Kittredge, *MP*, 10, 481-2; Lowes, *Wash. Univ. Studies* (1913), 3-18; Magoun, *MLN*, 52, 183-5; Neville, *JEGP*, 51, 167-79; Stillwell, *RES*, 48, 177-88; Whiting, *MS*, 47, 189-234.

GENRE: Romance.

SOURCE: Unknown; probably Ch had no single source but freely used material from many sources, such as oriental tales of Prester John, stories of the *Cléomadès* romance cycle, Hindu stories of faithless birds, accounts of oriental travels, etc.

DATE: Uncertain, but probably during *CT* period (see line 73).

GENERAL CRITICISM: Hin 210-4: probably based on lost French version of Tartar romance, perhaps of cycle based on Genghis Khan; probably dates before 1381 (prior to *KnT* which also has oriental coloring), showing preoccupation with rhetoric; plan of tale too extensive for *CT,* probably not written for Squire (despite line 73). Kit 204: "justly celebrated though fragmentary." Root 267: Ch probably broke off because he did not know how to end tale, which has fascination of a fragment with magical beginning, is happily suited to Squire. Getty: tale of purely romantic love fits Squire, is "the most fascinating story never told." Pat 210: romantic product of Ch's "ripest years." Braddy, *JEGP:* Ch probably planned oriental frame narrative like Persian *Thousand and One Days,* with Canacee's experience with falcon (making her think all men fickle) as frame for series of episodes before returning to Canacee and falcon at end (see 651-70). Fr 317-8: magic elements are "stock-in-trade" of many oriental writers. Stillwell: Ch broke off because tale did not suit his genius; throughout tale his irrepressible humor interferes with romantic mood, creates artistic confusion, finally makes him "realize that it is better to abandon his attempt to force an entrance into fairyland than to get stuck in a magic casement." Law 143: tale expresses "artificial and decorative concept of love." Neville: Squire hopes to outdo his father with tale more extravagantly romantic and complex than *KnT;* he takes love too seriously to share Knight's amused but kindly view of it, but he echoes *KnT* often (compare *KnT* 885-90, 1380, 892, 1334, 1449, 2961, 1429 with *SqT* 63, 73, 670, 289, 651, 401, 34, etc.); tale stresses chivalric ideals of love and *gentilesse* which contrast purposely with attitudes of Wife of Bath and Merchant. Brew 168: superb description in Part I is "perhaps the closest we shall ever get to a full description of a great 14th-century festival at Court"; tale's wonders are cut short, perhaps fortunately. Chapman: as model for plotting in Part I Ch used first part of *Sir Gawain and the Green Knight;* in both a strange knight rides into hall interrupting king's feast, addresses king courteously, is stared at as wonder from fairyland by courtiers, etc. Lum 177 disagrees with Stillwell that Ch broke off because materials did not suit his realistic interests; realistic passages are not comments by Ch but are given to Squire to fit tale to him (see Neville); other business kept Ch from finishing. Don 923: Ch probably grew impatient with tale, "a very respectable aristocratic romance, which few readers will wish longer."

INTRODUCTION TO THE SQUIRE'S TALE

V, 1-8
Host asks Squire to tell love story; Squire agrees.

3	*konnen* know	6	*lust* wish
5	*hertly wyl* good will		

1-3 Lum 176: Host's shrewdness in calling on gay Squire to banish unpleasant atmosphere of *MerchT.*

THE SQUIRE'S TALE, PART I

9-75

In Tartary ruled the noble king Cambyuskan, who had two sons, Algarsyf and Cambalo, and one daughter called Canacee. On his 20th anniversary as king Cambyuskan gives a great feast.

9	*Sarray* Tsarev (S. E. Russia)	47	*after the yeer* according to the calendar
10	*werreyed* made war on	59	*deys* dais
18	*lay* law	61	*halt* holds
20	*yliche* equally	67	*sewes* gravies
38	*rethor* master of rhetoric	68	*heronsewes* young herons
39	*colours longynge* fine phrases belonging	75	*firste* original subject

9-346 Cog 166: all of Part I shows boyish approach, fascination with courtly code, fits Squire of *Gen Prol*.

34-41 Hin 215: urbanity of actual style in tale suggests it may not have been written for a pilgrim. Stillwell: a comic touch, satirizing tedious rhetoric and perhaps also conventional descriptions in romances; similar touches in 89-109 (pun on *stile,* etc.). Lum 177-8: shows Squire's humility and knowledge of formal rhetoric, both noted in *Gen Prol* 109, 96.

37 Cog 167: Squire boyishly concerned about style.

38-41 Baum, *MLN:* "merely a rhetorical way of saying that Canace was indescribably, ineffably lovely."

69-72 Bennett: lines probably suggested by passage on Tartars eating strange meats in Sir John Mandeville's *Travels.*

76-167

During feast strange knight enters on brass horse, carrying glass mirror, and wearing gold ring and sword—all gifts for Cambyuskan from king of Arabia and India. Horse will take a man anywhere in the world in one day; mirror will reveal whether a man is true friend or foe; ring (for Canacee) enables one to converse with birds; the edge of sword will cut through any armor, and flat side will heal any wound.

77 *nobleye* state
88 *ful bisily* all agog
01 *vice* error
05 *sowne* imitate
06 *style* stile
20 *wilneth* desires
21 *wem* hurt
27 *writhyng* twisting

28 *koude* knew. *gyn* cunning device
31 *seel . . . bond* (seals and bonds to compel service of spirits)
50 *stevene* language
62 *the plat* the flat side
66 *glose* deceit

95-7 Whiting: Ch probably knew *Sir Gawain and the Green Knight*. Magoun disagrees; dialect of *Sir Gawain* perhaps too hard for Ch to read; he more likely drew reference to Gawain's courtesy from *RR* on which he also relied for glass-making in 254.

99-04 Kittredge: probable influence of Geoffrey de Vinsauf.

02-9 Lum 178: Squire's knowledge of rhetoric and his gaiety shown in pun on *stile* (both noted in *Gen Prol*).

168-262
Strange knight dismounts and joins feast. People gaze in amazement at horse which stands immovably. They wonder also and guess about the other gifts until the meal is finished.

74 *yfet* fetched
81 *remewed* removed
84 *wyndas* windlass. *polyve* pulley
88 *voyden* remove
90 *gauren* stare
95 *Poilleys* Apulian
04 *been* bees
05 *skiles* reasons

09 *Grekes hors Synon* horse of the Greek, Synon
14 *shapen hem* plot
16 *rowned* whispered
24 *gladly* usually
34 *queynte* curious
46 *algates* at any rate
54 *fern-asshen* ashes of ferns
56 *so fern* so long ago

91-5 Lum 178: professional comment on horse reflects Squire's training (see *Gen Prol* 94).

20-3 Shan 321: shows ways of ignorant folk in dealing with things beyond their ken.

25-35, 53-61 Stillwell: artistic confusion as Ch shifts from learned to common-sense tone, both unromantic; his interest in people leads him to linger over their speculations, but "to have the extras prick the bubble world of the principal actors with the pin of common sense" is artistically unsound.

263-346
After supper king entertains strange knight with a dance. Knight then instructs king in use of magic horse.

69	*parementz* rich hangings (i.e., the Presence Chamber)	91	*bit* orders. *hye* bring quickly
81	*feestlych* convivial	03	*route* crowd
90	*dresse* go	16	*trille* twirl. *stant* stands
		18	*nempne* tell

75-90 Stillwell: "light and tender humour" in these lines. Mal 230-1: here Squire calls himself dull, ignorant of love, in direct contradiction of *Gen Prol*.

40-2 Hin 229: horse apparently disappeared when bridle was removed, could be summoned by bridle.

PART II
347-408
Everyone having retired, Canacee rises early to test her ring and walks into the park to hear the birds.

50	*galpyng* gaping. *keste* kissed	76	*gladly wyse* usually inquisitive (confused sentence, meaning "Her governess, like these old women who," etc.)
59	*of which ther nys no charge* which have no weight		
60	*pryme large* fully prime (9 a.m.)	89	*soote* sweet
62	*mesurable* temperate	92	*trench* alley
65	*appalled* pale, enfeebled	93	*glood* glided
		01	*knotte* point

47-56 Stillwell: comic spirit here and in 362-7 ("Canacee didn't want to have a hangover") clashes with romantic mood of tale.

76 Baum, *PMLA*, 58: pun on *gladly wyse* (usually wise and glad to be thought wise).

01-8 Cow 174: plan of tale not in accord with this principle. Braddy, *JEGP:* lines strongly suggest Canacee-falcon episode was to be *knotte* of whole tale, probably framing device to be returned to at end, after intervening episodes. Francis: these prolix lines are probably "delicate parody of Ch's earlier asides to his audience on the subject of the dangers of prolixity" (especially in *KnT*), with humor turned back on its creator; Ch's audience was probably sophisticated enough to catch this (see also 278-301).

409-498

Canacee sees female falcon in tree weeping and beating herself. She asks cause of falcon's woe and offers to heal her wounds. Falcon swoons, falls from tree, agrees to tell her story.

09	*for drye* because of dryness	88	*bet* better
17	*evere in oon* continuously	91	(allusion to proverb "Beat
18	*prighte* pricked		the dog before [in front of]
29	*fremde* foreign		the lion," a device actually
35	*leden* language		used by lion-tamers to intimi-
42	*twiste* branch		date lions)
48	*furial pyne* furious pain	96	*to water wolde* would turn
54	*wreke* take vengeance		to water
56	*enchesoun* reason	98	*syk* sigh
83	*kitheth* shows		

28-9 Pres 271: "the one echoing cadence of the most mispraised poem of Ch."
48 Baum, *PMLA,* 56: pun on *furial* (furious and fiery).
50-3 Brew 169: true *gentilesse* of temper.
79 Lum 179: repeats *KnT* 1761, with other close parallels between 593, 325 and *KnT* 3042, 1089; these echoes suggest Squire's close association with his father the Knight.

499-631

"Near the home where I was reared lived a male falcon who falsely swore he loved me and courted me for years. Finally, I gave him all my love. One day he had to leave temporarily, but promised to return. However, he met and fell in love with a kite and deserted me."

00	*roche* rock	55	*galoche* shoe
04	*tercelet* male falcon	60	*at point-devys* to perfection
11	*greyn* scarlet dye	71	*worshipe* honor
12	*hit* hides	77	*twynne* depart
23	*wopen* wept	96	*to borwe* for a security
34	*that ootherwise noght* that I		(mild oath)
	gave nothing else	18	*newefangel* eager for nov-
37	*oon* alike		elty
54	*sophymes* deceits	31	*eft* again. *barm* lap

69-71 Neville: stress on freedom and dignity of both partners is rebuttal to Wife of Bath's argument for female sovereignty, connects tale with Marriage Group, anticipates *FranklT*.
24 Sk 5, 386: kite was known as base, cowardly hawk, unfit for hunting.

632-672

Canacee takes falcon home and nurses her back to health. Now I will leave the story of how the falcon regained her lover by help of Cambalus, and will turn to adventures and battles of the king and his sons.

44	*veluettes* velvets	49	*for despit* in scorn
48	*tidyves* small birds	58	*proces* story

67-9 Braddy, *MLN*: *brethren two* almost certainly means 2 *other brothers* (not Cambalo and Algarsif, obviously) whom Cambalo fights to win hand of his own sister in incestuous marriage, a situation for which there are Oriental analogues. Braddy, *JEGP*: perhaps incest motif persuaded Ch to break off tale.

The Franklin's Tale

COMMENTARIES: Gr 219-21; Ham 314;/ Don 924-7; ManCT 605-11; Rob 721-7; Sk 5, 387-400;/ Baum, 37, 122-33; Brew 170-2; Bron 61-3; Ches 160-3; Cog 123, 170-2; Cow 175-6; Dem 62-7; Dodd 248-50; Fr 319-24; Ger 33-54; Hin 237-60; Hodgson ed. *FranklT* (London, 1960); Kit 204-7; Lum 180-93; Mal 192-3; 232; Pat 220-6; Pres 272-6; Root 271-7; Sp 164-8; Tatlock, *The Scene of the Franklin's Tale Visited* (Ch Soc., 1914); Tho 93, 112-3, 129;/ Archer, *PMLA*, 50, 318-22; Baldwin, *PMLA*, 27, 106-12; Baum, *MLN*, 17, 376-7, and *PMLA*, 56, 225-46; Blenner-Hassett, *Spec*, 53, 791-800; Bradley, *JEGP*, 56, 624-30; Dempster and Tatlock, *SA*, 377-97; Donovan, *JEGP*, 57, 52-59; French, *MLN*, 45, 477-80; Gaylord, *DA*, 60, 3741-2; Gerould, *PMLA*, 26, 262-79; Harrison, *SP*, 35, 55-61; Hart, *Haverford Essays* (Haverford, Pa., 1909), 185-234; Hinckley, *MP*, 18, 39-48; Holman, *ELH*, 51, 241-52 (W); Howard, *MP*, 60, 223-32; Hunter, *MLN*, 53, 174; Kittredge, *MP*, 11-12, 435-67 (W, ST); Loomis, *SP*, 41, 14-33, and *Spec*, 58, 242-55; Lowes, *MP*, 18, 689-728; Lumiansky, *TSE*, 56, 5-13; Lyons, *ELH*, 35, 252-62; Manly, *PBA*, 26, 95-113 (ST); Owen, *JEGP*, 53, 294-311 (W, O); Prins, *ES*, 54, 158-62; Royster, *SP*, 26, 380-4; Schofield, *PMLA*, 01, 405-49; Sledd, *MP*, 47, 36-45; Tatlock, *Anniv. Papers for G. L. Kittredge* (Boston, 1913), 339-50.

GENRE: Breton lay, a short romance with Breton characters and setting, ultimately based on ancient folk tale known as "The Damsel's Rash Promise."

SOURCES: Main source very probably story of Menedon in Boccaccio's *Filocolo*, with suggestions from Geoffrey of Monmouth's *Historia Regum Britanniae* (for removal of rocks) and St. Jerome's *Adversus Jovinianum* (for Dorigen's complaint).

DATE: Uncertain; perhaps mid 1390's, but possibly written earlier and adapted for *CT*.

GENERAL CRITICISM: Schofield: tale not entirely harmonious, probably influenced by various sources. Hin 237-9: lapses in style (Dor's complaint and *wryte* in 1549) point to early date, no later than 1380, with tale later adapted for *CT;* same exaltation of one virtue at expense of others as in *ClT*—"Arv, in a passion of self-abnegation, fails to see that his first duty is to Dor"; appeal is not to common sense but to chivalric sentiment, and Arv's action is touching in this ideal context (casual promise more important than sacred rights); tale has great felicity of style. Kittredge: tale fits this individual Franklin (rich, socially ambitious, interested in *gentilesse*) in this situation. Dodd 248-59: Ch gives life and reality to courtly love conventions through characterization. Kit 207: Franklin utterly rejects courtly love idea that love and marriage are incompatible; love, not mastery, is vital principle in true marriage—this is his solution (stated in 760-805) and Ch's, refuting *WBT, CLT* and *MerchT*. Hinckley: in treating Dor's answer literally, Aur is not only naive, but forfeits all claim to *gentilesse* or even honor. Gaylord: Franklin shows "irony of one in quest of a *gentilesse* defined in terms of the letter but not the spirit." Root 274-5: chief beauty is "noble spirit" which finally compels Aur and magician to equal nobility. Cow 175-6: tale, not especially suited to teller, gives Ch's own wise compromise solution to marriage problem; something to be said for generosity of all 4 characters; Dor's complaint only flaw in charming tale. Dem 62: Ch's tale far superior in characterization and irony to Boccaccio's 2 versions. Pat 220-1: since Ch wished to stress Dor's love for Arv rather than Aur's passion, he used rocks device instead of Boccaccio's summer garden in winter as Aur's task, thus missing chance for ironic back-references to garden in *MerchT*. Loomis, *SP*: Ch got idea of connecting Breton lay type with theme of married love from *Orfeo*. Sledd: narrator, full of quiet humor, is prominent throughout; tale is tragicomedy with moral, serious but pleasant, told with artistic detachment without heavy pathos. Cog 170-2: Ch's last word on marriage, offering revolutionary solution; true theme is generosity and noble behavior, not limited to any one social class. Tho 93: Ch gives all possible views on marriage, but who is to say which is his? Holman: gentle, smiling tale, told with "unhumorous dignity," against courtly love and for marriage; triumph of conjugal love is complete reversal of courtly love system. Mal 232: tale fits teller as member of gentry but not as individual; Franklin serves as Ch's mouthpiece. Pres 274: tale fits Franklin exactly—his fussiness about food (1210-8), his common-sense rejection of magic (1129-34); since reader does not feel painful sympathy for Dor, he can consider relativity of evil without distraction. Blenner-Hassett: semi-legal tone of language in many passages fits Franklin and Ch himself; unfulfilled promises often basis for legal action in 14th century. Brew 170-2: pleasantest of CT, with sincere humanity and decency; Dor is central character; in ending Ch makes full allowance for pain and difficulty of each sacrifice for *gentilesse*. Lum 182-93: Ch shows Franklin as man of strong practical interests joined to social ambition; tale shows this ambivalence as Franklin wants both practical marriage and courtly love, tries to appeal to both gentry and common folk; tale's incongruities thus fit Franklin perfectly. Howard: Franklin's solution to marriage not Ch's, since he is shown as not wholly admirable in *Gen Prol,* and since his view conflicts with orthodox church view as in *ParsT* (wife subordinate to husband) which is more likely Ch's own. Don 924-7: optimism of tale suits sanguine Franklin, also his adaptation of courtly love to fit practical marriage ("bourgeois aspiration to aristocratic virtues"); tale shows Dor's impractical idealism finally coming to terms with reality; irony in idealism which puts her in situation that forces her to act in way directly contrary to her ideals. Baum 37, 128-33: marriage seems ideal but is saved only by "lucky last-minute gentilesse of a squire hitherto passionately urgent. Arv gave command, Dor obeyed, Aur withdrew: is this the formula for success in marriage?" The more Ch did to humanize artificial tale, the more "he exposed the underlying fallacies" and made it basically absurd (reality of Dor and Aur reduces Arv to a "plot-ridden fiction"). Hodgson 13-4: tale fits teller perfectly (high standards in food service, etc.); through Franklin Ch has voiced own wisdom, own view on marriage, "his own tolerant, half-humorous appraisal of life"; clerk is most subtly drawn character, but all 4 are developed far beyond corresponding figures in Boccaccio.

WORDS OF FRANKLIN TO SQUIRE AND OF HOST TO FRANKLIN

V, 673-708

Franklin praises Squire's story, wishes his own son were equally accomplished. Host interrupts rudely and orders Franklin to tell next tale. Franklin agrees.

76	*allow* commend	87	*vertuous* accomplished
77	*doom* judgment	88	*snybbed* rebuked
81	*deyntee* pleasure	05	*contrarien* oppose
83	*twenty pound* (rental value)		

73-94 Kit 204-6: Franklin feels wistful interest in *gentilesse,* aspires to found aristocratic family. Root 273: "there is something of pathos as well as fine generosity" in Franklin's praise of Squire, before Host (695) contemptuously rejects Franklin's "most cherished aspiration" (*gentilesse*). Ches 160-3 notes sharp reality of scene of Franklin commending Squire in contrast to own son—"it is as quiet and as real as Jane Austen," with a touch of comic pathos. Cog 123: tale intentionally cut short by interruption of Franklin, choking Squire with praises. Pres 272-3 agrees—"Ch intended Franklin's praise to be a blunderingly tactful interruption." Lum 184: Franklin's compliments to Squire reflect his social aspirations, were not meant to cut off Squire for fear he will run on too long (Cog). Bron 61-3: Franklin's "outgoing commendation" of Squire is "nearest approach to genuine friendly warmth" in all exchanges between pilgrims; most of drama of *CT* arises out of hostility and antagonisms among pilgrims.

95-08 Mal 192-3: Host's rudeness and Franklin's humility are unrealistic for actual 14th-century pilgrimage; "no innkeeper would have dreamt of behaving in this way toward a gentleman, and if he did so behave no gentleman would have put up with it"; but this is broad comedy, deliberate disregard for realities.

95 Ger 54 disagrees with Kit and Root on social aspirations of Franklin—franklins were already members of the gentry; Host interrupts simply because he is impatient at old gentleman's garrulity, not because of contempt for his genteel aspirations. Lum 184-5: Host indicates that he thinks Franklin is giving himself airs.

96-8 Lumiansky: *a tale or two* for each pilgrim suggests that by this time Ch had given up original scheme of 4 tales each and a return trip.

07-8 Lum 185: Franklin shamelessly flatters Host after meek apology.

THE FRANKLIN'S PROLOGUE

709-728

In ancient times the Bretons composed chivalric lays, one of which I shall tell though I lack skill in formal rhetoric.

11	*rymeyed* rimed	22	*Scithero* Cicero
16	*burel* unlearned	23	*colours* rhetorical ornaments
21	*Pernaso* Parnassus	26	*queynte* strange

09-13 Loomis, *SP:* Ch apparently well informed on Breton lays. Dem 62: Breton origin "one of Ch's little impostures."

16-28 Root 271: as self-made man, Franklin feels lack of gentility, shows excessive modesty. Baldwin: announcement of plain tale a skillful artistic device. Harrison: 3 possible reasons for inconsistency between Prologue disclaiming rhetoric and very rhetorical tale—Prologue may be meaningless gesture, may have been written for Franklin long after tale, or Ch may be playing with us. Rob 722: "modesty prologue" a conventional literary form. Lum 185-6: "modesty prologue" fits dramatic context, following Host's attack on Franklin's *gentilesse*.

23-6 Harrison: striking 3-fold play on *colours,* relating to vegetable life, painting, and rhetoric; this punning actually creates most brilliant of rhetorical colors, *traductio.*

THE FRANKLIN'S TALE

729-802

After long wooing, a Breton knight (Arveragus) wins a lady (Dorigen) in marriage. He says that he will never force her to obey him; she promises to be true and humble. This is the wise approach in marriage; force or restraint kills love. They settle down happily.

47	*maistrie* mastery	81	*constellacioun* fate (stars)
48	*kithe* show	82	*complexioun* disposition
52	*for shame of his degree* out	86	*kan on* is skilled in
	of regard for his rank	88	*suffrance* permission.
68	*of kynde* by nature		*bihight* promised

29-02 Lum 188: description of courtship and marriage agreements not in Boccaccio, added by Ch; Dor and Arv retain in marriage some of courtly love relationship.

44-70 Hodgson 79-81: Franklin here directly answers Wife of Bath on *maistrie,* using same words with same nuances; doubtless he is also voicing Ch's opinion.

60-02 Lyons: forbearance in marriage may be Ch's own view, but central theme is problem in *gentilesse* (who is most generous?), not marriage problem. Lum 188: in digressing on marriage Franklin is accomplishing both his aims—showing common-sense workable marriage and telling aristocratic tale of *gentilesse.*

64-6 Sp 164: "the final Chaucerian English wisdom on marriage."

92-8 Lum 189: "fine example of double-talk."

01 Sk 5, 389 notes Celtic names: *Pedmark* is Penmarch Point near Quimper, south of Brest in Brittany; *Kayrrud* (808) unidentified, probably means "red town"; Arv and Dor also are Celtic names.

803-894

After a year of bliss Arveragus leaves for two years to win glory in England. Dorigen pines for him at home, is finally persuaded to take walks on sea cliff where she curses the rocks as danger to ships.

09	*shoop him* prepared himself	64	*sikes* sighs
17	*siketh* sighs	65	*purveiaunce* providence
20	*destreyneth* afflicts	80	*merk* likeness
30	*graven* engrave	81	*chiertee* love
56	*warisshed* cured		

03-5 Hodgson 82-3: lines echo *MerchT* 1259-60, 1340-1, are intended as "antidote to the Merchant's venomous irony." Root 275: "sly ambiguity" of these lines.

07-13 Lum 189-90: Arv's going away to win honor, required by courtly love convention, is what causes trouble, nearly wrecks marriage; not in Boccaccio.

15-47 Baum 123-4: Dor's neurotic grief, with stress on her *hevynesse* and *rage,* prepares for her rash promise.

17-8 Root 275: ambiguity of *whan hem liketh.*

29-34 Donovan notes parallel (closer than Ovid) in *Anticlaudian,* I, i, by Alanus de Insulis.

57-94 Sp 166: Dor distressed both by fears for Arv's safety and by irrationality of rocks, "an emanation of evil," which later come to symbolize an even more dangerous threat to her marriage (Aur). Tho 129: Dor ponders God's inconsistency in allowing existence of evil forces that destroy mankind. Owen: Dor's prayer paralleled by Aur's for removal of rocks (1073-6), removal then becoming threat to marriage; both prayers show weakness—Dor's unwillingness to accept real world, Aur's failure to see Dor's love superior in quality to his passion. Don 924: "delightfully feminine speech" in which Dor asks Nature to rearrange creation to suit her notions.

895-966

Dorigen, still pining, goes to party in lovely garden in May. Aurelius, a young squire and her neighbor who has been secretly in love with her for 2 years, is also there.

00	*tables* backgammon	34	*prys* esteem
12	*verray* true	42	*withouten coppe* with diffi-
20	*moone* moan		culty, or in large draughts
28	*doom* judgment	44	*wreye* hide
32	*beste farynge* handsomest	54	*biwreye* reveal

38 Archer doubts Ch took name for Aur (a pagan) from Geoffrey of Monmouth's *Historia,* where he is famous Christian hero.

42 French: *withouten coppe* means to drink internally, secretly, the bitter draught—to suffer inwardly because of one's emotions.

967-1010

Aurelius reveals his love and begs Dorigen for mercy. She refuses

him, but then playfully promises to give him her love if he will
remove all of rocks on coast of Britanny.

73	*gerdon* reward	94	*lette* hinder
76	*grave* buried (in grave)	03	*deyntee* pleasure
78	*do* make	09	*inpossible* impossibility
92	*endelong* all along		

67-78 Baum 127: here and in 1031-79 Aur shows real despair and
touch of madness which humanize him (contrast prayers in *KnT*).
79-05 Lum 190: Dor shifts from wifely to courtly love attitude in
jokingly assigning task, then back to practical point of view.
80-98 Don 925: Dor draws analogy between Aur's bad behavior and
that of Nature in allowing cruel rocks to wreck ships; thus she unites
her 2 irritations in task she sets for Aur.
83-6 Holman: Dor's answer is "utter treason to the religion of love."
88-98 Dem 64-6: rocks have become obsession in Dor's mind, so
that in choosing Aur's task "the nature of it is dictated by her love
for her husband"; supreme irony, full of beauty and pathos, original
with Ch. Owen: superficial gentility of Dor's promise (made possible
by Arv's absence) contrasts with real gentility of ending; thus tale
criticizes some aspects of *gentilesse* in way not intended by Franklin,
too subtle for Host; on surface Dor agrees to adultery, but actually
task she sets is proof of love for Arv, guaranteed by permanence of
rocks she previously deplored as threat to him. Brew 172: profound
and poetic irony in fact that Dor's desire to save Arv from shipwreck
traps her into promise of love to Aur; not in Boccaccio.
00-5 Hodgson 90: lines show clearly that Dor did not intend Aur
to understand her literally, wanted him to forget whole idea, in direct
contradiction of courtly love convention.

1011-1086

Aurelius goes home in despair. He prays to Apollo to get his sister
Lucina (moon) to create high tide to cover rocks. Aurelius swoons
and is put to bed by his brother.

17	*orisonte* horizon	25	*knowes* knees
22	*asterte* escape	27	*breyde* started

33	*after* according to	45	*sheene* bright
35	*herberwe* abode	84	*thoght* anguish

18 Sk 5, 390: "humorous apology for a poetical expression." Hin 247: "curiously abrupt line" shows artistic immaturity. Root 272: after flight of rhetoric, Franklin's good sense and honesty bring him back to earth. Rob 274: astronomical way of defining time here satirized.

31-79 Pres 275-6: Aur's prayer is most eloquent speech in tale. Hunter: since Aur seeks to violate Dor's chastity, he cannot pray directly to Lucina (Diana), goddess of chastity; instead he asks her brother Apollo to influence her.

84-6 Root 275-6: playful assurance of author's own unconcern.

1087-1100

Meanwhile, Arveragus returns home to happy Dorigen.

87	*heele* health, prosperity	95	*oute* broad
94	*ymaginatyf* suspicious		

94-7 Holman: Arv's trust and lack of jealousy are totally against courtly love convention.

1101-1164

After Aurelius has been bedridden for 2 years of lovesickness, his brother recalls an old classmate at the university in Orleans who was expert in magic. Perhaps he can help.

13	*sursanure* wound healed on surface only	25	*magyk natureel* (legitimate science, not "black magic")
19	*lykerous* eager	41	*tregetoures* jugglers, magicians
21	*halke and herne* nook and cranny	50	*voyded* removed

18 Royster: Ch here uses common knowledge that Orleans in his day was gathering place for astrologers.

31-4 Root 272 (also Lum 191): Franklin's sound good sense makes him reject astrological magic. Tho 112-3: passage suggests Ch had doubts about astrology, at least in some applications; he apparently shared scepticism of enlightened minority.

43 Prins: *tregetoures* are magicians who can cause illusions or collective apparitions. Loomis, *Spec: tregetoures* may really mean artisans who were expert in fantastic stage effects for royal shows such as those given in Paris in 1378, 1398, featuring moving castles, moving boats, etc., of which eyewitness accounts and contemporary picture have survived.

1165-1238

Brother takes Aurelius to Orleans where they meet an expert in magic who shows them samples of his skill. After supper, this clerk agrees to remove the rocks for 1000 pounds.

70	*lissed* cured	96	*fauconers* falconers.	*ryver* bank of river where waterfowl were plentiful
74	*grette* greeted			
80	*dawes* days			
		23	*straunge* difficult	
		34	*to borwe* as a pledge	

02-4 Tatlock: magician prepares his visitors for high price with shrewdly chosen samples of skill.

1239-1296

Aurelius and brother return home with clerk. After long calculations, clerk succeeds and rocks seem to have disappeared for a week or two.

45	*hewed lyk laton* copper-colored	63	*conclusioun* experiment
53	*bugle* wild ox	67	*wene* imagine
54	*brawen* meat	71	*japes* tricks
60	*his herte* his own heart	73	*tables Tolletanes* astronomical tables

43-55 Sp 166-7: passage shows life at root of world even in winter, robust image of Janus drawing strength from both English farm life and Roman mythology; his realness contrasts with magician's illusions.

1297-1354

Aurelius meets Dorigen in temple, reminds her of her promise, and tells her all rocks are gone. Dorigen is stunned and goes home in despair. (Arveragus is temporarily out of town).

10	*salewed* greeted, saluted	37	*lith al to do* lies everything
23	*hight* promised		to make
36	*quyk* alive	41	*wende* supposed

1355-1456

Dorigen complains to Fortune of her fate. She recalls many stories of classical women who chose death rather than dishonor. She will do the same.

68	*thritty* thirty	93	*arace* wrench, tear
77	*been stirt* jumped	18	*if I may* if I can help it
78	*dreynte* drowned	36	*redressed* vindicated
88	*heet* called	45	*pardee* by God

67-56 Sk 5, 395-9: all examples taken from St. Jerome's *Adversus Jovinianum,* but Ch changes their order. Hin 239: long, dull list of chaste women, which holds up story without exculpating Dor, suggests artistic immaturity and early date for tale. Manly: fine tale nearly spoiled by 100 lines of rhetorical exempla; psychological analysis (as in *Troilus*) of Dor's real feelings would have been infinitely better. Pat 224: Ch gives complaint with humorous detachment, remembering that Wife of Bath listens to Dor's endless list of chaste wives. Sledd disagrees with Manly—deep pathos in complaint would stop tale in its tracks and blur moral; Franklin maintains emotional detachment as he does throughout; reader must sympathize but also feel sure nothing will go wrong, and complaint skillfully achieves this, showing Dor as frightened, but less and less intent on dying as she becomes increasingly illogical in tragicomic roll call. Lum 191: complaint shows Dor's "testing of one aspect of courtly behavior, her discarding it, and then adopting a more realistic and practical solution" (telling Arv). Bradley: here "mirrors" or ideal images of chaste wives are used to portray psychological drama and conflict in Dor. Don 925: having proved suicide is only answer, Dor does the sensible thing and tells Arv. Hodgson 31, 103-4: part of Ch's joke to use exempla from St. Jerome's *Adversus Jovinianum,* a book which Wife of Bath especially hated (favorite of her 5th husband); Ch may here be showing illogicality of frenzied woman, or perhaps he grew bored and let passage get out of control, or he may be ridiculing rhetorical convention of the complaint.

1457-1498

When Arveragus comes home Dorigen tells him all. He is distressed, but decides that Dorigen must keep her word and sends her secretly to Aurelius.

70	*as wys* as (is) certain	80	*brast* burst out
71	*and* if	86	*demen* judge
76	*ystiked* stabbed	93	*heep* large number
79	*trouthe* troth, one's pledged word	95	*jupartie* jeopardy, danger

72-98: Root 276-7: Middle Ages "admired such extreme conceptions of honor"; though truth did not require Arv's sacrifice, his is still a noble act and "begets nobility in others." Pat 225: though Dor and Arv reject *maistrie* at beginning of tale, here ironically Arv gives high-handed order forcing Dor to go to Aur; "how free is love when it is thus constrained to infidelity?" Sledd: Arv does not assume *maistrie,* since Dor has "tacitly placed the decision in his hands and he is guided by the demands of her honor more than his." Lum 192: Arv still clings to courtly principles, sends wife to Aur. Baum 124-6: Arv sacrifices wife to abstract, limited ideal of *trouthe*—"narrow logic supervenes over common sense and all human decency"; Ch here sacrifices realism and character of Arv to plot requirements (proof of *gentilesse*).

79 Schofield: if tale has definite moral, this line sums it up.

1499-1556

Aurelius meets Dorigen in main street. Tearfully she reveals that

Arveragus had ordered her to keep her word. Touched by husband's sense of honor and by Dorigen's misery, Aurelius releases her. She and Arveragus live happily ever after.

02	*quykkest* busiest	34	*serement* oath	
03	*bown* ready	44	*drede* doubt	
12	*bad* ordered	48	*weel apayd* pleased	
27	*sith* since			

99-1624 Sp 168: conclusion of tale suggests Franklin's aspirations toward *gentilesse* have basis in "his own genial humanity."

12-3 Pat 225: amusing irony of miserable Dor on way to garden, *My trouthe for to holde, allas! allas!* Lum 192: here Dor is conventional obedient wife, no courtly lady. Baum 124: perfect touch—"Ch has portrayed with complete success a gentle woman and loving wife driven almost to hysterical frenzy by perverse circumstances."

14-24 Baum, *MLN:* upon reflection Aur suddenly sees that taking Dor now would be low and churlish in comparison with generosity and *gentilesse* of Arv and Dor.

14-40 Owen: Arv's decision "forces Aur to see the 'obstacles' that have only seemed to vanish."

33-40 Blenner-Hassett: Aur uses some of stereotyped legal phrases employed in a "release" or "quit-claim." Baum 126: "needlessly legalistic terms" unfitted to passionate lover. Hodgson 104: legal diction appropriate to Franklin who had served at sessions and was friend of Man of Law; same terms were clichés of courtly love, thus suited to Aur.

1557-1620

Aurelius goes to clerk in despair and asks for two or three years to pay 1000 pounds due. He tells clerk whole story and is in turn released from debt.

62	*fordo* ruined	98	*als* also	
66	*but* unless	02	*apparence* magic	
75	*dayes* days of respite, time to pay	07	*leeve* dear	
		14	*cropen* crept	

13 Hodgson 25: clerk's echoing of Aur's words in releasing Dor "reflects his own humorous acceptance of the irony of the situation."
14 Donovan thinks clerk is calling Aur here a Fury who crept out of ground to attack virtue, but unsuccessfully; tale involves struggle in Aur between virtues and vices (sent by Furies) as in *Anticlaudian,* VIII and IX.

1621-1624
Question: Who was most generous—the knight, the squire, or the clerk?

22 *fre* generous

22 Lum 193: Dor should win since, in telling Arv of promise, she gave up "attitudes from courtly love that she brought into her marriage."

The Physician's Tale

COMMENTARIES: Gr 222; Ham 293-5;/ Don 927; ManCT 611-3; Rob 726-8; Sk 5, 260-4;/ Baum 19-20; Brew 158; Ches 156; Cow 149, 165; Dem 92; Fansler, *Ch and the RR* (N.Y., 1914), 31-5; Fr 266-8; Ger 85; Law 58; Lum 195-200; Pat 180; Pres 228; Root 219-22; Sedg 351; TatDC 150-6;/ Baum, *PMLA*, 58, 167-70; Manly, *PBA*, 26, 95-113 (ST); Shannon, *SA*, 398-408; Tupper, *JEGP*, 16, 61-7; Young, *Spec*, 41, 340-9.

GENRE: Historical tale.

SOURCE: Version in *Roman de la Rose* of original story from Livy's *History*, with some details taken directly from Livy.

DATE: About 1386-8.

GENERAL CRITICISM: Fansler 31-5: "finest English telling of the story." Root 219: tale not specially fitted to teller, perhaps written originally for *LGW;* Ch shifted focus of story from evil judge to Virginia, added passages on girl's beauty, advice to parents, pathetic dialogue between father and daughter. Cow 165: a legend of martyrdom rather than story of injustice. Ches 156: tale of stoic virtue of heathen Rome fits anti-clerical Physician. Law 58: tale "illustrates lechery through its antitype chastity." Brew 158: even fine death scene fails to redeem dull passages. Lum 198-200: pathetic moralizing tale is corrupt Physician's "bold attempt to perpetrate on the Pilgrims a bit of moral virtuosity"; Host is struck by contrast between chastity theme of tale and character of teller (see *PardT* 301-13). Baum 19-20: Ch ruins tragic tale "through carelessness or indifference." Don 927: no clear connection between teller and tale; though pathos and moralizing are skillfully handled, on the whole tale "shows Ch working rather routinely, without his characteristic originality."

THE PHYSICIAN'S TALE

VI, 1-117

According to Livy, a Roman knight called Virginius had a beautiful daughter who was 14 years old and a masterpiece of the goddess Nature. She was humble, discreet, modest, and she avoided bad company. All governesses and mothers and fathers should rear their children carefully to be like this girl.

20	*vicaire* vicar	99	*perisse* come to harm
43	*goost* spirit	02	*torent* torn to pieces
50	*facound* eloquence	15	*wele* wellbeing
63	*fleen* flee, escape	16	*unheele* misfortune
64	*treten of* deal with	17	*doctour* St. Augustine
79	*olde daunce* lovemaking		

1-109 Manly: most of passage purely rhetorical, "pretty crude," with no dramatic fusion of rhetorical elements.

5-38 Lum 197: stilted device of having Nature speak proudly of Virginia fits pompous Physician.

19-20 Pres 228: surprising couplet from one whose study was "little on the Bible."

22 Baum notes pun on *cure* (supervision or spiritual cure and medical cure).

30-71 Sedg 35: charming description of Virginia. Pat 180: description is conventional and vague.

35-120 Sk 5, 262: fine original passage, not in *RR* nor in Gower. Young: Ch probably found suggestions for whole passage, including lines on governesses, in Vincent of Beauvais' Latin treatise *De Eruditione Filiorum Nobilium,* a compilation of patristic doctrine on theme of the "consecrated virgin."

61-6 Pat 180: the one distinguishing touch in picture of Virginia, her tact in feigning sickness to escape wild parties.

72-104 Pres 228: "shrewd aside is the best thing in the tale."

72-92 TatDC 150-6: Ch may have had in mind fact that Katharine Swynford (his wife's sister) was governess to daughters of John of Gaunt, one of whom became involved in sexual scandal.

118-202

One day during trip to town with mother, this girl is seen by Appius, chief magistrate, who lusts after her. He bribes a scoundrel called Claudius to claim that the girl had once been his slave and was stolen by Virginius who is rearing her as his own daughter. Without evidence, Appius awards girl to Claudius.

25	*forby ther as* past where	63	*doomes* judgments
29	*for* despite	64	*pas* distance
33	*meede* bribe	75	*wite* know
46	*reed* plan	99	*deeme* judge
57	*sentence* contents	01	*warde* custody
62	*consistorie* court		

146-8 Dem 92: judge's premature glee is one of few instances of irony, which Ch generally avoided in stressing purity of Virginia rather than injustice of Appius.

203-257

Virginius, perceiving vile purpose, goes home and tells whole story to daughter Virginia. He must kill her rather than send her to dishonor. After pathetic scene, Virginius cuts off her head, takes it to Appius.

08	*leet . . . calle* had . . .	27	*the say* thee saw
	called	40	*Jepte* Jephthah
12	*al* although. *converte* turn	55	*of* off

207-53 Sk 5, 264: fine original passage; compare John Webster's play *Appius and Virginia,* iv, 1.
225-52 Ger 85: one of most pathetic passages ever penned, full of "tragic horror."

258-286

Appius orders Virginius hanged; but the people, suspecting truth, rise up and cast Appius in prison where he kills himself. Claudius is condemned to hang but Virginius takes pity on him and he is exiled. Wickedness, no matter how secret, is always revealed and punished.

60	*thraste* thrust	80	*agryse* feel terror
71	*demed* condemned		

The Pardoner's Tale

COMMENTARIES: Gr 222-5; Ham 295-6;/ Don 929-30; ManCT 612-23; Rob 728-32; Sk 5, 264-90;/ Bald 76, 109; Baum 45-59, 217-9; Brew 159-60; Bron 79-87, 100-3; Cow 166-7; Cog 158-62; Coghill and Tolkien eds. *PardT* (London, 1958); Cur 54-70; Dem 72-9; Ev 169-72; Fr 268-72; Ger 55-71; Hin 157-83; Kit 20-2, 166, 211-8; Low 195-6; Lum 201-23; Mal 14-6, 177-9, 211-3; Man 288-90; Pat 164-6; Pres 229-37; Root 222-31; Sedg 290; Sp 168-77; Tup 94-9;/ Baum, *PMLA*, 56, 225-46; Bushnell, *SP*, 31, 450-60; Candelaria, *MLN*, 56, 321-2; Chapman, *MLN*, 26, 506-9; Cross, *RES*, 51, 372-4; Curry, *JEGP*, 19, 593-606; Dempster, *SA*, 409-14; Ethel, *MLQ*, 59, 211-7; Francis, *PMLA*, 53, 1126-41; Friend, *JEGP*, 54, 383-8; Gross, *N&Q*, 53, 413-4; Hamilton, *SP*, 39, 571-6, and *JEGP*, 41, 48-72; Hemingway, *MLN*, 17, 57-8; Henkin, *MLN*, 40, 254-9; Kellogg, *Spec*, 51, 465-81; Kellogg and Haselmayer, *PMLA*, 51, 251-77; Krishnamurti, *MLR*, 44, 398; Miller, *Spec*, 55, 180-99 (ST); Norris, *PMLA*, 33, 636-41; Owen, C. A., *JEGP*, 53, 294-311 (W, O); Owen, W.J.B., *RES*, 51, 49-55 (W); Sedgewick, *MLQ*, 40, 431-58 (W); Sedgwick, *MLR*, 24, 336-7; Strang, *N&Q*, 60, 207-8; Swart, *Neophil*, 52, 45-50; Tupper, *JEGP*, 14, 553-65, and *SA*, 415-38; Weatherly, *MLN*, 35, 310-1.

GENRE: Moral exemplum in sermon framework.

ANALOGUES: Source is unknown, but many analogues exist of the tale which ultimately derives from oriental folk tale; there are incidental literary borrowings from *RR* (for Pard's confession), Pope Innocent III's *De Contemptu Mundi*, Maximian (for Old Man), etc.

DATE: Probably about 1390.

GENERAL CRITICISM: Sk 5, 275: Ch often quotes from *ParsT*, which must have been written earlier (compare 475, 482, 504, 529 with *ParsT* 591, 836, 819, 820, etc.). Hin 157-9: vigorous style suggests late date, seems revised for brilliant Pard, though perhaps originally meant for Parson (homily in 485-660 is wholly free of charlatanism); Ch wrote "drunken confession" to justify telling of superb moral tale by utter rascal (*WBT* 170-1 implies Pard was drunk at that point); one of most perfect tales in literature, supernatural powers combining with human cupidity to doom rioters, with mystery and terror of Greek tragedy, strangeness and beauty in Old Man ("a sort of prototype of the Ancient Mariner"). Tupper, *JEGP:* irony of tavern setting for sermon against tavern vices (drinking, lechery, gambling, swearing); tale deals with 2 of Deadly Sins (Gluttony, Avarice) of which Pard is most guilty, fits design whereby each pilgrim denounces his own special weaknesses. Kit 20-1: "matchless short-story" with superb structure and economy. Root 223-30: tale (told in tavern) is basically tragic and ironic "in the eagerness with which death is sought and the ease with which it is found," with dramatic structure (mostly in dialogue), sure but unhurried tempo without superfluous detail, "irresistible and inevitable as death and night." Man 288-90: great tragic tale, "one of the world's masterpieces," with every quality of ideal short-story; nowhere but in first scene of *Macbeth* is tragic atmosphere developed so swiftly. Cow 166-7: depraved rogue tells "Ch's most dramatic story" of mystery and horror with universal appeal, "a little masterpiece in the grim and gruesome." Dem 78-9: rioters' deliberate quest of Death (quickly forgotten) creates dramatic irony which is enjoyable apart from moral values; ambiguity of Old Man increases impressive mystery. Sedg 290: old plot by drunken Pard makes "best story in the book." Pat 166: Pard embodies blasphemy and deceit, lives in hellish isolation—"but his strength in the endurance of such a life is obviously, like a saint's, heroic." Sedgewick: research on tale has often lacked sense of proportion, resulting in 3 erroneous theories: the Flanders Heresy (tale is satire on greedy, hard drinking Flemings); the Tavern Heresy (tale is told to listening pilgrims in tavern, increasing irony); the Sermon Heresy (tale aims to be typical medieval sermon, but lacks logical structure and coherence). Cog 159-62: in character of Pard, "a monster of vanity and hypocrisy," Ch shows himself "the first and subtlest ironist in English" (ironies within the irony); like Iago, Pard says right things for wrong purposes, sees black as white; ironically and blindly, he rushes toward his own doom just as rioters in his tale do. Kellogg: sense of inevitable judgment of God emerges paradoxically from Pard's very defiance of Divine Providence (theme continued in tale from *Gen Prol*); Pard's character is prime example of spiritual degeneration of "mind averted from God," living not by God's will but by his own—"the eternal antithesis of the pride of Satan and the humility of Christ." Mal 211-3, 234: one of most powerful sermons in English literature, tale is also devastating exposé of Pard's mercenary character, is *only* one of *CT* which serves to characterize teller (opposed to Kit's view). Sp 168: Prologue and tale are unified dramatization of Pard, "one of Ch's maturest achievements." Ger 55-71: Pard's drunken condition explains histrionic garrulity and loss of control in confessions (Prol), confused style of sermon (not conforming to medieval pattern); but in tale proper Ch takes over, allowing no "drunken buffoonery" to mar its grim irony, yet still retaining voice of Pard "cleansed and elevated"; at end drunk Pard resumes hell-fire sermonizing and brazen sale of wares. Pres 160: "superb sermon from a revolting man," fully revealing his duplicity. Swart: whole performance from confession to attempted sale was premeditated as huge joke which fell flat; Pard thinks his chief sin is cupidity, but actually it is Pride (see *ParsT*). Brew 160: tale has good dialogue, touches of awe and horror unique in Ch, profound sense of mystery of life unusual in *CT;* irony in fact that Pard "enforces the moral lesson inadvertently by the very example of his own shamelessness." C. A. Owen: tale itself (like gold) is both warning against cupidity and instrument of Pard's greed and vanity in which he shows to intelligent audience "the full measure of his cleverness and cynicism." Ev 169-72: tale is beautifully organized and integrated for special purpose (characterization of Pard), giving illusion of a sermon. Lum 201-3: eunuch Pard, like bastard Edmund in *King Lear,* is bitterly scornful of society, finds compensations in outwitting normal folk, ignoring moral laws; he joined pilgrimage to get money from pilgrims by refinement of usual technique with peasants, but fails because he reverts to habitual methods at crucial moment. Miller: character of Pard relates to Scriptural view of eunuchry (Matthew, xix, 12) in 3 types—physical eunuch; holy man who is God's eunuch, denying himself for spiritual reasons; and unholy eunuch who is sterile in good works and spirit—Pard belongs to 3rd type (perhaps also to 1st) in sharp contrast to Parson (2nd type); traits of physical eunuch in *Gen Prol* would suggest to medieval reader qualities of spiritual eunuch developed in Pard's Prologue; another Scriptural symbol is Old Man (in original sin of Adam) who must die before New Man (redeemed by Christ) can be born. Don 930: despite "strong aura of the supernatural," tale's action is wholly naturalistic, with grim irony arising out of speeches of characters "who are constantly saying far more than they think they are." Baum 52: proud of success, Pard shows off with literary device of confession, is "led from one excess to another and then to complete deflation"; Curry's eunuchism theory not proved by text, only effeminacy (952-5 shows Host did not think Pard was eunuch); both Pard and Wife of Bath are "artistic creations, not real people," but Pard has vitality "almost enough to save him from our censure." Coghill and Tolkien 23-37: tale is told outside tavern where Pard stops; in Prologue he is impressing pilgrims with cunning, with no thought of victimizing them, an idea which comes to him only at end when he sees they are spellbound by sermon. Bron 84-7, 100-3: after confession, tale seems blasphemous mockery and attempted sale an affront to pilgrims' intelligence; perhaps answer lies in process of composition—Ch wrote tale first, ending piously with 915-8; then he added headlink and conclusion to give dramatic frame without violating psychological consistency; finally, as afterthought to develop Pard's character and lengthen tale to usual reading time (1-1¼ hour), he added confession which has baffled "several generations of critics suckled on psychological realism"; tale shifts from natural, real world to supernatural and allegorical "with such ease and confident mastery that we are hardly conscious of assenting to a miracle."

INTRODUCTION TO THE PARDONER'S TALE
VI, 287-328

Host expresses dislike of false judges and pity for Virginia whose beauty was her death. He asks God's blessing on physician and his remedies, then turns to Pardoner for merry tale to cheer him up. Pardoner wants drink first; at request of "gentils" he promises a moral tale—no ribaldry.

88 *nayles* (nails of Cross)   92 *sely* innocent

00	*prow* profit	09	*theen* thrive
04	*cors* body	12	*erme* grieve
05	*jurdones* chamber pots	13	*cardynacle* pain about the
06	*ypocras* cordial drink.		heart
	galiones medicines	14	*triacle* remedy
07	*boyste* box. *letuarie* reme-	21	*alestake* signpost of tavern
	dies		

87-19 Hin 159: Host's vehemence suggests he may be half drunk. Baum 46: Host, "sentimentally heartbroken" by *PhysT*, turns to Pard for comic relief.

01-13 Lum 198-9: Host makes ironic fun of Physician's hypocrisy in telling moral tale on chastity so unsuited to his real character as seller of aphrodisiacs.

21-2 Ger 57-9: Pard's reference to *alestake* and *cake* means Summoner's garland and cake (*Gen Prol* 666-8); Pard simply breaks off piece of Sum's loaf and takes swig of own ale from flask—no tavern; alarm expressed by *gentils* (324), confession, also "pointed reference to his tipsiness" in *WBT* 170-1—all suggest Pard is already half-drunk. Lum 210 rejects idea Pard is drunk.

23-8 Hin 158: objection of *gentils* suggests Pard had already been indulging in ribaldry, perhaps also in drink. Curry: *gentils* fear Pard will tell ribald tale because they "instantly translate his physical characteristics [eunuch] into terms of character." Gross: protest is "bluntly insulting," after obscenities of Miller, Reeve, Merchant; confession which follows is conscious ironic revenge for insult—telling of moral tale in immoral context. Baum 46: lines merely show Ch's readjustment after shifting tale from Parson to Pard (tale is an *honest thyng*).

27-8 Lum 210-1: Pard insists on stop for drink so he can fix pilgrims with eye, deliver sermon to assembled group undistracted by travel noises.

THE PARDONER'S PROLOGUE

329-346

When I preach in churches my text is always danger of loving money. But first I show my license, seals, and bulls to protect myself.

30	*hauteyn* loud	37	*lige lordes* bishop's
34	*Radix,* etc. Love of money is	38	*warente* protect
	root of evil	45	*saffron* give color to

29-492 Kit 213-5: Pard, on vacation, makes no effort to hide rascality, is "willing to pass for a knave, but objects to being taken for a fool"; hence his "cynical frankness" to pilgrims (showing that he knows that they already know what he is) is "dramatically inevitable." Root 223-4: Pard is "honest hypocrite" who does not deceive himself, reveals frauds because off duty, gives sample of oratory because pilgrims insist on moral tale. ManCT 613: frankness of confession is literary tradition, but Ch motivates it by Pard's drinking. Hamilton: evidence here and in *Gen Prol* favors view that Pard was Augustinian canon regular of St. Mary Rouncival hospital (Charing Cross, London), whence there is proof canons were sent out to beg alms by selling pardons through countryside. Fr 268: cynical confession seems wholly original with Ch. Kellogg: Pard's confessed contempt for others, hypocrisy, shamelessness, boasting of harm he does, etc.—all are treated under Pride in *ParsT*. Mal 178: devastating self-description gives superb dramatic effect at expense of verisimilitude, but Ch "makes no serious effort to be true to life" (disagrees with Kit). Sp 169: confession is literary convention like soliloquies in Elizabethan plays; even so, it is not excessively improbable as result of Pard's impudent exhibitionism and "tongue loosened by drink," and makes a "dramatization of spectacular boldness." Pres 232-3: seemingly crude repetitiveness in Pard's self-revelation is Ch's special technique for listening audience, a recurring chord sounded over and over to build up full horror of Pard's depravity as ironic context for "great and good sermon" he gives—a dramatic effect possible only to "a comedian of genius, and a master of his art." Brew 159: no evidence Pard is drunk; villain's confession is medieval satiric convention. Lum 212: Pard hopes by taking pilgrims into his confidence he will flatter their sophistication, win admiration for shrewdness, cause many to desire his convenient absolution.

30-1 Ger 60: seems to contradict goat-like voice of *Gen Prol* 688; probably Ch's view of Pard developed after he wrote *Gen Prol*.

35-43 Ger 61: confusion and fantastic exaggeration (bulls of popes,

cardinals, patriarchs, bishops) suggest "the talkative stage of intoxication."

37-40 Kellogg: Pard asserts "superiority of his evil will to God or Man," laughing at law which protects him; all his jokes show "terrible need to ridicule . . . sense of the presence of God from which he can never escape."

347-390

Then I show my fake relics: rags, bones. "Dip this sheep's shoulder bone in well and water will cure all diseases in cattle and jealousy in husbands. Come forward and make offerings, except those of you who are in horrible sin." Thus I make much money.

47	*cristal stones* glass cases		69	*mystriste* mistrust
48	*cloutes* rags		72	*miteyn* mitten
50	*in latoun* set in metal		89	*gaude* trick
68	*potage* soup			

51 Henkin rejects identification of *hooly Jew* with Jacob (Sk, Rob, from Genesis, xxx, 31), connects magic shoulder bone with pagan rites which Pard ascribes to holy Jew merely for effect on ignorant peasants.

60-5 Ger 62: "supremely muddled effrontery" shows Pard's drunken histrionics.

71 Hin 165: indicates Pard's natural hostility to priests.

77-90 Weatherly: blackmail device to force women to offer gifts lest they be suspected of infidelity, probably found in popular exemplum (see also Sedgwick).

89-90 Gross: through stress on his own hypocrisy here, repeated in 400-4, 424-33, 439-53, 461, and verbal repetitions of *wynne, avarice* and *coveitise* (389, 403, 440, 461; 400, 424, 428, 431, 433), Pard consciously succeeds in making himself "one of the most revolting characterizations in all literature"—as revenge on pilgrims for insult in 324.

391-434

I am very skillful in pulpit, warning ignorant people against greed so they will give freely. I care nothing about saving their souls; I just want their money. In holy guise I defame my enemies, satisfy my greed.

96	*bekke* nod	14	*asterte* escape	
97	*dowve* dove. *berne* barn	15	*defamed falsly* proclaimed	
98	*yerne* eagerly		as false or infamous person	
01	*free* generous	21	*under hewe* in the guise	
06	*a-blakeberyed* blackberrying	30	*twynne* turn away	
	(wandering)			

91-06 Sp 170: consciously a "spell-binder, in the guise of holiness," Pard holds up own pulpit image for admiration, incidentally shows contempt for *lewed peple*.

95-9 Low 195-6: "a picture so telling in its concrete realization of bodily action that one not only visualizes the movements but feels one's self incipiently reproducing them."

03-6 Cog 161: "he has taken the root of all evil to be his good . . . he is seeing black white."

06 Cross notes connection in south English dialect between "blackberrying" and "playing truant," so that Pard sees himself metaphorically as schoolmaster and his penitents as pupils.

07-8 Pres 229: this paradox from *RR* (5763-4) suggested chief irony of Prologue and tale; Ch develops hint into a "great study in the problem of evil."

12-9 Swart: Pard's "boastful self-respect and neglect of detail" here suggest slight drunkenness.

21-2 Pat 166: "most unsparing couplet" in all Ch.

29-32 Pres 229-30: "terrible irony of circumstance" in these words. Lum 213: Pard suggests to pilgrims that, though he is personally vicious, his pardons are as good as any (see also 459-60).

435-462

Do I want to preach in poverty like the apostles? No! I squeeze money from the poorest because I like wealth, good food, wine, women. Now having had my ale, I will tell moral tale, though vicious myself.

47	*countrefete* imitate	49	*page* servant
48	*wolle* wool	51	*al* although

36 Pres 231: one of Ch's "most hypnotic lines," highly appropriate to Pard.

39-53 Kellogg: Pard's refusal to serve God is perfect example of St. Augustine's definition of Pride; "the Pard sets himself up as his own end in place of God."

41 Kellogg: Pard's proud rejection of poverty is exact antithesis of Christ's humility as expressed in *WBT* 1179.

44-7 Hemingway: Pard here apparently confuses St. Paul the Apostle with St. Paul the Hermit who wove mats of palm leaves for clothing.

46 Baum, *PMLA,* notes pun on *ydelly* (inactively and vainly).

53 Cur 68 (also Ger 63): touch of bravado by eunuch Pard.

61 Lum 214: here Pard reveals his tale will also report on sly methods with peasants; thus he further flatters pilgrims by offering continued chance to laugh with him at peasants' gullibility.

THE PARDONER'S TALE

463-484

In Flanders there was a group of riotous young people who danced, gambled, swore, made love, and drank heavily in taverns.

65	*hasard* gambling. *stywes* brothels (stews)	77	*tombesteres* dancing girls
66	*gyternes* guitars	78	*fetys* shapely. *frutesteres* fruit girls
67	*dees* dice	79	*wafereres* cakesellers
74	*totere* tear to pieces	84	*luxurie* licentiousness
76	*lough* laughed		

63-84 Sp 171-2: lurid opening catches attention, its riotous images accompanied by Pard's "emotional orgy" of moral indignation and pseudo-religious feeling. Lum 214-5: Pard extends narrative bait before launching sermon; note skill of transition to sermon (77-84).

63 Hin 157, 167-8: setting in Flanders perhaps because Ch was using Flemish source (possibly a religious drama), or because of strong English bias against Flemings in 14th century. Norris: Flanders setting very apt because Flemings were notorious for drinking and cupidity, and their political and economic troubles in 1380's and 1390's provided effective moral lesson for Ch's England.

485-588

Gluttony is a terrible sin—caused Herod to slay John the Baptist, Adam to lose paradise. St. Paul preached against it. Drunkenness destroys discretion; beware especially of white wine of Lepe. Attila died drunk.

85	*unkyndely* unnaturally	34	*cod* gut	
96	*shrewe* ill-tempered person	37	*fynde* provide for	
03	*aboght* paid for	38	*stampe* grind in a mortar	
07	*drede* doubt	40	*talent* appetite	
10	*deffended* forbidden (Fr: defendu)	42	*mary* marrow	
17	*shorte throte* brief pleasure of swallowing	57	*honeste cure* care for honor	
22	*wombe* belly	87	*han justice* are in charge of justice	

85-660 Sp 172-3: sermon (a digression) not only treats themes tale will illustrate, but further dramatizes Pard himself who "unconsciously gloats over the sins he zestfully condemns." Don 929: Pard chooses exciting and entertaining sins (drunkenness, gluttony, swearing, gambling), easy to dramatize to illiterate audience; also, as with avarice, "he privately delights in his own experience with these vices" (Pard's sense of irony).

34-43 Sp 174: personification of belly and gullet (apart from rest of body) and idea of futile labor of cooks give "fantastic-comic effect."

39 Hin 172: Ch, following Pope Innocent's *De Contemptu Mundi,* means diversion of food from true function of nourishing (*substaunce*) to accidental attribute of pleasing appetite (*accident*).

54 Hin 173: *Sampsoun* pronounced so as to imitate snoring of drunkard. Swart: strange use of *Sampsoun* to depict drunken hiccoughs suggests Pard's own inebriation.

62-71 Hin 174: "a delicate and playful way of saying that the drinker who pretends to drink only the mild wines of Bordeaux and La Rochelle really drinks the strong Spanish wines, such as those of Lepe." Swart: strange addition of *Rochele* and *Burdeux* can only be explained as "logic of a man who is slightly drunk."

65-6 Krishnamurti notes possible pun on wine and vines here, often used interchangeably in Ch's London—audience would get joke. Bron 82: lines are "barb" aimed at Host for mixing cheap Spanish wine with French to increase profits; *other wynes, growynge faste by* is pointed reference to location of Tabard, just across London Bridge from Fish St. and Cheapside (564).

589-628

Gambling leads to lying, deceit, swearing, homicide, and financial ruin. Rulers like Chilon and king of Parthia had contempt for this vice.

91	*lesynges* lies	95	*repreeve* reproof
94	*catel* goods	10	*stal* stole

90 Swart: abrupt transition, lack of connection with preceding, then quick shift to *othes false* (629)—all suggest slight drunkenness in clever Pard.

629-660

Swearing oaths, especially blasphemous ones, is hateful to God.

37	*in doom* discreetly	43	*rather* ahead of
39	*firste table* first 5 command- ments	53	*cynk and treye* 5 and 3
		56	*bicched bones* cursed dice

51-7 Ger 66: scene of quarreling gamblers. probably based on reminiscence. Don 929-30 agrees that "gloatingly cynical" picture reflects Pard's personal experience, "so knowingly graphic as to exceed the limits of art."

51-2 Tupper, *JEGP:* oaths Pard mentions are almost same as those recently spoken by Host (288, 314); thus Pard has already convicted Host of sin before direct accusation in 942.

52-3 AHM: here Pard links gambling and swearing, suggesting that gambling leads to swearing and finally to homicide (657), thus preparing listeners for tale as exemplum—very skillful technique.

661-701

Three rioters, drinking in tavern, hear funeral bell and send boy to inquire. Boy says dead man was slain by Death who has killed a thousand by plague nearby. Rioters swear to kill Death.

66	*knave* boy servant	87	*henne* hence
67	*bet* faster	88	*hyne* laborer
73	*to-nyght* last night	90	*avysed* warned
74	*upright* straight	95	*digne* worthy
79	*pestilence* = bubonic plague	96	*al ones* of one mind

61-10 Dem 77: Ch shows "admirable skill" in using details of tavern scene in Flanders during plague "to create the proper atmosphere, an atmosphere of fear and sin."

61 Ev 170:   3 rioters actually not mentioned before.

75-83 Bron 101: words of boy lift us suddenly from naturalistic world of rioters to "realm of personified abstraction" (world of miracle plays).

75-6 Sp 175: "Death was a person to the medieval mind, with its deep-rooted personifying impulse."

79-10 Root 227-9:   fear of plague drives some to prayers, but rioters to dissipation and recklessness as they "rush madly toward the city of Death."

80-01 Miller: advice of *child* is true, but is literalized and thus perverted by rioters; in Scriptural symbolism the child's *dame* is the Church, source of doctrine; but rioters seek out literal Death.

702-776

Staggering forth in search of Death, they meet old man who wants to die but cannot till he finds a youth willing to exchange for his old age. Rioters demand whereabouts of Death; old man directs them to oak tree where they find heap of gold.

02	*plight* pledged	34	*cheste* clotheschest
09	*torente* torn to pieces	36	*heyr clowt* hair cloth
10	*hente* seize		(shroud)
14	*grette* greeted	43	*agayns* before. *hoor* hoar,
17	*with sory grace* bad luck to		white
	you!	56	*abye* pay for
28	*kaityf* captive	58	*oon of his assent* in his plot
31	*leeve* beloved		

11-67 Kit 215: Old Man is Death in person, though only by implication—"remarkable illustration of effective reticence." Root 229-30:
Old Man is ambiguous figure of "mystery as deep as the mystery of
death." Bushnell: Old Man derives ultimately from immortal wan-
derer of Buddhist legend, later personified as medieval Wandering
Jew with whom he shares meekness, piety, inability to die, restlessness; but Ch probably intended Old Man merely as "perfect foil"
to 3 rioters. Hamilton: Ch probably first conceived of Old Man as
spy of Death, added details from Maximian's elegy and legend of
Wandering Jew, increased irony by making him too old for worldly
desires (gold) as contrast to rioters; he is "Old Age as the Harbinger
of Death," resembling his master. Sp 176: Old Man has force of "allegorical Age (Elde)," connected with Death whose whereabouts
he knows. Kellogg: Old Man has dignity because he has humility,
symbolizing subjection to will of God. W.J.B. Owen: Old Man is
"an old man and nothing more"; no evidence he is Death or Death's
messenger, since he seeks Death himself. Pres 235: Old Man is multiple symbol of Death's messenger, Death himself, and Wandering
Jew (see 726). Pres 233-5: most impressive, mysterious, macabre
episode in Ch. Swart: Old Man is not Death, but Old Age presented
as mysteriously as possible by Ch. Miller: in Scriptural symbolism
Old Man is opposite of *child* (680-91); he is earthy element, the Old
Adam in us, which cannot die until human nature changes and the
redeemed New Man is born; Old Man points way to spiritual death
(see *ParsT* 213-6). Bron 102: Old Man is not symbol of Death, is
simply old man with "wisdom and gravity of his years" in contrast
to crass, headlong rioters. Strang disagrees with Owen; Old Man
is ambiguous but impressive allegorical figure, introduced by artful
Pard for momentary effect on audience; once audience becomes
absorbed in 3 rioters and gold, they do not care just *who* Old Man
was.

16-9 Bron 102: Young rioters are instantly revolted by sight of age
which "presumes to share life with those to whom life belongs."

29-31 Sp 176: Old Man "has the terrible primitive simplicity" of
aged peasant with elemental idea of death.

39-47 W. J. B. Owen: Old Man's "pitiful attempt to assert his
dignity is passed over in crushing silence."

45-7 W. J. B. Owen: irony of passage is pointless if Old Man is Death or his messenger.

59-65 W. J. B. Owen: Old Man has not seen gold, gives directions only to get rid of rioters, is eager to be on way in search of death (irony).

60-4 Miller: in Scriptural symbolism *croked wey* is road to spiritual death in false paradise of cupidity; *tree* is sterile tree of evil or death whose root is cupidity.

65 Candelaria: death was associated with oak tree in ancient myths; also Ch perhaps specified oak (not in analogues) because he was robbed at "fowle Ok" in Kent, Sept., 1390.

68-72 Sp 177: theme of avarice is resumed when rioters find gold, not Death.

72 C. A. Owen: gold makes rioters forget search for Death, but their greed ironically foreshadows their doom; "they no longer seek Death because they have found him."

777-836

Youngest rioter goes to town to fetch food and wine, while other two guard treasure till nightfall. They plot to murder youngest when he returns.

77	*taak kep* pay heed to		02	*fest* fist
78	*bourde* jest		12	*departed* shared
82	*wende* imagined		19	*conseil* a secret
90	*doon us honge* have us hanged		23	*biwreye* betray
93	*rede* advise		35	*shrewes* rascals

837-878

Meanwhile, the youngest plans to poison the other two. In town he buys poison from apothecary and puts it into two of three wine bottles with which he returns to oak tree.

42	*trone* throne		48	*leve* permission
45	*beye* buy		54	*quelle* kill

55	*hawe* yard	63	*montance* amount
58	*destroyed* harassed	65	*sterve* die
62	*confiture* concoction		

879-903

Two rioters guarding gold stab the youngest to death, then die themselves of poisoned wine. Murder is worst of all sins.

80	*cast* planned	88	*storven* died
85	*par cas* by chance	90	*canon* treatise. *fen* chapter

79-94 Kit 20: extraordinarily swift resolution of tale illustrates Ch's
"artistic economy." Sp 177: fact that Death is not a person after all,
but in this case the fatal result of Avarice comes as "last shock in the
tale's succession of disturbing surprises." Francïs: after slow development, swift shock of ending, on which whole effect depends, requires
that "narrative must keep pace with the reader's surmises concerning
the outcome."

83-4 Miller: false feast of rioters, "with its reversed sacramental
'breed and wyn,' serves to symbolize the subjection of these Cain-like
'brothers' to their earthly treasure," recalls Pard's snack at *alestake,*
shows consequences of cupidity.

95-03 Chapman: recapitulation of sermon, following exemplum;
whole tale conforms to rules of medieval sermon. Mal 16: eloquent
moral of story. Ev 171: final peroration against sins, followed by
benediction in 916-8. Baum 47: "grand climax" of Pard's "exhibition
sermon."

95-9 Ger 70: "rhetoric of the spell-binder to whom sense matters
little if the sound is right."

00-3 Bron 83: without Prologue, these lines would seem "genuine
piety"; Pard is hypocrite but not apostate—sincere note here "is not
necessarily cancelled by his vicious life."

904-945

"Good people, beware of greed. My pardons will save you from this
sin." Thus I preach. But I do have authentic pardons in my bag
which I will give any of you whenever you like for a price. Come
forward, Host, and make an offering, since you need pardon most.

05	*ware* avoid	37	*seuretee* security
06	*warice* cure	42	*envoluped* wrapped up
16	*leche* healer	45	*unbokele* unbuckle
36	*atwo* in two		

04-45 Don 930: Pard, like rioters, has seemed in firm control of his destiny but here suddenly comes to grief; it is "ironic destiny working through his own nature that impels the Pard to provoke his own social destruction among the pilgrims." Baum 217: possibly Pard changes tone in 916 only momentarily, then resumes speech to imaginary peasant audience; most likely Ch seized chance for rousing dramatic ending here "at some sacrifice of verisimilitude."

04-15 Kit 216: Pard is carried away by own eloquence and force of tale, gives usual summons for offerings, realizes error, and in 915 reminds pilgrims he is only giving sample of his oratory.

16-8 Hin 158: lines out of character, were probably left in by accident when Ch shifted tale from Parson to Pard. Kit 216: Pard's "cynicism falls away" in this benediction (still under spell of own tale) and he momentarily "suffers a very paroxysm of agonized sincerity." Cur 66-7 refutes Kit's moment of sincerity; rather it is merely preparation for "masterstroke of deception," hypnosis of pilgrims to sell relics despite earlier confession as crowning proof of his skill; "but he reckons without his Host!" Sp 177: "momentary sincerity." Ger 70: sincerity not really out of character (Pard is a man—wicked, but not a devil). Gross: here power of tale lifts Pard to "momentary exaltation," after which he tries vainly to resume plan of revenge on pilgrims for insult in 324 with "ironic offer" of pardons admittedly worthless. Bald 109: "one flash of painful sincerity." Lum 217-8: Pard's effort to reinforce solemn effect of tale to prepare pilgrims psychologically for sale of pardons. Bron 83: "the wish is sincere and devoid of irony."

19-45 Kit 217: "wild orgy of reckless jesting," mockingly offering relics for sale. Root 231 doubts Pard, on vacation, really expected to sell; he is "conscious artist in hypocrisy, who wishes to give a crowning example of his art." Sp 177: seeing tale has put fear of death in pilgrims, Pard promptly offers them "a kind of insurance policy." Swart: to flatter his own vanity, Pard must sell to pilgrims despite their knowledge of his frauds. Lum 220: Pard.breaks spell of sermon and benediction by foolishly reverting to usual crude sales methods. Bron 86: "so gross an affront to the meanest intelligence among the pilgrims is simply unimaginable."

41-5 Bron 81-2: Pard's offering relics to Host for bargain price of *grote* is jibe at innkeepers who were notorious for avarice and stinginess.

946-968

(Host explodes in anger, turns on Pardoner with brutal obscenity, threatens to castrate him. Pardoner is speechless with wrath. Host turns away. The Knight steps in to settle quarrel, forces Host to kiss Pardoner and make peace.)

47 *so theech* so may I thrive
(so thee ich)

52 *coillons* testicles

54 *lat kutte hem* let them be
cut

55 *toord* turd, piece of dung

46-68 Kit 166: "comic interlude with a tragedy behind it."

46-57 Cog 162: Host's "annihilating retort" expresses popular feelings toward pardoners. Ger 71: "utter grossness" of Host's reply shows extreme disgust at Pard's "brazen hypocrisy"; Host feels "it is like being attacked by a rat." Brew 159: brutal crudity of Host's retort is needed to voice reader's feelings toward "this cynical and depraved creature." Ethel: in taunting Pard for impotence (eunuchism), Host hits his most sensitive spot, which accounts in part for Pard's moral depravity, public bravado. Bron 82: utter contempt for the man (not relics) "as a living lie," rather than anger, inspires Host's grossness.

52-5 Cur 67: direct reference to Pard's eunuchism. Ger 59: Host did not think Pard was eunuch.

56 Lum 223: Pard is speechless with anger over reference to his eunuchism and with frustration over his own bungling of sale.

60-8 Swart: Knight forces Pard to pretend to be amiable and kiss Host; "can there be a more humiliating punishment for a professional and superior hypocrite than to be forced to be one?"

The Shipman's Tale

COMMENTARIES: Gr 225-6; Ham 283-5;/ Don 930-2; ManCT 624; Rob 732-4; Sk 5, 165-73;/ Brew 128; Cog 168; Dem 39-42; Fr 232-3; Ger 29; Kit 170-4; Law 62-4, 127-8; Low 167; Lum 70-7; Mal 217-18; Mus 199; Pres 206; Root 189; Sedg 284; Sp 178;/ Appleman, *N&Q,* 56, 372-3; Baum, *PMLA,* 56, 225-46; Chapman, *MLN,* 56, 4-5; Cline, *MLN,* 45, 480-2; Lawrence, *MLN,* 57, 87-8, and *Spec,* 58, 56-68; Silverman, *PQ,* 53, 329-331; Skeat, *MLR,* 10, 430-4; Spargo, *SA,* 439-46; Stillwell, *RES,* 44, 1-18; Tupper, *JEGP,* 34, 352-72.

GENRE: Fabliau, based on folk tale with motif of "Lover's Gift Regained."

SOURCE: Unknown, but probably a lost French fabliau; analogues have been found in Sercambi's *Novella 19,* Boccaccio's *Decameron,* viii, 1 and 2, ancient Indian, and modern European stories.

DATE: Probably early 1390's, before *WBT* (1393-4).

GENERAL CRITICISM: Root 189: though more delicate than *MillT* or *RvT,* this is basically more immoral since monk gets off scot-free; a "disagreeable picture of treachery and lust," but very skillful, realistic picture of bourgeois household. Kit 170-4: tale meant for Wife of Bath, fits her character in style and sentiment—frankly sensual, but "too hearty and too profoundly normal to be unwholesome"; tale almost as suited to Shipman who here satirizes merchants (see *Gen Prol*), with perhaps an implied hit at Pilgrim Merchant, and monks (Don John of tale very similar to Pilgrim Monk—both outriders). Tupper: tale (probably based on French fabliau) very appropriate to Shipman who steals merchants' French wines, tells gay tale of monk stealing merchant's wife, shows knowledge of fine wines (70-1) and practices of merchants; tale gains point from parallel with "mismated and debt-laden" Pilgrim Merchant; tale never meant for Wife of Bath since wife is made fool of as much as merchant, out of keeping with Wife's character. Sedg 284: relatively

uninteresting tale; "if the fo'c'sle of the *Magdelene* heard no better
yarns than that, I marvel that so many stout fellows went to sea."
Stillwell: tale has no purpose except to make people laugh. Law 62:
tale first written for woman, best fits Wife of Bath, involves marriage
but not question of sex supremacy (merchant has no suspicion of
trick). Sp 178: tale originally for Wife of Bath, thus juxtaposed with
PrT for 2 contrasting women's tales. Mal 218: transfer of tale from
Wife of Bath to Shipman shows tale written for its own sake, not to
characterize teller. Pres 206: wife surpasses corresponding figure in
Sercambi and Boccaccio in being "vain, feline coquette" of medieval
antifeminism, as monk is figure of medieval anticlericism. Silverman:
basic theme that "a husband had better be free with his wife or others
will be free with her" fits Wife of Bath perfectly; but tale also suited
to Shipman who is deceitful (*Gen Prol*) and expresses traditional
enmity between merchants and shipmen; commercialization of marriage relationship bitterly ironical, since wife's prostitution with
monk is followed by her offering herself to husband for money
which "seems also to be the merchant's compensation for his unwit-
ting graduation to cuckoldom," a twist not found in analogues, brilliantly summed up in puns in 416 and 434. Brew 128: shifting of tale
to Shipman shows *CT* was flexible, developing work—Ch ready to
adapt when good idea is succeeded by a better. Lum 74-7: tale fits
specifications given by Shipman in *MLT* 1185-90; wife's skill in
manipulating secret affair also suits Wife of Bath who is "quite capable of having her cake and eating it too;" Ch shifted tale (which has
no hint of female sovereignty theme) to Shipman when he conceived more complex idea of Wife of Bath. Chapman: tale ill suited
to Wife of Bath since antifeminist doctrine of women (from fabliau
tradition) shows clear male bias, originally meant for Shipman. Appleman rejects Chapman's argument, notes similarities between lists
of things women desire in *ShipT* 173-7 and *WBT* 925 ff., between
taillynge puns in *ShipT* 416, 434 and *WBT* 130, 153; tale fits Wife as
rebuttal to view of women in *MerchT,* was adapted from fabliau to
enhance characterization of Wife (merchant's wife does not deny
monk's repayment, but confesses and forces husband to forgive and
submit). Lawrence, *MLN,* refutes Chapman; tale shows triumph of
wife in appeasing husband with clever reply—no male bias. Mus 199:

though Shipman is from West of England, no trace of western accent in tale. Don 931-2; coldly brilliant fabliau, reducing all human values to money with "almost mathematical precision" (wife expensive because attractive, monk popular because generous with tips and gifts, and central issue of 100 francs is value of wife's sexual favors both to monk and husband); too sterile a situation for richly human Wife of Bath, better for neutral Shipman whose unawareness deepens irony. Lawrence, *Spec:* tale closest of Ch's fabliaux to standard French fabliau technique (swift narrative, no digressions or long descriptions as in *MillT,* much dialogue); idea that tale unsuited to Wife of Bath ignores her frank confession of women's frailties (refutes Tupper)—Ch altered tale to give more favorable view of wife, probably first meant it to follow *MLT;* "a little masterpiece of lively narrative and brilliant characterization," far more suited to Wife than to Shipman.

THE SHIPMAN'S TALE
VII, 1-19
A rich merchant of St. Denis (near Paris) had a beautiful wife who loved parties. Such husbands have to pay dearly to support and clothe us wives.

5	*dispence* expense	11	*sely* poor, hapless
6	*chiere* looks	19	*lene* lend

1-9 Cog 168: well constructed passages to open tale, with wit, imagery, and satirical theme.

1-19 Sk, 5, 168: feminine pronouns show tale originally meant for Wife of Bath (Pr and Second Nun unsuited). Tupper: pronouns do not eliminate man as original teller; he may be mimicking way a woman would talk; "in this way the passage becomes a conscious artistic touch, not an oversight." Low 166-7: feminine phrases not designed for bearded Shipman, "most fiercely masculine of the pilgrims," but surely for Wife of Bath.

5-19 Chapman: 5-10 present husband's view, 12-19 wife's; agrees with Tupper that witty Shipman (*good felawe* of *Gen Prol* 395) is simply mimicking woman's voice as contrasted with husband's in

5-10. Lawrence, *MLN,* disagrees that Shipman is witty mimic—*good felawe* connotes rascal or thief.

20-52

A young monk of thirty was frequent visitor at merchant's house and a close friend. This monk, Don John, was generous to the servants.

27	*evere in oon* all the time		43	*free* generous
29	*goode man* husband		48	*sitthe* afterwards. *meynee*
36	*cosynage* relative			servants

25-52 AHM: sexual misconduct of monks is frequent target of satire in medieval literature; possible ulterior motives in Don John's gifts to servants.

53-88

Merchant, planning business trip to Bruges (in Flanders, S.W. Belgium), invites monk to visit 2 or 3 days prior. On third day he shuts himself in office to check accounts.

61	*in alle wise* in any event		72	*volatyl* wild fowl
66	*graunges* granaries		76	*sadly* soberly
70	*malvesye* Malmsey wine		77	*countour-hous* counting-
71	*vernage* red wine from Italy			house, office

70-3 Lum 77: specific knowledge of wines fits Shipman in *Gen Prol.*

89-207

Monk rises same morning and meets wife looking pale in garden. He jokingly suggests that love has caused loss of sleep. She replies that she has no such luck; her life with merchant is miserable. Monk swears that he loves her and will never tell her secrets. She confesses love for monk, complains further of husband, and begs loan of 100 francs. Monk promises to bring money after husband leaves. He kisses her often and they separate.

91	*thynges* prayers	31	*porthors* breviary
94	*saleweth* greeted	54	*sikerly* certainly
97	*under the yerde* subject to	72	*nygardye* miserliness
	discipline	77	*buxom* submissive
99	*rathe* early	83	*slaundre* slander
03	*dare* lie still	94	*Genylon* Ganelon, betrayed
04	*fourme* fixed position		Charlemagne's army at
05	*forstraught* distracted		Roncesvalles
16	*reawme* realm	06	*chilyndre* sundial

151 Ger 29: monk's swearing by St. Denis is fitting since story takes place in town dedicated to him.

201-2 Don 931: rime of *frankes—flankes* is brilliant emphasis of sex-for-money theme of tale.

208-248

Wife orders dinner, then knocks at husband's office door. He says he has to work hard to retain his wealth, must go to Flanders next day. He asks her to guard house and goods well in his absence.

09	*pye* magpie	22	*alenge* wretchedly
14	*Quy la?* Who is there?	23	*messe* mass
	(Fr.). *Peter!* (an oath by St.	26	*chapmen* merchants
	Peter, not husband's name)	36	*queynte* sly
19	*sonde* sending	43	*curious* careful

24-38 Kit 173: at hearing this speech pilgrims probably wondered whether Pilgrim Merchant was "playing a pilgrimage to dodge his creditors"; unlikely that Merchant is in debt (*Gen Prol* 280-1), but Ch suggests this as possibility in any merchant's life.

27 Cline: *Seint Yve* is probably 12th-century French bishop of Chartres, since tale is set in France and all other oaths in it are appropriate to Frenchmen. (Cline does not explain identical oath in *SumT* 1943).

48 Dem 40: heavy irony, since we already know she will not lack silver.

in *MkT*); tale fits tender-hearted Pr with stress on pathos, shows Ch's devotion to Virgin and the "tender and credulous side" of his nature; anti-semitic feeling common to Ch's age. Mal 218-9: tale of murder and torture does not especially fit Pr who weeps at dead mouse and shows worldly traits in *Gen Prol;* a courtly tale would suit her better. Sp 178-80: Ch probably wrote tale for Pr, reverted to stanzaic form to strike note of religious exaltation; full of naive wonder and ecstasy, tale belongs to "world of medieval Christianized folk-belief"; pathos and human touches may be there to show "deeper instinctive humanity" of Pr. Pres 207-9: teller seems anonymous voice of "religious consciousness of the folk"; popular miracle of Virgin used as pulpit exemplum, with gentle, strong poetry, "painful and healing." Brew 151: tale brief but artistically flawless as *MillT,* with sweetness of mother and child, "devout wonder and gratitude at the miracle"; ironic that gentlest pilgrim tells tale which, to modern readers, is only cruel and fanatic one in *CT.* Lum 81: Ch has shaped material from source to give sense of Pr's personal belief. Schoeck: tale implies condemnation of ritual murder legend as "vicious and hypocritical," a view Ch shared with many enlightened people of the age and with church (popes issued bulls against superstitious persecution of Jews); Ch recognizes inhumanity of tale, does not condemn Pr, but shows understanding pity of her somewhat warped character. Mus 223: tale shows Ch's usual mixture of styles; realism "melts symbolically into the conventional frame without conflict or irony." Don 932: tale "a strange mixture of delicacy and horror," reveals failure of Pr's character, not Ch's; church itself did not approve of Pr's savage attitude toward Jews, and Ch was aware of this. Baum 75-9: tale "something less than completely serious," slight, delicate touches of exaggeration which show Ch's "smiling gravity" without loss of pathos, and match "reverent raillery" of Pr's portrait in *Gen Prol.* Bron 77-8: Kit's view of tale as showing Pr's "thwarted motherhood" is invalid superimposing of modern psychological interests on 14th-century poem; more probably Pr's celibate life was pleasant and fulfilling; tale suits her, the "overt streak of cruelty masked as pious hatred" is reverse side of her "shallow sensibility."

249-298
After dinner monk speaks privately to merchant and asks for loan of 100 francs. Merchant gives him the money and Don John leaves.

50 *lette* delay
62 *atemprely* temperately
76 *mile way* time it takes to walk mile

85 *chaffare* goods
89 *creaunce* borrow on credit

86 Dem 39: heavy irony, since it is clearly not monk's intention to spare in what he takes!

299-324
Next day merchant leaves for Bruges; following Sunday Don John comes to St. Denis. He gives wife 100 francs borrowed from husband and spends night with her, unsuspected by servants.

16 *bolt upright* flat on her back   17 *acord* agreement

02-6 Dem 40: passage partly aimed at contrasting merchant's sober ways with gaiety of others in his absence.

325-364
Merchant returns from Bruges, then goes to Paris to raise money. There he meets Don John who says he has repaid loan of 100 francs to wife.

28 *chaffare* purchasing
29 *chevyssaunce* borrowing
30 *reconyssaunce* legal bond

36 *chiertee* fondness
41 *yfeere* together
59 *tokenes* facts

35-64 Dem 40: fine scene of complex humor and emotions which suggests that Ch added importantly to fabliau outline; comedy of merchant as lender and borrower at same time, of monk's "shameless little piece of cheating" and of his delight in irony shown in parting words (363).

365-399
Merchant finishes business, goes happily home, and frolics with wife.
He scolds her for not telling him that monk had repaid 100 francs.

69 *papejay* popinjay (parrot)
71 *in that viage* from that trip
72 *costage* expenses
75 *bisette* employed

79 *maketh it ful tough* gives
her a vigorous tussling
90 *yvele apayed* ill pleased

75-9 Lum 75: reunion scene shows merchant far from impotent;
thus wife lied to monk in 170-1.
88-92 Dem 40: tremendous dramatic irony in "exquisite tact" of
duped husband toward wife's lover (and deceiver); "one of the most
cruel touches in this cruel story."

400-434
Wife denies she knew about loan, says she thought money was a
gift and spent it on clothes. Wife promises to pay merchant back in
lovemaking. Merchant forgives her.

05 *thedam* success
08 *prow* profit
11 *disjoynt* evil plight

16 *taille* tally (pun on "tail")
23 *to wedde* in pledge
31 *large* extravagant

30-2 Dem 41-2: irony centers on husband's attitude, but Ch breaks
away from typical fabliau pattern in not making duped husband
contemptible or grotesque; husband is worthy, successful, kind, and
dignified throughout, and thereby incongruity becomes the more
subtly cruel and ironical.
33-4 Lum 76: two elements (merchant's absorption in business and
wife's amorousness) are brilliantly brought together in final pun on
taillynge. Don 931: this second use of pun (see 416) notifies us that
proposition of tale (love can be bought with money) has been proved.

The Prioress's Tale

COMMENTARIES: Gr 226-8; Ham 285-7;/ Don 932-4; ManCT
624-8; Rob 734-6; Sk 5, 173-82;/ Baum 75-9; Bow 99-100; Brew
150-1; Bron 77-8; Brown, *A Study of the Miracle of Our Lady Told
by Ch's Prioress* (Ch. Soc., 1910); Cog 135-6, 159-60; Ev 157-8;
Fr 233-42; Ger 87-8; Kit 174-81; Leg 69-70; Low 165; Lum
80-2; Mad 52-9; Mal 218-9; Mus 223; Pat 170-1, 229; Pres 207-
9; Root 190-7; Shel 264-6; Sp 178-80;/ Brown, *MP*, 05-6, 467-91,
and *SA*, 447-85; Draper, *ESt*, 26, 238-51; Hostia, *CE*, 53, 351-2;
Manly, *PBA*, 26, 95-113 (ST); Rose Marie, *Cweal*, 40, 225-7;
Schoeck, ST, 245-58; Statler, *PMLA*, 50, 896-910; Tupper, *JEGP*,
34, 352-72; Yunk, *N&Q*, 60, 165-7.

GENRE: Miracle of the Virgin.

ANALOGUES: Over 30 analogues have been found, no one of
which seems to have been Ch's direct source.

DATE: Fairly late, probably mid 1390's.

VERSE FORM: Rime Royal (7-line stanza of iambic pentameter,
rimed a b a b b c c).

GENERAL CRITICISM: Root 190: tale shows Pr is earnestly religious; her affectations in *Gen Prol* are superficial; Ch's version of
tale differs from others in added stress on human side, less on
miraculous power of Virgin and malignancy of Jews. Leg 69-70:
Ch's early lyrical experiments bore fruit in later narratives such as
PrT where "he brings into play all the resources of a highly-trained
style in order to suggest a suave artlessness." Kit 181: in tale Pr
involuntarily reveals her inner nature in choosing most touching
and lovely of Miracles of Virgin. Shel 264-6: tender-hearted Pr who
gives "one of the most touching pictures of childhood to be found
anywhere," is also capable of bitter hatred and bigotry, prejudices
the age. Rose Marie: tale a "flawless gem," most artistic and sweet
human of miracle legends. Cog 135-6, 159-60: Ch's touch with children "has unselfconscious sweetness" (see also tragedy of Ugoli

WORDS OF HOST TO SHIPMAN AND PRIORESS
435-452
Host congratulates Shipman and comments on deceit of monks. Host then calls on Prioress courteously for next tale.

35 *dominus* (bad Latin for "domini")
38 *last quade yeer* loads of evil
years

42 *in* inn, house
49 *demen* judge

35-42 Sp 178:   Host cheered by having his notions of monks' behavior with wives confirmed by Shipman.

35 Lum 87:   error in *corpus dominus* (domini) suggests Host's pretentiousness.

39-42 Kit 174:   Host here raises a laugh at dignified Pilgrim Monk.

40-1 Tupper: these lines, pointing out that wife in *ShipT* came out as badly as husband, are evidence that Ch never intended *ShipT* for Wife of Bath—clearly a man's tale.

42 Lum 77:   Host, as innkeeper, is concerned as to sort of guests he harbors; he misses point that wife's boredom rather than monk's perfidy leads to cuckolding in *ShipT*.

47-52 Kit 175:   sweet impression Pr has made on pilgrims is beautifully suggested by Host's extreme courtesy, contrasting with rough badinage which precedes. Manly: brief conversation with Host endows Pr with "lasting beauty and sympathetic appeal." Low 165: Host, experienced innkeeper, adjusts tone of speech to individual pilgrims "with unerring nicety." Lum 80-1: Host's excessive courtesy may be sly dig at Pr's pride in good manners (see *Gen Prol*). Don 933: exaggerated politeness reminds us of Pr's frailty.

PROLOGUE OF THE PRIORESS'S TALE
VII, 453-487
Invocation to the Virgin: praise be to Christ and to His Mother. Gracious Maid and Mother, help me to tell my tale.

57	*bountee* excellence	76	*science* learned terms
59	*heriynge* praise	81	*wayk* weak
66	*boote* salvation	85	*unnethes* hardly

53-87 Root 191: invocation shows "sincere Christian humility." Hostia: last lines of invocation (481-7) savor of insincerity and false humility. Brew 150: invocation sets mood of "pious exaltation" of tale. Don 933: "Ch's most splendid prayer," using old symbols in fresh way.

53-75 Mad 52-3: first 4 stanzas are paraphrases of parts of services of Matins and Lauds.

54 ManCT 625: *quod she* shows Prologue, if not written for *CT,* was adapted for Pr; use of Rime Royal for words of Host proves they and tale written at same time.

467-73 ManCT 625: union of motherhood and virginity, so appealing to medieval love of mystery, was often illustrated by miracle of unburnt, burning bush. Pat 170-1: Ch used this passage (from St. Bernard's prayer in Dante's *Paradiso*) again in *SecNT* 36-42, but here the lines sing.

THE PRIORESS'S TALE

488-515

City in Asia has Jewish quarter with street leading to Christian school. One of students is widow's son of 7 years who walks to school daily by this street.

91	*usure* usury	03	*clergeon* schoolboy
93	*wende* walk	04	*wone* custom
97	*heep* large number	12	*sely* good. *alday* always

88-9 AHM: remote setting apt, since Jews had been expelled from England in 1290, not to be readmitted until 17th century.

91 Yunk: *Lucre of vileynye* does not mean "greed of filthy lucre" as editors gloss it, but is term in canon law (*turpe lucrum*) meaning "shameful profits from sales."

95 Brown, *MP:* two types of medieval schools—grammar schools teaching Latin, and elementary schools with no Latin; this one is probably grammar school, aimed at training children to take part in

church services. Ev 157-8: *litel* used as subtle motif of verbal repetition in tale (*litel scole, litel clergeon, litel child, litel bok lernynge,* etc.); singing of *Alma Redemptoris* is second repeated motif.

00 Brown, *MP:* *rede* often used to mean "read Latin."

03 Brown, *SA:* age of 7 years not found in any known analogue, was added by Ch to heighten pathos. Brown, *MP:* *clergeon* means young clerk, not chorister-boy (Sk's gloss); school he attended was too large for choir school.

516-557
From older schoolmate little boy learns song to Virgin, *Alma Redemptoris,* and sings it on way to school.

19	*antiphoner* book of responsive chants	22	*koude* knew
20	*ner* nearer	29	*knowes* knees
		41	*shent* punished

17 Brown, *MP:* *prymer* not elementary reader (Sk's gloss), but a development from psalter to which prayers and devotional exercises had been added, in ordinary use as school text in Latin.

25 Brown, *SA:* *felawe* added to tale by Ch to teach anthem, make possible dialogue with *clergeon;* adds human action and feeling to older miracle.

36 Brown, *MP:* *felawe* explains he cannot read Latin as if older boys could.

39-43 Pat 229: irony in boy's fearing he may be beaten for learning *Alma Redemptoris!*

48-9 Sp 180: child acquires (by absorption in worship) "the passivity of an instrument" (*it passed thurgh his throte*).

558-634
Jews, enraged by song, hire killer who cuts boy's throat and dumps him in privy. Mother seeks boy frantically, crying his name in Jewish quarter. Miraculously boy sings *Alma Redemptoris* despite cut throat, and is found. Many Jews are jailed, tortured, and executed.

60	*swal* swelled	08	*heere* here (we see)
72	*wardrobe* privy	11	*upright* on his back
79	*sowded* united	20	*leet bynde* had imprisoned
80	*evere in oon* always	29	*dooth to sterve* has put to
81	*quod she* said Prioress (slip		death
	on Ch's part)	31	*observe* tolerate
00	*frayneth* asks	33	*hors* horses (pl.)

70-3 Baum 77: coming from dignified, mannerly Pr, these lines are astonishing, show Ch's gentle satire.

70 Hostia: references to *cursed* Jews shows Pr's bigotry; note irony that child does not curse Jews, praises Virgin instead; also, tale honors Mary, a Jewess.

72 Draper: in 14th-century castles *wardrobe* was room used both as privy and as storeroom for clothes, etc.; here used as euphemism for simple privy.

81 Lum 82: *quod she* strongly suggests Ch had Pr well in mind.

93-8 Ger 87-8: in few lines Ch expresses intensity of mother's suffering, pathos increased by implied parallel with sorrow of Mother of God "which is all the more effective because it is not put into words"; verse has noble music, keyed to *Alma Redemptoris*.

11-72 Sp 180: "curiously physical ritualistic element," foreign to modern mind, results from medieval acceptance of the miraculous without rejection of role of natural body.

28-34 Bow 99-100: Pr's blandness in describing torture of Jews conflicts with soft-heartedness over animals (*Gen Prol* 142-5), suggests defect in her character.

635-690

While being prepared for burial, boy still sings *Alma*. Abbot asks how; boy says he sings to glory of Virgin who laid miraculous kernel on his tongue. Abbot removes kernel, boy dies, people praise Virgin. O Hugh of Lincoln, also slain by Jews, pray for us.

36	*laste* lasted	45	*halse* beg
40	*spreynd* sprinkled	58	*forlete* give up
44	*conjure* implore		

62　*greyn* kernel of grain, or
　　perhaps precious stone
　　(pearl, symbolizing Virgin)

75　*gruf* face down. *plat* flat
77　*covent* monks of convent
83　*leve* grant

42-3 Kit 174-5: reference to abbot and monks not satire but quiet defense of monks, answering reflections against them in *ShipT* and in Host's rude and flippant comments; there may be bad monks in world, but Pr knows only good ones. Lum 81: Pr's gentle disapproval of Don John in *ShipT* and perhaps also of pleasure-loving Pilgrim Monk.

62 Mad 58-9: *greyn* may be consecrated Host, or a prayer bead.

Sir Thopas

COMMENTARIES: Gr 228-31; Ham 287-9;/ Don 934-7; ManCT 628-34; Rob 736-40; Sk 5, 182-200;/ Bald 67-8, 75; Baum 79; Brew 151-2; Ches 10-2, 157; Cog 150-2; Cow 160; Ev 11, 142-4; Fr 242-4; Kit 181-3; Law 129-30; Leg 152; Lum 83-92; Mal 170-2; Pat 168; Pres 209-12; Root 199-203; Sedg 45; Sp 180-2; Shel 227; Winstanley ed. *PrT and Thop* (Cambridge U.P., 1922);/ Camden, *RES*, 35, 326-30; Donaldson, *EIE*, 51, 116-40; Ficke, *PQ*, 28, 82-5; Francis, *PMLA*, 53, 1126-41; Herben, *Spec*, 37, 475-87; Kimpel, *ELH*, 53, 77-86; Knott, *MP*, 10, 135-9; Knowlton, *JEGP*, 24, 83-93; Lawrence, *PMLA*, 35, 81-91; Linn, *MLN*, 36, 300-11; Loomis, *PQ*, 35, 371-3, and *MLN*, 36, 311-3, and *SA*, 486-559; Lumiansky, *PQ*, 47, 313-20; Magoun, *PMLA*, 27, 833-44; Manly, *MP*, 10, 141-4, and *Essays and Studies*, 28, 52-73; McCracken, *Expl*, 59, item 57; Melton, *PQ*, 56, 215-7; Moore, *JEGP*, 54, 532-45; Patch, *ESt*, 31, 351-9; Roppolo, *MLN*, 48, 365-71; Ross, *MLN*, 30, 172-4; Strong, *MLN*, 08, 73-7, 102-6.

GENRE: Burlesque romance.

ANALOGUES: Metrical romances in general are satirized, but parallels have been noted especially in *Libeaus Desconus, Guy of Warwick, Thomas of Erceldoune, Amis and Amiloun, Sir Beves of Hamptoun, Sire Degaré*, and several others.

DATE: Uncertain, but probably during *CT* period, written expressly for dramatic situation.

VERSE FORM: Prologue is in Rime Royal, linking with preceding *PrT* in same meter; Tale is mainly in 6-line stanza, riming a a b a a b, with iambic tetrameter for a-lines and trimeter for b-lines, with variations in 790-826, 881-90.

GENERAL CRITICISM: Sk 5, 183: in tale Ch uses favorite meter of "long-winded ballad-makers," with many sly echoes in phrasing. Strong notes many parallels in situations and phrasing of famous English romance *Guy of Warwick*. Manly, *MP:* no bitter satire, but

249-298

After dinner monk speaks privately to merchant and asks for loan of 100 francs. Merchant gives him the money and Don John leaves.

50 *lette* delay   85 *chaffare* goods
62 *atemprely* temperately   89 *creaunce* borrow on credit
76 *mile way* time it takes to
   walk mile

86 Dem 39: heavy irony, since it is clearly not monk's intention to spare in what he takes!

299-324

Next day merchant leaves for Bruges; following Sunday Don John comes to St. Denis. He gives wife 100 francs borrowed from husband and spends night with her, unsuspected by servants.

16 *bolt upright* flat on her back   17 *acord* agreement

02-6 Dem 40: passage partly aimed at contrasting merchant's sober ways with gaiety of others in his absence.

325-364

Merchant returns from Bruges, then goes to Paris to raise money. There he meets Don John who says he has repaid loan of 100 francs to wife.

28 *chaffare* purchasing   36 *chiertee* fondness
29 *chevyssaunce* borrowing   41 *yfeere* together
30 *reconyssaunce* legal bond   59 *tokenes* facts

35-64 Dem 40: fine scene of complex humor and emotions which suggests that Ch added importantly to fabliau outline; comedy of merchant as lender and borrower at same time, of monk's "shameless little piece of cheating" and of his delight in irony shown in parting words (363).

365-399
Merchant finishes business, goes happily home, and frolics with wife.
He scolds her for not telling him that monk had repaid 100 francs.

69	*papejay* popinjay (parrot)	79	*maketh it ful tough* gives
71	*in that viage* from that trip		her a vigorous tussling
72	*costage* expenses	90	*yvele apayed* ill pleased
75	*bisette* employed		

75-9 Lum 75: reunion scene shows merchant far from impotent;
thus wife lied to monk in 170-1.
88-92 Dem 40: tremendous dramatic irony in "exquisite tact" of
duped husband toward wife's lover (and deceiver); "one of the most
cruel touches in this cruel story."

400-434
Wife denies she knew about loan, says she thought money was a
gift and spent it on clothes. Wife promises to pay merchant back in
lovemaking. Merchant forgives her.

05	*thedam* success	16	*taille* tally (pun on "tail")
08	*prow* profit	23	*to wedde* in pledge
11	*disjoynt* evil plight	31	*large* extravagant

30-2 Dem 41-2: irony centers on husband's attitude, but Ch breaks
away from typical fabliau pattern in not making duped husband
contemptible or grotesque; husband is worthy, successful, kind, and
dignified throughout, and thereby incongruity becomes the more
subtly cruel and ironical.
33-4 Lum 76: two elements (merchant's absorption in business and
wife's amorousness) are brilliantly brought together in final pun on
taillynge. Don 931: this second use of pun (see 416) notifies us that
proposition of tale (love can be bought with money) has been proved.

The Prioress's Tale

COMMENTARIES: Gr 226-8; Ham 285-7;/ Don 932-4; ManCT 624-8; Rob 734-6; Sk 5, 173-82;/ Baum 75-9; Bow 99-100; Brew 150-1; Bron 77-8; Brown, *A Study of the Miracle of Our Lady Told by Ch's Prioress* (Ch. Soc., 1910); Cog 135-6, 159-60; Ev 157-8; Fr 233-42; Ger 87-8; Kit 174-81; Leg 69-70; Low 165; Lum 80-2; Mad 52-9; Mal 218-9; Mus 223; Pat 170-1, 229; Pres 207-9; Root 190-7; Shel 264-6; Sp 178-80;/ Brown, *MP,* 05-6, 467-91, and *SA,* 447-85; Draper, *ESt,* 26, 238-51; Hostia, *CE,* 53, 351-2; Manly, *PBA,* 26, 95-113 (ST); Rose Marie, *Cweal,* 40, 225-7; Schoeck, ST, 245-58; Statler, *PMLA,* 50, 896-910; Tupper, *JEGP,* 34, 352-72; Yunk, *N&Q,* 60, 165-7.

GENRE: Miracle of the Virgin.

ANALOGUES: Over 30 analogues have been found, no one of which seems to have been Ch's direct source.

DATE: Fairly late, probably mid 1390's.

VERSE FORM: Rime Royal (7-line stanza of iambic pentameter, rimed a b a b b c c).

GENERAL CRITICISM: Root 190: tale shows Pr is earnestly religious; her affectations in *Gen Prol* are superficial; Ch's version of tale differs from others in added stress on human side, less on miraculous power of Virgin and malignancy of Jews. Leg 69-70: Ch's early lyrical experiments bore fruit in later narratives such as *PrT* where "he brings into play all the resources of a highly-trained style in order to suggest a suave artlessness." Kit 181: in tale Pr involuntarily reveals her inner nature in choosing most touching and lovely of Miracles of Virgin. Shel 264-6: tender-hearted Pr who gives "one of the most touching pictures of childhood to be found anywhere," is also capable of bitter hatred and bigotry, prejudices of the age. Rose Marie: tale a "flawless gem," most artistic and sweetly human of miracle legends. Cog 135-6, 159-60: Ch's touch with children "has unselfconscious sweetness" (see also tragedy of Ugolino in *MkT*); tale fits tender-hearted Pr with stress on pathos, shows Ch's devotion to Virgin and the "tender and credulous side" of his nature; anti-semitic feeling common to Ch's age. Mal 218-9: tale of murder and torture does not especially fit Pr who weeps at dead mouse and shows worldly traits in *Gen Prol;* a courtly tale would suit her better. Sp 178-80: Ch probably wrote tale for Pr, reverted to stanzaic form to strike note of religious exaltation; full of naive wonder and ecstasy, tale belongs to "world of medieval Christianized folk-belief"; pathos and human touches may be there to show "deeper instinctive humanity" of Pr. Pres 207-9: teller seems anonymous voice of "religious consciousness of the folk"; popular miracle of Virgin used as pulpit exemplum, with gentle, strong poetry, "painful and healing." Brew 151: tale brief but artistically flawless as *MillT,* with sweetness of mother and child, "devout wonder and gratitude at the miracle"; ironic that gentlest pilgrim tells tale which, to modern readers, is only cruel and fanatic one in *CT.* Lum 81: Ch has shaped material from source to give sense of Pr's personal belief. Schoeck: tale implies condemnation of ritual murder legend as "vicious and hypocritical," a view Ch shared with many enlightened people of the age and with church (popes issued bulls against superstitious persecution of Jews); Ch recognizes inhumanity of tale, does not condemn Pr, but shows understanding pity of her somewhat warped character. Mus 223: tale shows Ch's usual mixture of styles; realism "melts symbolically into the conventional frame without conflict or irony." Don 932: tale "a strange mixture of delicacy and horror," reveals failure of Pr's character, not Ch's; church itself did not approve of Pr's savage attitude toward Jews, and Ch was aware of this. Baum 75-9: tale "something less than completely serious," with slight, delicate touches of exaggeration which show Ch's "smiling gravity" without loss of pathos, and match "reverent raillery" of Pr's portrait in *Gen Prol.* Bron 77-8: Kit's view of tale as showing Pr's "thwarted motherhood" is invalid superimposing of modern psychological interests on 14th-century poem; more probably Pr's celibate life was pleasant and fulfilling; tale suits her, the "overt streak of cruelty masked as pious hatred" is reverse side of her "shallow sensibility."

WORDS OF HOST TO SHIPMAN AND PRIORESS
435-452
Host congratulates Shipman and comments on deceit of monks. Host then calls on Prioress courteously for next tale.

35 *dominus* (bad Latin for "do-   42 *in* inn, house
    mini")   49 *demen* judge
38 *last quade yeer* loads of evil
    years

35-42 Sp 178:   Host cheered by having his notions of monks' behavior with wives confirmed by Shipman.

35 Lum 87:   error in *corpus dominus* (domini) suggests Host's pretentiousness.

39-42 Kit 174:   Host here raises a laugh at dignified Pilgrim Monk.

40-1 Tupper: these lines, pointing out that wife in *ShipT* came out as badly as husband, are evidence that Ch never intended *ShipT* for Wife of Bath—clearly a man's tale.

42 Lum 77:   Host, as innkeeper, is concerned as to sort of guests he harbors; he misses point that wife's boredom rather than monk's perfidy leads to cuckolding in *ShipT*.

47-52 Kit 175:   sweet impression Pr has made on pilgrims is beautifully suggested by Host's extreme courtesy, contrasting with rough badinage which precedes. Manly: brief conversation with Host endows Pr with "lasting beauty and sympathetic appeal." Low 165: Host, experienced innkeeper, adjusts tone of speech to individual pilgrims "with unerring nicety." Lum 80-1: Host's excessive courtesy may be sly dig at Pr's pride in good manners (see *Gen Prol*). Don 933: exaggerated politeness reminds us of Pr's frailty.

PROLOGUE OF THE PRIORESS'S TALE
VII, 453-487
Invocation to the Virgin: praise be to Christ and to His Mother. Gracious Maid and Mother, help me to tell my tale.

57	*bountee* excellence	76	*science* learned terms
59	*heriynge* praise	81	*wayk* weak
66	*boote* salvation	85	*unnethes* hardly

53-87 Root 191: invocation shows "sincere Christian humility." Hostia: last lines of invocation (481-7) savor of insincerity and false humility. Brew 150: invocation sets mood of "pious exaltation" of tale. Don 933: "Ch's most splendid prayer," using old symbols in fresh way.

53-75 Mad 52-3: first 4 stanzas are paraphrases of parts of services of Matins and Lauds.

54 ManCT 625: *quod she* shows Prologue, if not written for *CT*, was adapted for Pr; use of Rime Royal for words of Host proves they and tale written at same time.

467-73 ManCT 625: union of motherhood and virginity, so appealing to medieval love of mystery, was often illustrated by miracle of unburnt, burning bush. Pat 170-1: Ch used this passage (from St. Bernard's prayer in Dante's *Paradiso*) again in *SecNT* 36-42, but here the lines sing.

THE PRIORESS'S TALE

488-515
City in Asia has Jewish quarter with street leading to Christian school. One of students is widow's son of 7 years who walks to school daily by this street.

91	*usure* usury	03	*clergeon* schoolboy
93	*wende* walk	04	*wone* custom
97	*heep* large number	12	*sely* good. *alday* always

88-9 AHM: remote setting apt, since Jews had been expelled from England in 1290, not to be readmitted until 17th century.

91 Yunk: *Lucre of vileynye* does not mean "greed of filthy lucre" as editors gloss it, but is term in canon law (*turpe lucrum*) meaning "shameful profits from sales."

95 Brown, *MP:* two types of medieval schools—grammar schools teaching Latin, and elementary schools with no Latin; this one is probably grammar school, aimed at training children to take part in

church services. Ev 157-8: *litel* used as subtle motif of verbal repetition in tale (*litel scole, litel clergeon, litel child, litel bok lernynge,* etc.); singing of *Alma Redemptoris* is second repeated motif.

00 Brown, *MP: rede* often used to mean "read Latin."

03 Brown, *SA:* age of 7 years not found in any known analogue, was added by Ch to heighten pathos. Brown, *MP: clergeon* means young clerk, not chorister-boy (Sk's gloss); school he attended was too large for choir school.

516-557

From older schoolmate little boy learns song to Virgin, *Alma Redemptoris,* and sings it on way to school.

19	*antiphoner* book of responsive chants		22	*koude* knew
20	*ner* nearer		29	*knowes* knees
			41	*shent* punished

17 Brown, *MP: prymer* not elementary reader (Sk's gloss), but a development from psalter to which prayers and devotional exercises had been added, in ordinary use as school text in Latin.

25 Brown, *SA: felawe* added to tale by Ch to teach anthem, make possible dialogue with *clergeon;* adds human action and feeling to older miracle.

36 Brown, *MP: felawe* explains he cannot read Latin as if older boys could.

39-43 Pat 229: irony in boy's fearing he may be beaten for learning *Alma Redemptoris!*

48-9 Sp 180: child acquires (by absorption in worship) "the passivity of an instrument" (*it passed thurgh his throte*).

558-634

Jews, enraged by song, hire killer who cuts boy's throat and dumps him in privy. Mother seeks boy frantically, crying his name in Jewish quarter. Miraculously boy sings *Alma Redemptoris* despite cut throat, and is found. Many Jews are jailed, tortured, and executed.

60	*swal* swelled	08	*heere* here (we see)
72	*wardrobe* privy	11	*upright* on his back
79	*sowded* united	20	*leet bynde* had imprisoned
80	*evere in oon* always	29	*dooth to sterve* has put to
81	*quod she* said Prioress (slip		death
	on Ch's part)	31	*observe* tolerate
00	*frayneth* asks	33	*hors* horses (pl.)

70-3 Baum 77: coming from dignified, mannerly Pr, these lines are astonishing, show Ch's gentle satire.

70 Hostia: references to *cursed* Jews shows Pr's bigotry; note irony that child does not curse Jews, praises Virgin instead; also, tale honors Mary, a Jewess.

72 Draper: in 14th-century castles *wardrobe* was room used both as privy and as storeroom for clothes, etc.; here used as euphemism for simple privy.

81 Lum 82: *quod she* strongly suggests Ch had Pr well in mind.

93-8 Ger 87-8: in few lines Ch expresses intensity of mother's suffering, pathos increased by implied parallel with sorrow of Mother of God "which is all the more effective because it is not put into words"; verse has noble music, keyed to *Alma Redemptoris*.

11-72 Sp 180: "curiously physical ritualistic element," foreign to modern mind, results from medieval acceptance of the miraculous without rejection of role of natural body.

28-34 Bow 99-100: Pr's blandness in describing torture of Jews conflicts with soft-heartedness over animals (*Gen Prol* 142-5), suggests defect in her character.

635-690

While being prepared for burial, boy still sings *Alma*. Abbot asks how; boy says he sings to glory of Virgin who laid miraculous kernel on his tongue. Abbot removes kernel, boy dies, people praise Virgin. O Hugh of Lincoln, also slain by Jews, pray for us.

36	*laste* lasted	45	*halse* beg
40	*spreynd* sprinkled	58	*forlete* give up
44	*conjure* implore		

62 *greyn* kernel of grain, or
perhaps precious stone
(pearl, symbolizing Virgin)

75 *gruf* face down. *plat* flat
77 *covent* monks of convent
83 *leve* grant

42-3 Kit 174-5: reference to abbot and monks not satire but quiet defense of monks, answering reflections against them in *ShipT* and in Host's rude and flippant comments; there may be bad monks in world, but Pr knows only good ones. Lum 81: Pr's gentle disapproval of Don John in *ShipT* and perhaps also of pleasure-loving Pilgrim Monk.

62 Mad 58-9: *greyn* may be consecrated Host, or a prayer bead.

Sir Thopas

COMMENTARIES: Gr 228-31; Ham 287-9;/ Don 934-7; ManCT 628-34; Rob 736-40; Sk 5, 182-200;/ Bald 67-8, 75; Baum 79; Brew 151-2; Ches 10-2, 157; Cog 150-2; Cow 160; Ev 11, 142-4; Fr 242-4; Kit 181-3; Law 129-30; Leg 152; Lum 83-92; Mal 170-2; Pat 168; Pres 209-12; Root 199-203; Sedg 45; Sp 180-2; Shel 227; Winstanley ed. *PrT and Thop* (Cambridge U.P., 1922);/ Camden, *RES*, 35, 326-30; Donaldson, *EIE*, 51, 116-40; Ficke, *PQ*, 28, 82-5; Francis, *PMLA*, 53, 1126-41; Herben, *Spec*, 37, 475-87; Kimpel, *ELH*, 53, 77-86; Knott, *MP*, 10, 135-9; Knowlton, *JEGP*, 24, 83-93; Lawrence, *PMLA*, 35, 81-91; Linn, *MLN*, 36, 300-11; Loomis, *PQ*, 35, 371-3, and *MLN*, 36, 311-3, and *SA*, 486-559; Lumiansky, *PQ*, 47, 313-20; Magoun, *PMLA*, 27, 833-44; Manly, *MP*, 10, 141-4, and *Essays and Studies*, 28, 52-73; McCracken, *Expl*, 59, item 57; Melton, *PQ*, 56, 215-7; Moore, *JEGP*, 54, 532-45; Patch, *ESt*, 31, 351-9; Roppolo, *MLN*, 48, 365-71; Ross, *MLN*, 30, 172-4; Strong, *MLN*, 08, 73-7, 102-6.

GENRE: Burlesque romance.

ANALOGUES: Metrical romances in general are satirized, but parallels have been noted especially in *Libeaus Desconus, Guy of Warwick, Thomas of Erceldoune, Amis and Amiloun, Sir Beves of Hamptoun, Sire Degaré,* and several others.

DATE: Uncertain, but probably during *CT* period, written expressly for dramatic situation.

VERSE FORM: Prologue is in Rime Royal, linking with preceding *PrT* in same meter; Tale is mainly in 6-line stanza, riming a a b a a b, with iambic tetrameter for a-lines and trimeter for b-lines, with variations in 790-826, 881-90.

GENERAL CRITICISM: Sk 5, 183: in tale Ch uses favorite meter of "long-winded ballad-makers," with many sly echoes in phrasing. Strong notes many parallels in situations and phrasing of famous English romance *Guy of Warwick*. Manly, *MP:* no bitter satire, but "good-humored rollicking burlesque," brilliant and high-spirited, in which we can "clearly see Ch at play, having no end of fun with the romances and his readers and himself." Root 200-2: burlesque of "matchless poetic skill," with subtle humor in recurring tone of *petite-bourgeoisie,* but not exaggerated into farce, close enough to the real thing to be mistaken for it. Knowlton: Thopas a "small town booby" who has read romances, a rural squire type like Shakespeare's Sir Andrew Aguecheek or Sheridan's Bob Acres. Magoun: tale has definite plot, good deal of action, much of which is similar to *Ile d'Or* episode in romance of *Libeaus Desconus.* Cow 160: "a nonsense romance" of sheer raillery, its humor and sharp satire best appreciated after reading romances listed in 897-900. ManCT 628-9: Ch brilliantly succeeds (through device of Host's interruption) in mocking wordy longwindedness and "general futility" of the poorer romances without boring reader to death—tale is both prolix and brief; Ch's primary aim was probably not so much burlesque of romances as satire on bourgeois knights of Flanders (Londoners hated Flemings). Camden: since Thopas is burlesque of heroic knight, Ch makes him effeminate through features which denote fearfulness in physiognomy —hair and beard *lyk saffroun* (730) showing timidity, *fair and gent* (715) and *sydes smale* (836), both phrases used of women only; other effeminate traits are white complexion, red lips, dainty nose; his cowardly behavior confirms these signs. Lawrence refutes Winstanley's identification of Thopas with Philip van Artevelde (Flemish leader) and Manly's view that tale is satire on Flemings; bourgeois qualities, not limited to Flemings, are merely one way of ridiculing knight errantry in romances. Pat 168: tale's "raucous gaiety" contrasts with pathos of *PrT.* Ches 10-2, 157; supreme irony in fact that Ch, creator of whole *CT,* gives himself only unpoetic tale, "a gabble of the worst doggerel in the book"; this irony far outshines the burlesque of bad romances, is "laughter in the grand style, *pace* Matthew Arnold," and illustrates (behind the surface simplicity) Ch's true greatness. Cog 151: the first parody in English and one of most brilliant and critical, "a piece of cunning literary mockery of current popular taste." Law 129: "wild parody" of absurdities in some current romances. Mal 171: a "gem" of brilliant parody, cleverly terminated before it becomes labored. Sp 181: a piece of "most delicately discerning literary criticism" which, though brief, miraculously gives "an impression of interminableness." Pres 209 doubts that this "miniature *Don Quixote*" was meant as satire of Flemish knights. Brew 151-2: tale contains satire of tail rime romances and of Flemish knights, and sheer farce; Ch brilliantly parodies outdated habits and poetic clichés. Kimpel: narrator (not Ch) is dull witted and "unintentionally funny," thus adding to humor of tale. Francis: tale is parody not only of romances but also "of its author's own garrulity." Moore: apart from burlesque of romances and dig at Flemings, tale is also satire of ignorant, inept minstrels whose performance was even worse than worst literary romances (note mannerisms recalling public recitals in 712-4, 880-93, etc.). Bald 75: delightfully "muted burlesque." Ev 142: Ch's subtlest satire in sensitive mimicry of romance meter. Lum 83: whole tale (also *Mel*) aimed at genial ridicule of Host by exposing his lack of critical taste. Rob 736-7: fact that Ch wrote excellent romances himself is no argument against his satire of romance absurdities here; satire is both literary and social (perhaps against Flemings). Baum 79: a playful "high comedy of criticism," with satire against Flemings at best a subordinate motif. Don 934-6: brilliant burlesque of plot and of oral style of minstrel romances with "dogtrot rhythm"; knightly hero is really "drabbest sort of late 14th-century burgher," whose action (or inaction) is told in "most horrendously emphatic meter."

PROLOGUE TO SIR THOPAS

VII, 691-711

Host turns jokingly to Chaucer, notes his ample waistline, asks for merry tale. Chaucer says he will tell only rime he knows.

94	*at erst* for first time	03	*elvyssh* elf-like
01	*popet* puppet, dainty little person	10	*ye* yea

91-11 Root 199: by speaking in the stanza of *PrT* Host "pays subtle tribute to the potency of the spell" cast by it. Bald 67-8: here Ch shifts skillfully from 3rd person omniscient point of view to that of 1st person spectator and participant.

Rob 736: only headlink in Rime Royal in *CT*.

91-2 Kit 181: whole boisterous company falls silent under profound effect of *PrT*.

93-11 Knott: notion of reserved and serious Ch, taken from Host's jibes, is sheer myth; here Ch (with rest of pilgrims) is momentarily awed by *PrT;* when Host "with characteristic indelicacy, blunders out a crudely humorous reference to the obvious emotion of the poet's face," Ch quickly recovers and gives us exuberant *Thop,* quite in keeping with sociable Ch of *Gen Prol.* Kit 183: real Ch is affable man of *Gen Prol;* here, on the road, he has been effacing himself, keeping in background as listener and reporter so as not to miss any detail. ManCT 628: this picture of Ch not to be taken as truly characteristic. Lawrence disagrees with Knott—Host simply arouses Ch from temporary fit of abstraction. Lumiansky agrees with Knott on consistency of Ch here and in *Gen Prol,* but disagrees with view that Ch is overcome by *PrT;* rather whole company's mood has been cheered by Host *before* he describes Ch. Roppolo: *at erst* (694) means "not until then" (supporting Lumiansky's interpretation). Sp 180-1: a portrait of Ch which agrees with those in *House of Fame* (by eagle) and Prologue to *LGW,* as "gentle, elusive, scholarly (but not ascetic), humane personality . . . humorously aware not only of himself but of others." Kimpel: humble, stupid, but well-meaning narrator here (as in *House of Fame, Parliament of Fowls, LGW*) is a literary device. Bald 67: none of pilgrims recognizes Ch; this "deliberate artistic dualism" of Pilgrim Ch and Poet Ch "immeasurably enriches the tales." Rob 736: reticent, aloof Ch here is inconsistent with social-able Ch of *Gen Prol;* moving *PrT* may explain difference.

96-7 Lum 89: perhaps Ch stares at ground "to prevent the Host's seeing merry twinkle which has come into his eyes at the prospect of the joke he plans."

00 Sk 5, 182: line means Ch is as corpulent as Host. Rob 736 agrees, adds that this hint is confirmed by *Lenvoy a Scogan* 31.

03 Root 199-200: *elvyssh* is exact word for "peculiar elusiveness of Ch's playful-serious nature." Sedg 45: *elvyssh* suggests "ironical, quiz-zical expression" of roguish fun under quiet exterior. Lum 89-90: Ch appears *elvyssh* because he is enjoying private joke he plans on Host.

07-9 Lum 90: Ch "assumes an ironic mock humility," hoping Host will find *Thop* (burlesque of Host's favorite kind of literature) disgusting.

SIR THOPAS, THE FIRST FIT (Canto)
712-796

Sir Thopas, a brave knight, was born at Poperinghe, Flanders. He is handsome, well dressed, good at wrestling and at love. One day he rides in forest, rests, has dream that elf-queen will be his lover.

15	*gent* graceful	37	*river* waterfowl	
25	*payndemayn* fine white bread	47	*hepe* hip (of dogrose)	
		52	*launcegay* short lance	
27	*rode* complexion	61	*cetewale* ginger	
31	*raughte* reached	62	*clowe-gylofre* clove	
32	*cordewane* Cordovan leather	67	*sparhauk* sparrowhawk	
34	*syklatoun* costly cloth	69	*thrustelcok* male thrush	
35	*jane* small coin	89	*goore* robe	

12 Sk 5, 184: a typical beginning for metrical romances, requesting silence for oral recitation.

17 Sk 5, 183: a fine name for "such a gem of a knight." Ross: topaz was known in 14th century as cure for sensuality; since Flemings in London (where many were prostitutes) and in Flanders were notorious for lechery, perhaps Ch chose ironic name of Thopas to enhance satire on Flemings.

18-9 Don 935: hero's nationality emphasizes his lack of chivalric traits.

20 Lawrence: Ch chose Poperinghe as part of satire—most prosaic of towns, whereas reader expects romantic birthplace. AHM: Ch probably chose Poperinghe for its funny sound and also possibly to recall ancient obscene joke about the Poppering pear (resembling male organs) later referred to by Mercutio in *Romeo and Juliet,* II, i, 35-8; *in the place* may mean "in the market place or town square," rather than "manor house" (Sk) or "right there" (Rob), thus satirically reinforcing Thopas's bourgeois background.

24-35 ManCT 630: bourgeois details in description—leather shoes, Bruges hose, robe costing *many a jane* (halfpenny), comparisons of face with bread, complexion with cloth dye, beard with food coloring —all "suggest the tradesman" and fit theory of satire on Flemish bourgeois knights.

24-5 McCracken: pun on *doghty* (doughty or valiant and "dough-like"), paralleling *doghty swayn* and *payndemayn* (fine bread).

27-9 Ev 142: Ch uses emphatic tail-lines skillfully for anticlimaxes here and in 742-4. Cog 152 notes unequaled imbecility of these "inspired" lines.

36-47 Cog 151: passage illustrates "pungent silliness" of *Thop* in contrast to "dreary silliness" of similar lines in popular romances.

45 Don 935: hero's chastity, which Ch exaggerates into effeminacy, is "unusual if not absolutely impossible in a knight of popular romance."

59-71 Pres 210: utter nonsense, anticipating nonsense rimes of Edward Lear.

72-96 Patch (also Rob 738): humor in fact that Thopas has *never seen* his lady love, a reversal of usual order.

72 Donaldson: *love-longynge* was degraded term (implying fleshly desire), inappropriate to courtly idealism, used by Ch only here and in description of Absolon (*MillT* 3349).

84-96 Ev 11: Ch here mocks common failure in romances to prepare properly for entrance of supernatural beings.

88-9 Donaldson: *goore* was sexual term in vernacular literature, and this is surely intended here as well as surface meaning of "cloak."

797-890

He seeks elf-queen in fairyland, meets threatening giant, Sir Olifaunt, challenges him to duel. Giant drives Thopas away with stones from slingshot; Thopas goes home, puts on armor for fight with giant.

01	*pryve woon* secret dwelling-place	52	*mazelyn* maplewood bowl
10	*child* young warrior	55	*comyn* cummin
23	*mawe* belly	56	*trye* choice
43	*jolitee* beauty	57	*leere* flesh
		58	*lake* linen

60	*aketoun* short tunic	75	*jambeux* leg-armor.
63	*hawberk* breast and back-plate		*quyrboilly* boiled leather
		78	*rewel boon* whale ivory
71	*charbocle* carbuncle (stone)	90	*fonde* try

10-3 Ev 142-3 notes Ch's mimicry in "bathetic slowing down of pace which comes with the single-stressed line."

18-9 Don 935: Thopas "a most reluctant hero," refusing to fight unarmed, but later putting on "an extraordinary amount of defensive armor"—very unknightly.

27-32 Loomis, *MLN:* brilliant burlesque of Biblical story of David and Goliath, with Goliath using slingshot.

33-4 Pres 211: "exquisite imperatives" in style of minstrel romances.

57-87 Manly, *Essays and Studies,* argues that whole passage is absurd, full of errors. Linn refutes this view, showing that wearing of *aketoun,* breeches and shirt, hauberk, and habergeoun, are paralleled in many serious romances; but real "crowning absurdity" is omission of indispensable sword and spurs which were also symbols of knighthood. Herben also disagrees with Manly; facts of 14th-century armor show passage is "fairly realistic description of the successive stages of arming"—no absurdity except possibly in "overelaboration of detail." Rob 739: passage is "pretentious and absurd"—also tedious.

64 Ficke: *Jewes werk* refers to fact that Jews in Middle Ages were famed as metal workers and armorers. Loomis, *PQ: Jewes werk* was probably suggested by passage on armor from Jerusalem in stanzaic version of *Guy of Warwick.*

71 Melton: *charbocle* is not decoration on shield, but means sword with jewelled pommel decorated with carbuncle; this is Thopas's missing sword on which he swears on *ale and bread.*

THE SECOND FIT

891-918

Sir Thopas, surpassing heroes of romances, sets forth on journey to meet giant; sleeps in the open.

93	*spelle* tale	08	*shonde* shame
95	*love-drury* passionate love	09	*auntrous* adventurous
04	*glood* glided	12	*wonger* pillow

13 *baiteth* feeds. *dextrer* war-   17 *under wede* in armor
    horse

HOST STOPS CHAUCER'S TALE OF SIR THOPAS
   919-966
(Host breaks in, swears he is fed up with this worthless rime, asks for
something else perhaps in prose. Chaucer agrees to tell short moral
tale in prose with many proverbs. He asks to be allowed to finish this
one.)

23 *drasty* filthy   39 *daungerous* hard to please
24 *biteche* consign to   57 *tretys* treatise
33 *in geeste* in alliterative verse 64 *murye* pleasant
35 *doctryne* instruction

19-66 Knowlton: Host fails to see wit or burlesque in *Thop,* is then
trapped into *Mel;* Lawyer would have seen and appreciated this joke
—*Thop* is perhaps an answer to his criticism of Ch's meter (*MLT*
46-50). ManCT 634: Host is disgusted with lack of action in tale,
wants rapid series of adventures. Shel 227: Host's outspoken words
show his "soundness as a literary critic." Law 129-30: Host "is about
as able to appreciate such delicate satire as a bull is to admire a
flower." Sp 181: complex comedy in fact that *Thop* (offered as best
Ch can do), "taken at its face value by the company, is not tolerated."
Mal 171: by device of "stinting" Ch avoids laboring his clever parody
and running it into the ground, puts blame on Host for its fragmentary state. Lum 91: Host sees in *Thop* only ignorance of good
poetic practice.

33 Moore interprets *geeste* as prose narrative rather than as alliterative verse (Rob).

34-5 Lum 92-3: in asking for something in prose of *murthe* or
doctryne Host plays into Ch's hands; burden of responsibility for
Mel is thus shifted to Host.

36-66 Root 203: Ch shows "angelic sweetness of temper" at interruption, but takes ample revenge by telling *Mel.*

37, 57, 63 Lum 94-5: phrases *litel thyng, litel tretys,* etc., are consciously ironic.

The Tale of Melibee

COMMENTARIES: Gr 231-2; Ham 289-90;/ Don 937; ManCT 634; Rob 740-5; Sk 5, 201-24;/ Baum 79, 129, 153; Bron 65, 115-6; Cow 162; Fr 244-7; Ger 99; Kit 170; Law 87, 130-3, 151; Leg 152; Lum 194; Mus 93, 207; Pat 189, 223, 240; Pres 212; TatDC 188-97; Tho 91;/ Baum, *JEGP*, 46, 38-42; Bühler, *Spec*, 49, 410-2; Hotson, *SP*, 21, 429-52; Ker, in *Eng. Prose Selections*, ed. Craik (London, 1893), 40-3; Landrum, *PMLA*, 24, 75-100; Langhans, *Anglia*, 29, 235-68; Lawrence, *Brown*, 100-10; Moore, *JEGP*, 54, 532-45; Severs, *PMLA*, 35, 92-9, and *SA*, 560-614; Stillwell, *Spec*, 44, 433-44; Tupper, *JEGP*, 34, 352-72.

GENRE: Moral allegory in prose.

SOURCE: French *Livre de Melibée et de Dame Prudence* by Renaud de Louens (sometime after 1336) which is condensed paraphrase of Latin *Liber Consolationis et Consilii* (1246) by Albertanus of Brescia. A text of French version survives in *Le Ménagier de Paris*, compiled in 1392-4, but Ch probably used a somewhat different text. Tale is a close translation from the French.

DATE: Uncertain, but probably late 1380's.

GENERAL CRITICISM: Ker: tale an orgy of mediocrity, example of worst medieval literary vices, "pathos, forced allegory, spiritless and interminable moralizing"; "monstrous virtue" of Prud akin to patience of Griselda, to point of honor in *FranklT;* yet Ch "had always, in some corner of his being, the average mind of the fourteenth century," and tale expresses representative "ideas and tastes of millions of good souls." TatDC 197: *Mel*, with formal arguments, appeals to precedent and authority, well suited to Lawyer. Kit 170: tale mainly taken up with "pitilessly long-winded arguments" of Prud. Hotson: tale, with "its masterly brief for the case against war," was probably a political tract to dissuade Ch's patron John of Gaunt from entering private war in Spain by invading Castile in 1386 to avenge private wrong; after several of Gaunt's enemies in parliament voted for this war to get Gaunt out of way, he went to Spain and Ch's own fortunes suffered as a result; this interpretation would date tale in winter of 1385-6. Cow 162: "a feeble tract," colored by Quaker-like hatred of war. Tupper: tale originally meant for Lawyer. Severs, *PMLA:* only printed text of French version in *Le Ménagier de Paris* is not as close to Ch's text as are several unpublished MSS (especially MS fr. 1165) in Bibliothèque Nationale in Paris which give readings Ch used and are not in *Ménagier;* Ch probably used French *MS* source for *all* details, did not have to rely on Latin at all; arguments based on Ch's supposed changes (such as those of Hotson and Landrum) collapse, since all these readings appear in French MS sources. Pat 189, 223: view of wife's influence is seriously radical, though Ch here surrounds edifying moral tale with humorous setting. Lawrence: though tale is "thin stuff" as narrative, it has qualities highly esteemed in Middle Ages, with theme not so much patience in adversity as peace and civil justice in preference to war, a very timely topic both in Albertano's strife-torn North Italy and Richard II's England, though Ch probably valued it for its own sake and for relevance to marriage discussion (roles of husband and wife reversed in *NPT,* leading to theme of female sovereignty in *WBT*); Hotson's theory certainly wrong, since tale is translation of popular work of previous century with no direct reference to invasion of Castile; tale not to be viewed as revenge on Host for interrupting *Thop*—"certainly the poet was not punishing his readers for the sins of the Host." Stillwell: Ch aimed tract not at Gaunt, but at political squabbles over 100 Years' War. favoring peace policy of Richard II, warning against Richard's instability (*ire* and *hastifnesse*), advising him on choice of councilors (a sore point), praising prudent advice of women (such as Queen Anne); it contains "some of the healthiest platitudes in our literature," especially timely in 1386-8. Fr. 245: tale, if intended as joke, was rather heavy one. Tho 91: tale held attention of 14th century, since outspoken pilgrims heard it through. Law 87, 131-3: tale held values for Ch's age difficult to appreciate today; it is important because, though heavy and didactic, it provided germ of Marriage Discussion, liveliest debate in *CT*. Pres 212: tale can be taken as "huge joke," but only by modern reader who skips it. Moore: though Ch was probably aware of artistic deficiencies, he meant tale to show vast gap between serious literature and "minstrel drivel" (*Thop*). Lum 94: most routine literary fare, contrasting with highly original *Thop;* tale, "whatever else it is, certainly is the second half of the joke used by the Pilgrim Ch to make evident the Host's lack of literary taste." Mus 93, 207: Middle Ages found philosophy more pleasing in dialogue than in direct exposition; was wife ever "so learned or so pedantic" as Prud? Baum 153: serious discussion of ethical problems, useful collection of common views of pious, well educated people, certainly not meant to be funny. Don 937: tale not meant as elaborate hoax in revenge for interruption of *Thop;* but, whereas its advice is serious, its lack of imagination suits demonstrated character of pilgrim Ch (as distinguished from poet Ch). Bron 65, 115-6: a "weighty preachment," meant seriously; Ch gave it to himself because he greatly admired it.

THE TALE OF MELIBEE

VII, 967-1003

Three old enemies (the world, the flesh, and the devil in moral allegory) enter through the windows of Melibee's house (body) and injure his daughter Sophie (wisdom) through the 5 senses. Melibee is in despair. His wife Prudence comes to rescue, urges him to stop grieving and call a council of friends.

74	*as ferforth as* as far as	93	*forgoon* lost. *boote* remedy
75	*nat forthy* nevertheless	97	*flees* fleece
82	*warisshe* recover	02	*lynage* relatives
88	*attempree* moderate.		
	deffended forbidden		

03 Bühler: Biblical proverb of which Ch must have been especially fond, since he used it also in *MillT* 3530 and *MerchT* 1485-6.

1004-1050

In council, surgeons and physicians say they will work to heal daughter (diseases often cured by contraries); neighbors urge immediate war against foes; lawyer favors self-defense and further deliberation, but the young call for war; old man advises caution, is drowned out by others. Mel decides on war.

05	*semblaunt* appearance	20	*wreken* avenge
12	*withholde* retained in service	26	*propre* own
15	*ententif bisynesse* devoted care	27	*garnisoun* garrison
		28	*demen* judge
19	*empeireden* impaired, injured. *agreggeden* aggravated	32	*algates* nevertheless
		34	*weaxen* increases

04-50 Lawrence: "best scene in the story, vividly set forth, and not overloaded with quotations until Dame Prud begins to speak"; occasional eloquence and conviction "break through the crabbed prose."

1051-1113

Prudence urges caution, offers advice. Mel objects that council has already decided; also, women's advice is traditionally untrustworthy. Prud refutes both arguments with copious examples. Mel agrees to hear and follow her advice.

51	*shoop hym* planned, prepared	66	*bihight* promised. *weyve* neglect
52	*for alle gerdons* for the good of all	68	*thar* need. *but* unless
56	*wyse* wise men	72	*noght ne kan* does not know
62	*Car il est escript,* etc. For it is written, the gossip of women can conceal nothing except what they don't know.	89	*hele* conceal
		03	*forme fader* first father
		04	*to been a man alloone* for a man to be alone
63	*Apres, le philosophre dit,* etc. Afterwards, the philosopher says, in bad advice women surpass men: and for these reasons I must not take your advice at all.		

62-3 Sk 5, 206: Ch apparently skipped these lines in translation, but they are needed for sense here and are supplied from French text. For Ch's rendition of ideas see 1084-5, 1090.

1114-1260

Prud opens her argument against war and vengeance by discussing general principles for choosing councilors. "First ask God's help and drive anger, greed, and impulsiveness from your heart. Keep your own opinion secret and ask advice of truest and wisest friends. Avoid fools, flatterers, reconciled enemies, drunkards. Consider possible results and fear not to change course." Mel asks about councilors in present case. "You called too large and mixed a group; you erred in revealing your own view at outset and in deciding too quickly."

18	*dresse* direct		15	*distreyneth* grasps
53	*seeld* seldom		22	*sadly* steadily
65	*delivernesse* agility		23	*repreve* shame
77	*egre* sharp		33	*covenably* fittingly
93	*dronkelewe* addicted to drink		43	*chargeant* burdensome
			48	*anientissed* annihilated
03	*alderfirst* first of all		51	*talent* wish

1261-1348

Prud comments on Mel's wise councilors: "Physicians and surgeons gave good advice, should be rewarded. Evil is cured by goodness, not by more evil. Lawyers were right in urging you to protect yourself against further attack; best protection is in Christ and in love of your subjects. Old councilors were wise in advising more deliberation."

64	*mannyssh* human		15	*lete* omit, give up
72	*gerdoned* rewarded		19	*contrewayte embusshementz* watch against ambushes
77	*warisshed* cured			
94	*amonesteth* recommends			
97	*warnestoore* fortify, provision			

1349-1426

Prud discredits advice of neighbors, reconciled enemies, flatterers, and young men. Mel is virtually alone, whereas his enemies are 3 and have many close relatives. War against them may be long and costly. Prud explains allegorical meaning of attack against Mel ("a man who drinks honey" of worldly delights): the deadly sins have wounded his soul through 5 senses.

71 *taken but litel reward* have little reason

75 *syb* akin, related

76 *ny* closely, nearly

01 *It letted nat in as muche as in hem was.* They delayed no longer than they could help.

18 *misericorde* mercy

24 *wittes* senses

1427-1539

Mel argues that crime is discouraged by fear of vengeance. Prud replies: "Leave vengeance to legal authorities or to God. Moreover, your foes are too strong for you. You should suffer this woe in patience as punishment for your own weaknesses, following example of Christ and saints. Private revenge is sin."

33-4 *Et a ce respont dame Prudence,* etc. And to this replies dame Prudence, "Certainly," says she, "I grant you that from vengeance comes much of bad and of good; but vengeance does not belong to each individual but only to the judges and to those who have jurisdiction over wrongdoers."

35 *singular* individual

50 *brotil* insecure

62 *sompne* summon

66 *mowe* be able to

77 *putte* suppose for sake of argument

81 *woodnesse* madness

91 *Yet sette I caas* Yet if I put (suppose) the case that

02 *sewe* follow, pursue (cp. Fr: suivre)

33-4 Sk 5, 216-7: here again Ch inadvertently skipped a passage, supplied from French text.

1540-1675

When Mel states that wealth gives him power for vengeance, Prud lectures on wise use of money: "Wealth is a blessing if honestly acquired and wisely spent. Avoid both miserliness and extravagance; cherish God, good conscience and reputation. Do not trust to money in war; only God can give victory." Mel is now convinced that war is unwise, asks for positive advice.

41	*coupable* guilty. *entre-metteth* interferes	00	*chyncherie* miserliness
43	*outherwhile* sometimes	18	*swelweth* swallows
51	*avanten hym* boast	21	*debonairetee* graciousness
56	*net-herdes* cowherd's	44	*loos* praise, fame (cp. Latin: laus)
61	*of lynage* by birth	64	*ne plus que,* etc. no more than he is certain that he is worthy of God's love
65	*overthrowynge* rebellion		
70	*algates* nevertheless		
76	*sokyngly* gradually	70	*goodly* honorably
93	*enchesoun* reason		

1676-1768

Prud urges Mel to make his peace with God and with enemies. Mel at first balks, then agrees to let Prud negotiate privately with foes. She meets them, advises them to repent. They readily agree to do so and to put themselves in Mel's power, begging Prud to influence him to be merciful. Prud promises.

82	*bryge* strife	96	*mystyde* be unlucky
84	*meke me* humble myself	11	*konne* know
85	*nat my worshipe* beneath my dignity	43	*mowen* are able

1769-1831

Prud reports result of meeting to Mel who calls another council. Council agrees to peace proposal and Mel summons enemies. They arrive, admit guilt, ask forgiveness, agree to accept Mel's judgment on punishment. Mel appoints day for passing judgment.

96	*messages* messengers	10	*skile* cause
07	*borwes* pledges		

1832-1888

Mel tells Prud he intends to punish foes by confiscation of property and exile for life. Prud argues for clemency, urging that Mel does not need foes' wealth and should not stain reputation by cruelty. Mel is convinced; on appointed day he forgives enemies completely, as he hopes to be forgiven by God.

32	*freyned* inquired	61	*appeseth him* is appeased
45	*renovelle* renew	70	*skiles* arguments

The Monk's Tale

COMMENTARIES: Gr 232-5; Ham 291-2;/ Don 937-40; ManCT 635-6; Rob 745-50; Sk 5, 224-47;/ Baum 20,81-3; Brew 154; Bron 72-6, 97-100; Cog 158; Farnham, *Med. Heritage of Elizabethan Tragedy* (Univ. of Cal., 1936), 129-36; Fr 247-57; Kit 174; Low 166; Lum 97-104; Mal 169-73, 219-22; Man 261-2; Pres 215-20; Root 203-7; Sp 182-4;/ Aiken, *Spec,* 42, 56-68; Babcock, *PMLA,* 31, 205-13; Bloomfield, *JEGP,* 52, 301-13; Braddy, *PMLA,* 35, 69-80, and *MLN,* 47, 173-5; Johnson, *PMLA,* 51, 827-43; Jones, *MLN,* 37, 570-2; Kenyon, *JEGP,* 16, 282-8; Malone, *ES,* 50, 209-15; Norris, *MLN,* 33, 146-8; Patch, *MLR,* 27, 377-85; Rickert, *MP,* 27, 79-82; Robertson, *ELH,* 52, 1-37; Root, *SA,* 615-44; Savage, *Spec,* 49, 357-75; Seaton, *MLR,* 46, 196-202; Schlauch, *Spec,* 45, 133-56; Silverstein, *MLN,* 32, 148-50; Socola, *JEGP,* 50, 159-71; Spencer, *Spec,* 34, 295-301; Young, *SP,* 43, 494-501.

GENRE: Series of "tragedies."

SOURCES: *RR* for general plan and for Nero and Croesus; Boccaccio's *De Casibus Virorum Illustrium* for general plan and for details in several of the tragedies; Boccaccio's *De Mulieribus Claris* for Zenobia; Bible for Sampson, Nebuchadnezzar, Belshazzar, Holofernes, and Antiochus; Dante's *Inferno* for Ugolino; possibly Machaut's *La Prise d'Alexandrie* for Peter of Cyprus; other tragedies seem to derive from mixed literary sources or from oral accounts (for Modern Instances); scattered passages show probable influence of Boethius, Vincent of Beauvais, Ovid, etc.

DATE: About 1374 for ancient tragedies, with Modern Instances probably added later (that on Bernabo cannot have been earlier than 1386 since he died Dec. 19, 1385).

VERSE FORM: Stanza of 8 lines of iambic pentameter, rimed a b a b b c b c (same as Spenserian stanza without final Alexandrine).

GENERAL CRITICISM: Kenyon: of 17 tragedies, 5 (Adam, Samson, Hercules, Zenobia, Holofernes) show ascendancy of women over men, leading into direct treatment of theme in *NPT*. Root 206-7: Ch probably planned 100 tragedies under influence of Boccaccio but gave up after 12 or 13, later using these in *CT* as dramatically fitting dignity of Monk; but reactions of Knight and Host show Ch realized their "unspeakable monotony." Patch: tragedies show sentimentalism of Monk who "knows how to squeeze the juice even out of pathos and to feel the respectable luxury of piety." Man 261-2: Ch substitutes "gloomy, uninteresting person" for gay, brilliant Monk of *Gen Prol*. Babcock: of 3 traditions of medieval tragedies—Roman (Ovid, Boethius, Boccaccio), clerical (Innocent III's *De Contemptu Mundi,* etc.), and non-clerical (*RR,* etc.)—Ch was working in non-clerical tradition derived from Roman goddess Fortuna through *RR;* only 5 of 17 tragedies follow Boccaccio at all. Braddy, *PMLA:* whole tale can be dated by Modern Instances since these were not added later (*NPT* 2782 echoes last line of Croesus, *MkT* 2766), probably about 1374-5 after first Italian trip (influence of Dante in Ugolino). Farnham 129-36: "obvious imitation" of Boccaccio, unsuited to Ch, a "most sterile confinement" of his spirit, though partly attributable to dramatic characterization in *CT;* Monk accepts Boccaccio's theory of tragedy as "manifestation of man's powerlessness in an irrational world" ruled by whimsical Fortune. Jones: whole tale is in form of medieval sermon, with individual tragedies as exempla. Aiken: more important as source than Boccaccio is Vincent of Beauvais' *Speculum Historiale,* probably source for details in 8 of tragedies, especially in Sampson, Nebuchadnezzar, Nero, Caesar. Fr 248: Ch clearly realized defects of tale. Savage: tale well fits pompous, self-satisfied Monk of *Gen Prol,* with Modern Instances reflecting view of a man who is all for modernity. Socola: tale shows original development by Ch of concept of Fortune from impersonal abstraction (Hercules, Nebuchadnezzar, Belshazzar, Zenobia, and 4 Modern Instances) to strong personality in last 6 tragedies; this development supports placing of Modern Instances between Zenobia and Nero, unifies tale, and suggests Ch took some pains with it. Sp 182: unexpectedness of such a tale from Monk (now in "purely professional role") is surely part of comedy of *CT.* Johnson: for Biblical tragedies Ch relied little on Boccaccio, probably used Bible directly, and Vincent of Beauvais; but prime source, with almost all of Biblical material (and 2 unique parallels), was French *Bible Historiale* (1291-4) by Guyart Desmoulins. Pres 216-7: except for Ugolino, tale is "minor penance" for modern readers; Monk does his best with edifying materials which might have convinced pilgrims had he himself been convinced. Robertson: tale shows medieval definition of tragedy—man of high degree falls because he seeks false worldly satisfactions, turns from God, loses free will, becomes slave to Fortune who turns against him. Brew 154: apart from Ugolino, tragedies are "too bare to be moving." Don 938-9: tale shows Fortune as utterly whimsical and malignant, making no distinction between virtue and vice ("God disappears entirely"); thus tale is "infected with a real pessimism, a despairing disgust with life," which is distortion of genuine monastic ideal of ordered universe. Bron 72-6: giving tragedies to Monk is one of Ch's "most inspired coups," adding new dimension to Monk's character and ironic drama to *CT* as Monk tries to counteract impression given in *ShipT* and in Host's barbed remarks about monks by digging up sober and heavy tale, rich in impressive allusions to authority; seen in dramatic context, tale is "lifted to a level of complex vision that can hardly be matched in its kind until the arrival of Sterne."

THE PROLOGUE OF THE MONK'S TALE
VII, 1889-1990

Host wishes tale of Melibee's patient wife could have been heard by his wife (Goodelief). She is very jealous, violent, and strong. Host calls on Monk for next tale, notes Monk's fine physique and jokingly deplores his celibacy. Best manly specimens are all in holy orders, cannot beget children. Monk offers to start by telling 100 tragedies.

92	*corpus Madrian* body of Madrian (unidentified saint?)	42	*wel farynge* goodlooking.
			for the nones for that position (*governour*)
04	*rampeth* flies	45	*tredefowel* treader of fowls (a rooster)
05	*wrek* avenge		
11	*overlad* put upon	47	*engendrure* procreation
14	*me dighte* take myself	50	*and* if
34	*penant* penitant	55	*borel men* laymen
36	*celerer* cellarer	62	*lussheburghes* spurious coins

89-1990 Bron 76: after *Mel* Host is "boisterous as a boy just released from the school-room," turns to Monk fully expecting something cheerful, "only to be dashed with another load of depressing doctrine" —one of most delectably ironic moments in *CT*.

89-96 Root 203-4: Host has "true middle-class Englishman's love for moralizing, if not for morality." Lum 95: Ch has maneuvered Host into "finding moral application to his own marital situation in a story preaching mastery for the wife, a state which the Host would hardly favor."

92 ManCT 635: *corpus Madrian* seems to be error, part of characterization of Host. Norris: oath may not refer to obscure saint but to Virgin Mary, Mother of God ("Madre" in Italian), which Host may have picked up from Italians in London and is here flaunting (inaccurately). Lum 87: error suggests Host's pretentiousness.

94 Rickert: *Godelef* was fairly common name in Southwark and district, here ironically related to phrase meaning "dear to God" or to phrase of affection used by Wife of Bath in *WBT* 431. Seaton: Ch named Host's wife ironically after St. Godeleva, popular virginmartyr of Flanders, who was known as miracle of wifely patience.

95-23 Root 204: Host's wife is "a sort of *bourgeois* Lady Macbeth." Low 166: Host is lordly with pilgrims, but cowed at home; "never did browbeaten husband unpack his heart with more soul-satisfying words." Malone: henpecked husband and muscular, domineering wife are ancient types of broad comedy or farce; Goodelief is "a literary wife," whose every feature is conventional, "and she is all the funnier for that."

26-65 Root 204: Monk keeps dignity with unruffled patience despite Host's jibes. Baum 81: Host "offensively bids for another bawdy tale" (like *ShipT*) in words recalling Monk in *Gen Prol*. Bron 74: Monk cannot allow Host's insults to his vocation and dignity go unanswered; he patiently waits for revenge.

29 Kit 174: a pointed attempt to connect Monk with wayward monk of *ShipT*.

44-8 Lum 101: rude tone is reflected in use of familiar pronouns— *thou, thee, thy.*

54-64 Lum 101: Host deliberately tries to aggravate Monk in hopes of an entertaining explosion of wrath.

61 Baum 82:   reference to Venus recalls *fair prelaat* of *Gen Prol* who *loved venerie.*

63-4 Lum 101:   Host's apology is obviously no apology at all.

65 Bron 74:   Monk's admirable self-control here shows "genuine character."

65-90 ManCT 635-6:   here Monk seems "sedate and bookish," utterly different from Monk in *Gen Prol* (has Ch forgotten?) Lum 102: Monk takes dignified revenge against Host's jokes by plunging into dreary tragedies.

65-8 Mal 219:   Monk's readiness to give *a tale, or two, or three* suggests loquaciousness, foreshadows length of tale.

70 Sk 5, 226:   reference is certainly to Edward the Confessor.

71-2 Farnham 129:   *hundred* may be used without specific meaning, or perhaps Ch had once planned "a sort of *Decameron*" of 100 tragedies.

73-82 Mal 221:   "admirable medieval definition" reflects Monk's erudition.

THE MONK'S TALE

1991-1998
I shall lament those who fell from high estate to misery.

92   *harm* suffering

91-8 Mal 221:   erudition shown here and in whole tale does not fit portrait in *Gen Prol.*

LUCIFER

1999-2006
Lucifer, though an angel, sinned and fell into hell.

01   *dere* hurt   05   *twynne* escape

99-06 Farnham 132:   Monk's accounts of Lucifer and Adam surprisingly brief in view of their significance in Christian belief; his "pedantic concern" (99-00) over fact that Lucifer was not human is unnecessary since fall of Lucifer is essential prelude to human tragedies.

Robertson: not a true tragedy, but necessary since Satan's influence is what persuades man to abandon reason, subject himself to Fortune.

ADAM

2007-2014

Adam, for disobedience, was driven out of earthly paradise.

07 *feeld of Damyssene* (future   10 *welte* ruled
     site of Damascus)

07-14 Robertson: Adam first man to abandon reason, becoming "first fool of Fortune"; all rest of tragic "heroes" follow in his steps.

SAMPSON

2015-2094

Sampson, consecrated to God, ended in suicide, betrayed by wife. He slew thousands of enemies, burned crops, ruled Israel for 20 years. Then he told secret of strength to Delilah, was blinded and imprisoned, later pulled down temple killing Philistines and himself.

15	*annunciat* foretold		49	*plyght* torn
25	*torente* tore to pieces		55	*ciser* strong drink
35	*cornes* crops		66	*barm* bosom
36	*olyveres* olivetrees		74	*queerne* hand-mill
44	*wang* molar		79	*caytyf* captive
46	*Judicum* Judges (Book of)		83	*foul affray* terrible assault
48	*maugree* despite			

15-94 Sk 5, 228-9: based mainly on Bible rather than Boccaccio.

HERCULES

2095-2142

Mighty Hercules, famed for killing lion and for many other great feats of strength, was finally slain by poisoned shirt sent by his sweetheart Dianira.

01	*rafte of* stole from	31	*blaked* blackened
04	*frete* devour	36	*any throwe* for any time
15	*reawme* realm	37	*of prees* turbulent
16	*lette* oppose	40	*glose* deceive

03 Sk 5, 232: Ch here confuses story of king Busirus of Egypt (who sacrificed foreigners till Hercules slew him) with that of Diomedes of Thrace (who fed mares with human flesh till Hercules slew him and gave body to mares).

36-9 Farnham 134: passage is closest Monk ever comes to philosophic effort to fix human responsibility for tragedy.

NEBUCHADNEZZAR

2143-2182

King Nebuchadnezzar of Babylon twice conquered Jerusalem, enslaved Israelites including Daniel. Yet this great king lost power, was reduced by God to level of beasts.

48	*vessel* plate (Fr. vaiselle)	66	*tweye* (error for "three," i.e.,
52	*leet do gelde* had castrated		Shadrach, Meshech, Abed-
56	*expowned* explained		nego)
58	*fyn* result. *sowned* signified	78	*wit* sanity
62	*loute* bow down		

BELSHAZZAR

2183-2246

His son Belshazzar, proud and idolatrous, saw handwriting on wall which Daniel explained: God had humbled his father and would likewise destroy him. That night Belshazzar was slain.

84	*regne* kingdom	22	*figure* human form
04	*siked* sighed	33	*weyest noght* have no
13	*wreche* vengeance		weight

85 Socola: Ch probably aimed at father-son tragedy, with father redeemed after fall, but son failing to profit by example; this double tragedy summed up in 2239-46.

ZENOBIA

2247-2374

Zenobia, Queen of Palmyra, was great hunter in youth, married Prince Odenake, had two sons. She and husband conquered many kingdoms subject to Rome. She ruled strongly after Odenake's death until Emperor Aurelian defeated and captured her, displayed her in Rome.

54	*his* (error for "hir")	28	*propre* own
62	*weelde* control	32	*werreye* make war
67	*wight* strong	60	*chaar* chariot
96	*lettrure* learning	70	*starke stoures* stern battles
05	*perree* jewels	72	*vitremyte* woman's cap
21	*proces fil in dede* things turned out	74	*hire cost for to quyte* to earn her keep

47-74 Robertson: a sympathetic tragedy, with Zenobia showing some virtue and wisdom; but excessive devotion to gifts of Fortune results in fall, loss of potential for good.

72 Young: *vitremyte* probably means not merely fragile glass headdress (Sk's gloss), but a "hood of glass" signifying that Fortune has deluded Zenobia (to "make a hood of glass" for someone, or to "glaze his hood," means to deceive him in folk idiom).

KING PEDRO OF SPAIN

2375-2390

King Pedro, after glorious reign, was betrayed and slain by own brother.

84	*lymrod* lime-twig. *gleede* red coal	89	*meede* bribes
86	*wikked nest* = pun on name of Sir Oliver de Mauny (OF *mau ni,* bad nest)	90	*brike* trap

75-90 Braddy, *PMLA:* Ch probably got story of murder from his friend Sir Guichard d'Angle who fought in Spanish campaign and had reason to be embittered against Du Guesclin, Mauny, and Don

Enrico (Pedro's killers). Savage: probably dates 1371-4, shortly after murder (1369) and marriage of Pedro's daughter Constance to John of Gaunt (1371); as pensioner of Gaunt, Ch sympathized with Pedro, probably got story orally from Don Fernando de Castro, follower of Pedro, present at murder, later sheltered by Gaunt in England in 1375.

KING PETER OF CYPRUS

2391-2398

King Peter captured Alexandria, but was slain by own nobles.

92   *maistrie* skill
96   *by the morwe* early in morn-
      ing

91-8 Braddy, *MLN:* for some reason Ch deliberately distorted well known facts (Peter not killed in bed), and adopted fictitious version from Machaut's *La Prise d'Alexandrie.*

BERNABO VISCONTI, DUKE OF LOMBARDY

2399-2406

Bernabo was slain by own nephew.

02   *cloumbe* climbed

99-05 Sk 5, 240-1:   Ch knew Bernabo Visconti personally, having been sent to negotiate with him in 1378. Farnham 131-2: a remarkable addition to tragedies, "made out of the day's news."

UGOLINO, EARL OF PISA

2407-2462

Through revolt, treacherously started by Ruggieri, Bishop of Pisa, Ugolino was imprisoned in tower with 3 children and slowly starved to death. Dante tells story in full.

33	*potage* soup		46	*wyte* blame
37	*wombe* belly		57	*carf* cut
38	*levere* more desirable		61	*devyse* describe

07-62 Root 207: tale, full of pathos and tragic power, successfully reproduces Dante's "matchless art," is "shining exception" to dullness of tragedies. ManCT 636: "most interesting" of *MkT*, probably latest written. Spencer: Ch shifted Dante's focus from Ugolino to children, from tragic horror and moral force of Dante to pathos through realistic detail (children's speeches, etc.) with no moral significance— simply another example of Fortune's reversals. Farnham 135-6: most lyrical, moving, and (in a sense) best of tragedies, but sentimental rather than tragic (Dante); Monk leaves Ugolino innocent to fit thesis that world is "realm of causeless misfortune." Pres 217-20: here Ch closely approximates *terza rima* of Dante, his stanza resembling 7 lines of *terza rima* with extra rime in middle; rest of *MkT* is "poetic exercise." Baum 20: Ch alters story from Dante "almost beyond recognition"—artistic failure. Don 940: Dante's Ugolino has "all the pity and terror of a Greek tragedy," while Ch's version has only pity, is too sentimental; "nothing could better demonstrate the besetting vices of medieval tragedy" than Ch's version.

12-4 Sp 183: small, helpless children, metaphor of birds, blame on Fortune—all added by Ch.

23-54 Pres 219-20: Ch's sublime compassion for suffering childhood; lines reflect Monk's "moment of genuine religious emotion."

31-42 Sp 183: Ch's humanity shown in child's acceptance of death, "a simple bareness of statement that leaves the fact salient."

EMPEROR NERO

2463-2550

Nero, proud, luxurious, and vicious, burned Rome, killed senators, brother, mother, and wise teacher Seneca. But his fortune changed, people rose against him, and he killed himself in garden.

67	*septemtrioun* north		11	*hadde of acustumance* was accustomed
69	*brouded* embroidered			
79	*delicasie* amusement		17	*tormentise* torture
86	*tolde* cared		25	*trice* drag
90	*domesman* judge		29	*dight* hurried
94	*wade* go		46	*girden of* strike off
02	*uncowple* unloose itself			

63-50 Robertson: Ch wastes little pity on Nero; he fully deserves what he gets (in contrast to some others).

65 Fr 255: reference to Suetonius is misleading, since Ch relied almost wholly on *RR* and Boethius.

78 Socola: here concept of Fortune as personal, individualized being begins.

19-50 Socola: view of Fortune as former friend, now turned laughing foe, fits conventional medieval personification of Fortune as proud, vindictive, malignant goddess.

HOLOFERNES

2551-2574

Mighty Holofernes, who forced people to deny their faith, was slain in sleep by Judith.

57 *likerously* wantonly
60 *for lesynge* for fear of losing

61 *reneyen his lawe* renounce his faith
69 *berne* barn

KING ANTIOCHUS

2575-2630

Proud Antiochus hated Jews, led army against them. God struck him with invisible wound, causing putrefaction and death.

92 *of* by
94 *greithen* prepare. *chaar* chariot
98 *let* thwarted

01 *boot* bit (byten)
11 *totar* tore to pieces
24 *wlatsom* loathsome

ALEXANDER

2631-2670

Greatest of all conquerors, Alexander ruled most of world for 12 years. His huge ambition ended in death by poison.

42 *fredom* nobility
45 *entente* purpose
47 *pris* praise

61 *sys* six (high throw in dice).
    aas ace (one)

2671-2726

Caesar rose from low estate to supreme power, defeating Pompey. After triumph he was stabbed to death by Cassius in Roman capitol.

94	*fyn* end	12	*estaatly honestee* dignified decency
97	*Brutus Cassius* (error for Brutus and Cassius)	25	*have hire in awayt* be watchful of her
02	*boydekeyns* daggers		

97 Silverstein: Ch's error in viewing Brutus and Cassius as one man is traditional blunder at least as old as 9th-century commentary on Vergil.

19-20 Fr 256: Ch probably drew on as yet unidentified medieval source rather than on authors named.

2727-2766

Croesus, saved from fire by rain, swore vengeance against Cyrus. He refused to be warned by dream and was finally hanged.

27	*Lyde* Lydia (in Asia Minor)	51	*galwes* gallows
31	*welkne shadde* sky poured	57	*plat* bluntly
45	*towaille* towel	64	*unwar* unlooked for

61-6 Jones: these lines are Monk's closing summary, repeating his opening definition of tragedy, "although the Knight is evidently unaware of this, as is the Host," Pres 217: in abrupt ending Ch was perhaps "dramatizing the exhaustion of his Monk's patience."

65-6 Cog 158: lines are "up to the standard of *Troilus*."

The Nun's Priest's Tale

COMMENTARIES: Gr 235-8; Ham 292-3;/ Don 940-4; ManCT
636-46; Rob 750-5; Sk 5, 247-59;/ Brew 155-8; Ches 13-6; Cog
154-7; Cow 164-5; Cur 219-40; Dem 68-71; Ev 172-4; Fr 22, 63,
257-65; Hin 121-56; Kit 13-4, 164; Law 134-5; Lum 105-17; Mal
169-73; Mus 237-43; K. Petersen, *On Sources of NPT* (Boston,
1898); Pres 170, 220-3; Root 207-18; Sisam ed. *NPT* (Oxford,
1927); Sp 185-93; Wells 712-3;/ Aiken, *Spec*, 35, 281-7; Baum,
PMLA, 58, 167-70; Brown, *MLN*, 20, 479-82; Curry, *ESt*, 24, 24-60;
Dahlberg, *JEGP*, 54, 277-90; Dieckmann, *MLN*, 38, 177-80; Donovan, *JEGP*, 53, 498-508; Hamm, *MLN*, 54, 394-5; Hemingway,
MLN, 16, 479-83; Hitt, *MissQ*, 59, 75-85; Hotson, *PMLA*, 24, 762-
81 (W); Hulbert, *SA*, 645-53; Kaske, *ELH*, 57, 249-68; Kenyon,
JEGP, 16, 282-8; Law, *PMLA*, 22, 208-15; Lecompte, *MP*, 17, 737-
49; Manly, *PBA*, 26, 95-113 (ST); Manning, *JEGP*, 60, 403-16;
Owen, *JEGP*, 53, 294-311 (W, O); Severs, *SP*, 46, 22-41; Sherbo,
PMLA, 49, 236-46; Steadman, *Isis*, 59, 236-44; Tatlock, *PMLA*, 35,
100-39; Tupper, *Nation*, 13, 354-6.

GENRE: Beast fable.

SOURCE: An episode from the French beast epic *Le Roman de
Renart*, or a retelling thereof.

DATE: Probably late 1390's.

GENERAL CRITICISM: Hin 121-5: Ch probably influenced by fables
in Dutch or Flemish, and for mock-heroic by Nigel Wireker's *Speculum Stultorum;* excellent characterization is original, homiletic parts
added to fit Priest; Pope's *Rape of the Lock* is tale's only rival in
English mock-heroic. Tupper: cock and fox fable subordinated to
uxoriousness of Chaunt, servant of Venus. Kit 13-4: tale in form is
preacher's exemplum expanded until it swallows sermon; perfect
mock-heroic using every trick of academic rhetoric. Kenyon: Ch intended tale as part of Marriage Group, linking *Mel* and *MkT* with
WBT (Wife's rebuttal to Priest); tale is antidote to *MkT* as requested

by Host and is Priest's answer to view of women's advice in *Mel* (with traditional roles of Chaunt and Pert on dreams reversed); common theme in *Mel,* parts of *MkT,* and *NPT* is, specifically, woman's power over man, leading into *WBT.* Root 208-17: Priest not characterized—thus Ch himself seems teller, with genial and elvish humor; Ch changed fable, delaying entrance of fox, expanding dream discussion, heightening description and characterization; Chaunt a great creation, real and interesting, human yet always rooster, strutting and pedantic, yet kindly and likable. Hotson: Ch made changes in and additions to fable to create a "touch-and-go allusion to contemporary events" which gives tale new zest. Cur 219-20: Pert, practical and unimaginative, correctly diagnoses Chaunt's trouble according to medieval medicine; Chaunt, pompous and imaginative, argues dream forecasts future, and reader feels difference of opinion comes from difference in temperament. Manly: fulsome rhetoric is brilliant and amusing parody of *MkT* (100% rhetoric), but here rhetoric used dramatically as speech of characters who seem real. Cow 164-5: strikingly original, with emphasis changed to make Chaunt hero instead of fox—full of vigor, wit, and mock-heroic dignity. Severs: main theme is badness of woman's advice. Fr 265: "a sprightly bit of nonsense" with touches of satire and burlesque. Ches 13-6: Ch, with intensely English humor, revels in absurdity of cock acting like man, gets "huge enjoyment out of metaphysical chicken." Cog 154: Priest well suited in retinue of Prioress who loves animals. Law 134-5: Priest, under thumb of woman (Prioress), ridicules Pert's slender learning and bad advice, thus countering moral of *Mel;* Ch altered tale to fit marriage discussion. Sp 185: greatest and wisest of *CT,* with central theme of pride; mock-heroic brilliance of cock contrasts with realistic background (poor widow). Pres 222: masterly fusion of diverse ideas, apparent ease concealing superb artistry. Brew 155-8: one of Ch's most perfect comic tales; "this kind of joyful burlesque is the play of the mind." Owen: tale is first a ridicule of vanity, but Priest joins other pilgrims in discussing poverty (*MLT, WBT*), women's advice (*MerchT*), rhetoric (Host, *SqT*), marriage; also, in contrasting widow and Chaunt, he makes "veiled comment" on his own situation with Prioress ("a misogynist dependent on a woman"). Donovan: tale is allegorical sermon on "alertness to moral obligation," with Chaunt as any holy man, fox as devil and heretic (as in bestiaries), widow as Church which shelters Chaunt, Pert as sensuality which blinds him; Chaunt is saved by recovery of moral alertness; tale counteracts *MkT*'s stress on man's helplessness in hands of Fortune. Dahlberg agrees with Donovan, goes farther; fox also stands for friars (often symbolized as foxes) in struggle against secular clergy (Chaunt) who are in slothful state, in danger unless they open eyes; Ch favors secular clergy against friars. Sherbo: Priest was muscular and virile. Lum 105-13 sees Priest as timid and frail, under "petticoat rule," expressing anti-feminist view—Chaunt's amorous interest in Pert overcomes own better judgment. Mus 238-42: tale constantly shifts focus, gaily contradicting itself on marriage ("Chaucerian multiple perspective"), offering no conclusions; it is allegory of the Fall, "leaving Man, somewhat wiser, still in possession of his paradise, or his chicken yard." Don 940-4: though wholly comic, tale gives far more serious and mature view of human responsibility than *MkT;* in one way, in "godlike detachment" from scene, Priest resembles Ch, lovingly and humorously observing human affairs. Steadman: Chaunt's traits reflect medieval scientific ideas about cocks—choleric (movements of choler in body causing precise crowing every 3 hours), generous, devoted to wives, proud, strutting, learned; Ch used natural history as new source of humor. Hitt: Chaunt, not Pert, is main target of satire which strikes at worldly pride, deflating puffed up Chaunt.

THE PROLOGUE OF THE NUN'S PRIEST'S TALE
VII, 2767-2820

Knight stops Monk's tragedies as too depressing. Host agrees, asks Monk for more cheerful tale. Monk refuses; Host then calls on Nun's Priest.

71	*a greet disese* very painful	03	*substance* ability
92	*daun Piers* master Peter	18	*attamed* broached, opened
98	*slough* mud		

67-79 Kit 164: Knight interrupts as natural leader of group, with "same sense of duty he would display in battle." Mal 169-73: surprising that Knight, shown earlier as "soul of courtesy," should be rude here, "not perfect after all"; Ch wished to avoid repeating Host's interruption of *Thop;* Knight shows taste of a child, literary naiveté which cannot abide tragedy, must have happy endings; whole passage is amusing, dramatic way to break off *MkT.* Kaske disagrees with Mal—Knight is not rude, but courteous as possible in situation, calling Monk *good sire;* passage stresses contrast (already developed in *Gen Prol*) between ideal Knight, dedicated to his calling, and worldly, corrupt Monk (negation of monastic ideal); Knight interrupts distorted Boethian philosophy of *MkT* (showing Fortune as blindly fickle and meaningless), as contrasted to true Boethian philosophy of *KnT* (Fortune part of ordered universe, with ill luck often sent to good men to "exercise" them); *MkT* is *greet disese* to Knight because it is not philosophically true or sound. Don 939-40: rude interruption of Monk is "Ch's revenge on his own pompous creation," shows he was aware of "fatal flaw" in tragedies.

94, 05 Lum 104: references to bells and hunting show that Monk of *MkT* is same as Monk of *Gen Prol.*

08-15 Sherbo: Host's rude tone and comment on Priest's poor horse suggest Priest was not confessor for important nunnery, but merely bodyguard and attendant to Prioress (see also 3447-60). Lum 107-8: Host picks on timid Priest to relieve pent-up irritation over *MkT,* uses familiar pronouns (*thou,* etc.) and contemptuous *sir John.*

20 ManCT 636: line shows John was actual name of Priest ("Sir John" was used for any priest). Lum 109: *sweete preest* suggests femininity, does not fit idea of brawny priest.

THE NUN'S PRIEST'S TALE

2821-2881

Poor old widow lives in cottage with daughters. In yard she keeps 7 hens and rooster Chauntecleer who crows magnificently, has favorite hen Pertelote.

21	*stape* advanced	36	*cote* cottage
27	*catel* property	45	*seynd* broiled. *ey* egg
29	*foond* provided for	46	*deye* dairy woman
31	*keen* cows	53	*logge* lodge

54	*orlogge* clock	
60	*batailled* crenelated	
75	*lith* limb	

79 *My lief,* etc. My love has gone into the country.

21-46 Root 214: view of daily peasant life with narrow interests contrasts with lordly intellectual scope of Chaunt.

32 Hin 126-7: cottage had 2 rooms, bedroom (bower) and dining room (hall), with chickens roosting in hall (see 2884); no chimney, hence sooty. ManCT 637: cottage was more likely single room (hall) with garret (bower) for sleeping.

47 ff. Mus 239-40: from sober, restrained setting, Chaunt's magnificence gradually emerges, "then bursts like a rocket into a shower of color."

59-64 Hotson: Chaunt's colors—gold, azure, black, etc.—are those of Henry Bolingbroke (political allegory of quarrel between Bolingbroke and Mowbray and his follower Colfax, the fox, in 1398).

62 Brew 156: Chaunt's "body, like his speech, is a blaze of colours."

2882-2969

One morning Chauntecleer groans in sleep, tells Pertelote of bad dream in which he is attacked by animal (fox). She chides him for cowardice, says dream comes from indigestion—he needs laxative.

87	*drecched* vexed	
96	*swevene recche aright* interpret dream favorably	
98	*mette* dreamed	
08	*hertelees* coward	
17	*avauntour* boaster	
30	*lemes* flames	

32	*contek* strife	
41	*ne do no fors of* attach no importance to	
50	*prow* benefit	
65	*gaitrys* dogwood	
66	*herbe yve* buck's-horn	

82-69 Root 216: Pert's kindly solicitude, wifely confidence in home remedies; she humors Chaunt's weakness for pedantry.

88 Hin 130: *roore* is mock-heroic touch; in 4368 Chaunt is compared to *a grym leoun.*

89-69 Curry: Pert's analysis of Chaunt's trouble is scientifically accurate, according to medieval medicine.

00-1 Hin 131: legal phrase.

02-4 Hotson: colors of fox resemble sign of Mowbray (gold truncheon tipped with black), enemy of Bolingbroke.

12-20 Pres 170: Pert wants perfect courtly lover.

21-2 Hamm: Pert's empirical view of dreams is that of Aristotle, opposed to Plato's which Chaunt favors.

40-1 Hin 132-3: *Disticha* of Dionysius Cato was elementary Latin schoolbook, showing Pert's reading very limited.

43 Mus 241: Chaunt's magnificence shifts from courtly love into "most unromantic, domestic familiarity."

61-7 ManCT 640: choice of herbs is sound; medieval wives prided themselves on such knowledge.

2970-3156

Chauntecleer retorts that dreams foreshadow future. He tells of man whose friend was murdered in stable and appeared to him in dream telling full details. He gives stories of man who foresaw shipwreck in dream which came true, and of St. Kenelm of Mercia who foresaw his own murder. Citing other Biblical and classical proofs, he rejects laxatives.

76 *thee* thrive

89 *streit of herbergage* short of accommodation

08 *abrayde* started

10 *keep* notice

34 *lette* delay

43 *ministres* magistrates

53 *wlatsom* loathsome

55 *heled* concealed

59 *pyned* tortured

60 *engyned* racked

61 *biknewe* confessed

72 *agayn* toward

78 *agayn* just before

84 *viage* voyage. *lette* give up

93 *maze* delusion

96 *forslewthen* waste

01 *casuelly* accidentally

17 *for traisoun* for fear of treason

18 *litel tale hath he toold* he took little heed

36 *actes of remes* histories of kingdoms

54 *telle . . . no stoor* set no value on

70-83 Curry: despite Chaunt's show of learning, he knows little of philosophy or psychology of dreams; "his puerile mind is capable of grasping only the thread of a marvelous story."

84 Baum: *gretteste auctour* is play on name of Valerius Maximus, whose name means "greatest," and who is source for Chaunt's first exemplum.

15 Dahlberg: line suggests Christ who was 3 times denied by Peter (dreamer) before the cock crew; function of cock (priest in allegory) is to waken others to danger.

50-7 Hotson: secret murder in foreign town may refer to murder of Gloucester by Colfax and Mowbray at Calais.

24 Hin 137:   *In Affrike* is Ch's mistranslation of "Africanus," the surname of Scipio.

38-40 Hemingway: Croesus exemplum shows Chaunt's pedantic discussion is meant as burlesque of *MkT;* self-important Chaunt is reminiscent of Monk, just as *rethor* in 3207 may be sly reference to him; also 3252-8 echo *MkT* 2091-2 (Sampson).

53-6, 63-6 Brew 156:   Chaunt shows typical husband's irritation at being told to take medicine, together with patronizing smugness over superior learning.

3157-3214

Attracted by Pertelote's beauty, Chauntecleer follows her from perch into yard despite his own argument, lords it over hens.

63-4 *In principio,* etc. In the beginning, woman is man's ruination.	76 *real* royal
	78 *trad* trod, copulated with
	97 *stevene* voice
72 *fley* flew	07 *rethor* master of rhetoric

57-71 Owen: in this crucial passage Chaunt uses deceitful flattery on Pert, same technique later used against him by fox; his smug pedantry and wife's charms blind him to danger.

63-6 Kenyon: Priest's and Chaunt's ironic rebuttal of proverb cited by Prud in *Mel* 1106; Chaunt's "humorously gallant interpretation" shows Pert's power over him. ManCT 641: Chaunt's joke becomes epic irony, for true meaning of Latin turns out to be *siker* indeed. Brown: Chaunt here is sharply sarcastic to simple Pert. Sp 188: Chaunt takes mean advantage of Pert's ignorance, heightens his own bookish absurdity.

70-86 Dem 69-71: Ch creates original dramatic irony in Chaunt's new self-confidence through victory in argument; "because he has so brilliantly demonstrated that he should be afraid, he is not afraid any more!"

87-98 Sk 5, 250: date is May 3; calculation of prime is exact for 9 a.m. Hin 139-40 agrees, thinks tale written 1381 because May 3 in that year fell on Friday (see 3341).

05-9 Lum 116: repetition here of formula of Monk's "tragedies" is satire on Monk's sententiousness, resembling Chaunt's.

3215-3266
Fox sneaks into yard, lies treacherously in wait for Chauntecleer. Women's advice is often bad.

15	*col-fox* fox tipped with black	40	*bulte* sift
17	*heigh ymaginacioun* divine foreknowledge	43	*forwityng* foreknowledge
21	*wortes* cabbages	53	*with sorwe* (an imprecation, comparable to "confound her!")
22	*undren* noon		

15 Hotson: *col-fox* may be political reference to Nicholas Colfax, follower of Mowbray, murderer of Gloucester, also guilty of treason (see 3227-9).

24 Baum: pun on *gladly* (gladly and habitually).

27-50 Root 217: Ch uses mock-heroic to keep "airy fabric" of tale from collapsing too suddenly (also in 3338-74).

34-50 Donovan: passage gives cosmic setting for struggle between moral alertness (Chaunt) and devil (fox).

52-9 Lum 114-5: lines sum up main point of tale; in next (3260-6) Priest softens argument slightly to avoid offending Prioress, but *auctors* he refers to were strongly antifeminist. Severs: exact parallel with Adam. Law 135: Priest momentarily lets antifeminist feelings run away with him.

56-3337 Sp 189-91: whole passage becomes tragi-comic allegory of the Fall of Adam (Chaunt), through advice of Eve (Pert) and temptation of Serpent (fox) in Garden of Eden (yard).

56-9 Hin 145: unfair to accuse Pert; Chaunt went into yard because he wanted to, having first snubbed Pert; 3260-5 show that this view of situation is Chaunt's, not Ch's.

65 AHM: *Thise been the cokkes words*—not so; they are the Priest's.

66 Mus 239: "most deliciously ambiguous line in Ch."

3267-3354

Chauntecleer sees fox, is frightened; fox says he admires rooster's voice and merely comes to hear him sing as his father before him (with eyes shut, neck out). Chauntecleer, flattered, sings; fox grabs him by neck, runs for woods.

67	*soond* sand	26	*losengeour* flatterer
69	*agayn* in	33	*for the nones* for that pur-
81	*erst* before		pose (of imitating father)
00	*brouke* enjoy	35	*gargat* throat
06	*wynke* close (eyes)	37	*sewed* pursued
15	*nyce* foolish	40	*roghte* heeded
21	*countrefete* imitate		

84-3330 Donovan: temptation speech of fox (devil) is interrupted by Priest (25-30) to affirm warning—main point of tale.

93-4 Dieckmann: reference to Boethius's *De Musica* is ironical, since by Ch's time this work was regarded as cold and outmoded, thus revealing Chaunt's ignorance.

95-7 Hin 147-8: exquisitely satiric *double entendre*.

22-4 Brew 156: in Chaunt's shuddering with delight at flattery, Ch gives fine picture both of way bird flutters and of "reactions of a certain type of person when flattered."

34 Hotson: *daun Russell* perhaps refers to Sir John Russell, one of 5 hated favorites of Richard II.

38-54 Sp 191-2: passage full of parodies of academic rhetorical devices and scholastic philosophy.

47-51 Manly: Geoffroi de Vinsauf one of chief rhetoric textbooks known to all educated men in Ch's day; Ch reveals "enormous absurdity" of Geoffroi's rhetorical outburst on Richard I. Cog 156: Ch puts Geoffroi to "loving and preposterous use." Brew 157: Ch aims not to ridicule rhetoric (which he constantly uses himself), but to laugh at Geoffroi's bad poetry. Ev 172-4: comic incongruity of using rhetorical devices of high and tragic poetry to comment on farmyard disaster; without rhetorical amplification tale would have nothing but bare bones.

3355-3446

Hens shriek in horror; widow, daughters, barnyard animals all chase fox with great clamor. Chauntecleer advises fox to shout defiance at them. When fox opens mouth to do so Chauntecleer escapes into tree, refuses to be coaxed down. Thus we see danger of flattery.

57	*streite* drawn	90	*dokes* ducks. *quelle* kill
60	*clos* yard	98	*bemes* trumpets. *box* box-
62	*shrighte* shrieked		tree
75	*sely* poor	12	*maugree youre heed* despite
78	*syen* saw		all you can do
88	*breeke* would break	16	*delyverly* nimbly
89	*yolleden* yelled	26	*shrewe* curse

55-74 Sp 192-3: superb mock-heroic climax, followed by actual chase of fox—"moral disorder, the universal chaos of the Fall, conceived as a commotion in an English farmyard."

75 Mus 240: shock effect of transition from rhetoric and heroics back to humble farmyard.

83 Hin 154: *Talbot* and *Gerland* are also dogs, not men (see *dogges* in 3386).

94-6 Ch's only reference to Peasants' Revolt of 1381.

18-35 Severs: Ch adds fox's final effort at deceit, reverses order of concluding morals, all to stress fact that cock has learned lesson beyond any doubt.

EPILOGUE TO THE NUN'S PRIEST'S TALE

3447-3472

Host praises tale, jokes coarsely about Nun's Priest's physique and sexual potency.

48 *stoon* testicle
50 *seculer* layman
51 *trede-foul* treader of fowls, i.e., a lecher
55 *whiche braunes* what muscles
59 *brasile* dye from brazilwood. *greyn of Portyngale* cochineal

47-62 Tupper: Host's description makes both Monk (*MkT* 1932-64) and Priest fit total scheme of domination of Venus in tales. Owen: double irony in Host's failure to see point of tale (Priest's veiled misogyny) and suggestion that Priest, if layman, would be prodigious treader of hens. Lum 110-1: Host's references to Priest's brawn and sexual powers resemble *MkT* 1932-64, but here Host is ironical; Priest is really thin and pale; note ring of irony in exaggerations in 3450-4 (Sherbo takes exactly opposite view of passage).

54 Hin 156: *Ya* is Flemish and Dutch form, suggesting that Ch used Flemish and/or Dutch sources for tale.

61-2 Tatlock regards lines as genuine; Rob 755 judges them probably "a spurious attempt at patchwork."

The Second Nun's Tale

COMMENTARIES: Gr 239-41; Ham 315-6;/ Don 944-5; ManCT 647; Rob 755-9; Sk 5, 401-14;/ Brew 52-3; Cog 135; Fr 324-7; Ger 4, 19, 98, 242; Gerould, *Saints Legends* (New York, 1916), 239-44; Giff 29-48; Mad 27-60; Mus 216-7; Pat 169-73; Pres 279-81; Root 277-8; Sp 193-4;/ Brown, *MP*, 11, 1-16; Eliason, *MLQ*, 42, 9-16; Emerson, *PMLA*, 26, 252-61; Gardner, *UTSE*, 47, 77-83; Gerould, *SA*, 664-84; Henshaw, *MP*, 28, 15-16; Hostia, *CE*, 53, 351-2; Jones, *MLR*, 37, 283; Lowes, *PMLA*, 11, 315-23, and *MP*, 17, 193-202; Manly, *PBA*, 26, 95-113 (ST); Reilly, *MLN*, 54, 37-9; Tatlock, *PMLA*, 30, 169-79; Tupper, *MLN*, 15, 5-12.

GENRE: Saint's life.

SOURCE: *Legenda Aurea* by Jacobus Januensis (a Voragine), with some features from a Latin version of the Greek life by Simeon Metaphrastes; Ch either combined these two accounts himself, or used a lost Latin version which incorporated both.

DATE: Probably early, shortly after 1373 (imperfectly adapted later for *CT*), though some would date it as late as 1383.

VERSE FORM: Rime royal (7-line stanza of iambic pentameter, rimed a b a b b c c).

GENERAL CRITICISM: Root 277-8: serious tale very appropriate to teller, with spirit of religious exaltation and "irresistible force of Cecilia's sweet personality"; inconsistencies in 62, 78 show it was not written for *CT*, probably 1373-4. Gerould 242: though Ch sticks strictly to legend he makes Cecilia "as vivid against the background of miracle as are all the personalities of his maturer work." Manly: Ch fails to visualize main characters who remain mere names. Tatlock: finest version of the legend, showing Ch's serious Christianity, recreating spirit of early church. Jones: tale is in form of medieval sermon on saint, delivered on saint's day, lacking only benediction and prayer at end. Pat 169-73: "piety shines in the awkward enthusiasm of the story," but Ch perhaps less interested in holiness of Nun (and Prioress) than in incongruity of her human weakness in showing Cecilia "slanging the Judge." Eliason: tale perhaps intended as second tale of Prioress; rubrics in MSS inconsistent and ambiguous; *Gen Prol* 163-4 may have been added by scribe to account for what he mistakenly thought was a second nun. Cog 135: teller cannot compare with Prioress as narrator of visionary things. Sp 193-6: tale more bookish, less folksy than *PrT;* probably early stanzaic work slightly adapted for *CT.* Pres 279-80: tale perhaps a "pious addendum" to marriage debate (stress on extreme chastity in wedlock); artistically far below *PrT,* with stanzaic rhythm getting out of control; theory that Ch meant to characterize teller as more humble and devout than Prioress very doubtful, based on incompleteness of text. Ger 4, 19: tale shows strength of Ch's own religious faith beyond any dramatic aim since he did not cancel "telltale reference to himself" in 62; from uninspired Latin prose Ch created original "poem of exquisite tone and temper." Brew 52-3, 172: tale is close translation, but has real warmth, quiet piety, occasional freshness, is "honest, pious, rather restrained and colourless," contrasts with robust *CYT.* Hostia: Second Nun more objective than Prioress, does not curse Roman persecutors as Prioress does Jews, has truer religious character. Giff 29-48: tale shows careful craftsmanship and economy, with 3 overlapping themes—central theme of *bisynesse* in God's work (64-6, 112, 195-6, 258-9), chastity and martyrdom (87-8, 220-9, 243-56, 270-80, 388), and spiritual sight (100-1, 106-12, 252-9, 400-4, 498-504, etc.); possibly tale was written in 1383 especially for Richard II's visit to Norwich in honor of nomination of Archbishop Adam Easton as cardinal and priest of Santa Cecilia in Trastevere (Rome); if Ch wrote tale for monks of Norwich from whose ranks Easton came, *unworthy sone of Eve* in 62 and reference to church in 550 (not in other versions) seem very fitting. Mus 216-7: tale contrasts more than coincidentally with *CYT,* as St. Cecilia, cool in bath of flame, contrasts with alchemists, "the blackened, sweating believers in earth, whose fire blows up in their faces." Don 944-5: as saint's life tale lacks complexity of fictitious *ClT* in showing sufferings of saintly person.

THE SECOND NUN'S PROLOGUE

VIII, 1-28

Idleness is a grievous sin, easy to slip into. To warn us against it, I shall tell legend of St. Cecilia.

5	*leveful* lawful	12	*lappe* hem of garment
7	*hente* seize	19	*slouthe* sloth. *lees* leash
9	*biclappe* catch	25	*after* following

1-28 Mad 53-4: invective against idleness echoes monastic *Rule of St. Benedict*. Brew 53: opening stanza clumsy and conventional.

29-84

Invocation to Mary: Merciful mother of Jesus, help me tell the story of thy maiden Cecilia's death.

38	*wone* dwell	62	*sone of Eve* (failure to revise?)
45	*tryne* threefold		
46	*out of relees* without ceasing	63	*bileve* faith
47	*heryen* praise. *wemmelees* spotless	78	*write* (should be "tell"—failure to revise)
58	*flemed* banished		

29-77 Sk 5, 403: free translation of Dante, *Paradiso*, xxxiii, 1-21. Brown: strong influence of church hymns to Virgin as well as Dante; whole invocation written at one time, far superior to rest of Prologue and tale, probably a later addition (line 78 follows smoothly from 28). Tupper: most direct source is "The Hours of the Virgin," part of the *Prymer* or *Lay Folk's Prayer Book*. Lowes, *MP,* notes influence of Alanus de Insulis and Macrobius, in addition to Dante and church hymns. Ger 4, 98: invocation is Ch's own, despite debt to Dante—general pattern derivative, resulting product original, "one of the noblest and most beautiful passages of devotional poetry in our tongue," most poignant lyric in Ch except for songs of Troilus and of Antigone in *Troilus*. Hostia: invocation poetically superior to Prioress's, better constructed, more felicitous, with spirit of true humility.

Brew 53: "Dante's virtue shines through, clear, direct, elevated," contrasts with clumsy opening stanza of Prologue, showing extent and importance of Ch's debt to Dante.

43-4 Cog 135: lovely lines improved from Dante.

62 Gardner: Ch here uses word-pattern from *Salve Regina,* recited daily by nuns, wholly appropriate to teller here (*sone* means descendant of either sex).

78-84 Giff 31: lines are very appropriate if Ch was writing for monks of Norwich who would know more about saint's life than he.

85-119

Interpretation of name Cecilia: Cecilia means "heaven's lily," or "way to the blind," or "heaven and Lia" (active life), or "wanting of blindness," or "heaven of people."

91	*soote* sweet	09	*goostly* spiritually
01	*thewes* morals	19	*highte* was called
03	*leos* people (Greek)		

85-119 Sk 5, 405: all 5 etymologies are wrong; actually name is feminine of Caecilius, name of members of Roman family descended from ancient Italian hero Caeculus (diminutive of *caecus,* blind).

THE SECOND NUN'S TALE

120-140

Cecilia, of noble Roman family, wears hair-shirt and prays during her wedding to young Valerian.

33	*haire* hair-shirt	40 *biddynge* praying

33 AHM: hair-shirt was worn next to skin as means of self-punishment, mortification of the flesh to subdue physical desires; this kind of extreme asceticism was greatly admired in Middle Ages.

141-182

At night she tells Valerian an angel guards her virginity; he will die if he touches her. Valerian wants to see angel. Cecilia sends him to St. Urban (pope in hiding) for baptism.

45	*conseil* a secret	59	*gye* keep
47	*biwreye* reveal	82	*twynne* depart

51-68 Tatlock: stress on continence in marriage may come from apocryphal Acts of Peter (by pseudo-Linus), where Peter is shown converting Roman prefect's concubines and many matrons to continence, resulting in his martyrdom to which angels bring crowns of lilies (extreme chastity) and roses (see 220-1).

52 Mad 59: based on Catholic teaching of guardian angel (Psalm 91).

183-217
Valerian finds Urban, then is confronted by angel and confesses his faith. Angel vanishes; Urban baptizes Valerian.

86	*buryeles* burial-places.	
	lotynge hiding, lurking	05-6 When he (Valerian) saw him; and he (old man) then lifted up him (Valerian); and then he (Valerian) began thus to read in his (old man's) book.
92	*hierde* shepherd	
96	*thral* servant	
		14 *sother* truer
		15 *thynke* imagine

01 Sk 5, 408: old man is St. Paul, passage Valerian reads being translation of Eph. iv, 5-6.

218-241
Returning home, Valerian finds angel with Cecilia. Angel gives to both crowns of heavenly flowers. Valerian asks that his brother be converted to the truth.

21	*corones* crowns	34	*boone* request
29	*lese* lose		

20-1 Lowes, *PMLA,* explains meaning of 2 crowns of lilies and roses as traditional church symbols of virginity (lily) and martyrdom (rose). Tatlock: crowns of flowers are carry-over from pagan garlands symbolizing victory.

242-289

Brother Tiburce arrives, is amazed at sweet smell of flowers in winter. After conversation with Valerian and Cecilia, Tiburce is converted.

43	*undernoom* perceived	76	*chambre* marriage-chamber.
50	*depper* deeper		*weyve* forsake
64	*at erst* for the first time	77	*shrifte* confession
68	*reneye* renounce	86	*deve* deaf

46-8 Cog 135: one of few moments of loveliness in tale.

60-5 Sp 194: "beautiful and profound metaphysical recognition."

70-83 Emerson: St. Ambrose was source of 2 crowns image, also palm of martyrdom.

71 Henshaw: *preface* refers not to any preface in St. Ambrose's writings, but to *prefatio* of the Ambrosian mass for St. Cecilia's day which is almost identical to Ch's passage (274-83).

290-357

Cecilia accepts Tiburce as ally and sends him to Urban for baptism. Tiburce at first fears he may be caught and burned, but is encouraged when Cecilia explains eternal life. He is baptized by Urban and afterwards is often visited by angel.

06	*til* to	29	*sowled hem* given them
08	*wonder* dede strange thing		souls. *drede* doubt
	to do	39	*engyn* imagination
11	*halkes* nooks	43	*come* coming
20	*skilfully* reasonably		

09-18 Giff 47: contrast of earthly fire and cosmic energy (compare celestial fire of 118) heightens intensity.

52-3 Reilly: Tiburce was not only baptized, but Pope Urban gave him sacrament of confirmation, *goddes knight* being term used for those who had received confirmation.

358-399

Valerian and Tiburce are finally arrested, brought before prefect Almachius, and ordered to sacrifice to Jupiter on pain of death. They are taken to house of officer Maximus, whom they convert with preaching. Cecilia arrives at night with priests who baptize whole household. Shortly after, Valerian and Tiburce refuse to sacrifice to Jupiter and are beheaded.

63	*apposed* questioned		79	*woxen* become
66	*swape* strike		80	*yfeere* together
69	*corniculer* clerk		95	*encense* offer incense
73	*tormentoures* executioners		98	*hevedes* heads
76	*reve* take away			

400-409

Maximus preaches and converts many with vision of brothers' souls going to heaven. Almachius has him beaten to death. Cecilia buries him alongside brothers.

05	*dide hym tobete* had him beaten	06	*lete* give up

410-511

Almachius then orders Cecilia to sacrifice, but she converts officers. In court, Cecilia defies Almachius, refuses to deny Christianity, preaches to him of his pride and blindness.

20	*sterve* die		67	*woodeth* raves. *advertence* pronouncing judgment
23	*alderfirst* first of all			
33	*freyned* asked		68	*unsely* unhappy
47	*withseye* deny		86	*naked* helpless
49	*nobleye* nobles			
63	*confus* confused. *nycetee* folly			

91-2 Fr 324-7: Ch apparently condensed source, dropping speech of Cecilia (present in other versions), so that Almachius scolds her for evil words against his gods whom she has not yet mentioned.

98-04 Mus 216-7: here Cecilia anticipates Yeoman's teaching in *CYT* 1412-21.

512-531

Almachius orders Cecilia taken home and burned in bath of flames. Cecilia sits coolly in bath, unharmed. Almachius next orders beheading and Cecilia's neck is cut half through.

18	*betten* kindled	25	*sonde* messenger
23	*lete* yield		

532-553

For 3 days Cecilia survives, preaching to the people. St. Urban buries her secretly and raises a church on site of her house.

33	*ycorven* cut	45	*do werche* make
39	*fostred* converted, educated in the faith	47	*deknes* deacons
40	*moebles* movable possessions	48	*fette* fetched
41	*bitook* entrusted	51	*halwed* hallowed

40-53 Giff 38-9: if Ch wrote tale to recognize Easton's nomination as cardinal priest of Santa Cecilia in Rome, he could not have ended more effectively.

The Canon's Yeoman's Tale

COMMENTARIES: Gr 241-2; Ham 316-7;/ Don 945-6; ManCT 647-53; Rob 759-62; Sk 5, 414-34;/ Cog 172-3; Fr 327-33; Leg 183-4; Low 192-3; Lum 227-35; Mal 222; Man 235-52; Mus 215-21; Pres 281-3; Root 280-3; Sp 196-8; Tho 114-5;/ Aiken, *SP*, 44, 371-89; Baum, *MLN*, 25, 152-4, and *PMLA*, 56, 225-46; Damon, *PMLA*, 24, 782-8; Duncan, *MP*, 40, 241-62; Hamilton, *Spec*, 41, 103-8; Lowes, *MLN*, 13, 229; Spargo, *SA*, 685-98.

GENRE: Anecdote of fraudulent alchemist, prefaced by detailed exposé of alchemical practices.

SOURCE: Unknown, but most probably a current anecdote; Ch must have derived much of his knowledge from alchemical treatises, but none of these has been positively identified.

DATE: Sometime in 1390's.

GENERAL CRITICISM: Root 281-2: tale is exposé of alchemy by a victim, and thus has personal bitterness not to be attributed to Ch himself; fullness of Ch's information shows he had studied alchemy (intellectual curiosity), but believed search futile. Damon: far from attacking alchemy, Ch probably sympathized with it and was an adept himself. Baum, *MLN:* Part II may have been written separately as *jeu d'esprit* for special occasion, then adapted for *CT;* 1342-8 and 1388-1481 are totally inappropriate for Yeoman; tale probably dates from *CT* period. Man 235-52: realistic details of alchemy (implying Ch's profound knowledge of the science) and bitterness of tone suggest Ch himself may have dabbled in alchemy and been cheated, possibly by alchemist Canon William Shuchirch of King's Chapel, Windsor (first proposed by H. G. Richardson in *Trans. of Royal Hist. Soc.,* 1922); possibly tale was written for canons at Windsor (see 992-1011); Ch's borrowings of small sums in 1390's may have resulted from investments in alchemical experiments. Leg 183-4: tale brilliantly illustrates character of Yeoman, who is unsure whether he admires or hates master, is duped but still clings to illusions, dazzled by exotic science but broken in health and finances, shifting from delusion to anger to common sense, "giving vent to all sorts of contradictory feelings." ManCT 647-8: mature dramatic skill shows Ch probably planned this incident from the first. Duncan: most of Part I describes process of *silver citrinacioun,* turning silver to gold, or at least *coloring* it to look like gold, by fusing silver with refined compounds of sulphur (such as orpiment) or mercury, with preliminary step of sublimation of orpiment and mercury in 750-83; of about 80 chemical terms in tale, all but 6 are illustrated in 13th-century alchemical treatises of Geber. Aiken: terms in Part I suggest Ch was not adept at alchemy himself (he makes 2 or 3 errors), but that he had some technical understanding (far beyond general knowledge) almost all of which he could have got from Vincent of Beauvais' *Speculum Naturale.* Cog 172: tale is "rough and breathless, the utterance of a sharp but 'lewed' wit." Tho 114-5: Ch's exposé shows "independent judgment of a man who was far from gullible." Mal 222: character of Yeoman is "of incidental interest only." Pres 282: most remote and difficult of *CT* for uninstructed reader. Lum 228-9: though Yeoman aims at exposing alchemists who dupe innocents like himself, he unintentionally shows his own greed and stupidity. Mus 219: technical imagery powerfully evokes "feeling of matter as matter." Don 946: tension in Yeoman (as in confirmed gambler) "between disgust and hope is evident in everything he says."

THE CANON'S YEOMAN'S PROLOGUE
VIII, 554-598
A Canon and his Yeoman overtake the pilgrims after a fast ride on sweating horses. They explain that they wish to join pilgrimage for sake of company.

56	*atake* overtake		66	*male* bag
59	*pomely grys* dappled gray		74	*laas* string
61	*priked* spurred		77	*clote* burdock
64	*peytrel* collar		80	*stillatorie* still
65	*pye* magpie		81	*paritorie* nettles

54-971 Root 282: Yeoman's speech is rambling, disordered, confused exposition, resulting from "pent-up scorn"—just the effect Ch aimed at. Man 238-9: Yeoman's jumbled account shows Ch's "consummate art" in picture of "ignorant helper who has no clear understanding of the mysterious undertakings in which he has borne a part, and an impression of the wild irrationality of this pursuit of the impossible."

54-98 Don 945: breathlessness of arrival of Canon and Yeoman gives urgency to Yeoman's story of fraud and attractiveness of alchemy.

59-80 Low 192-3: view of Yeoman who sweats "magnificently, gloriously," is a masterpiece; to Ch "nothing was common or unclean."

69-73 Lum 229 notes skill with which narrator builds interest in 2 newcomers.

599-683

Yeoman tells Host his master is wonderfully skilled at alchemy. Host then questions canon's shabby clothes. Yeoman changes tune and reveals that Canon has failed in search of secret through years of misery and frustrated hopes.

07	*leere* learn	58	*hernes* corners	
09	*prow* profit	65	*harde grace* bad luck	
14	*passyng* surpassing	68	*prie* peer	
21	*wite at* learn from	69	*multiplie* transmute base metals to gold	
32	*worshipe* dignity			
33	*overslope* gown	70	*blondren* blunder. *pouren* stare	
35	*baudy* dirty. *totore* tattered			
41	*thee* thrive	82	*slit* slips	

99-26 Man 236: Yeoman here uses "patter he is accustomed to use to kindle the interest and credulity of strangers and prepare the way for his master's swindling."

40-51 Lum 230: shows Yeoman's disturbed mental state, full of complaints only withheld by fear of master. Don 945: Yeoman feels sudden revulsion from contrast between "brilliantly accomplished man he is praising and the dirty, sweating Canon to whom the praise is supposed to apply."

70 Baum, *PMLA:* pun on *pouren* (stare and pour).

78-83 Sp 196: passage "testifies to the persistent strength of the delusion."

684-719

Canon overhears Yeoman's exposé, orders him to keep quiet. Yeoman refuses; Canon angrily rides away. Yeoman now can speak freely.

91	*sawe* speech	05	*quelle* kill
94	*abye* pay for	07	*biheete* promise
98	*thretyng* threatening	10	*ernest* serious thing

10-4 Lum 231: two opposing forces in Yeoman (disgust with himself and fascination with alchemy) have built up tension which causes rebellion; tale is his method of resolving inner conflict.

THE CANON'S YEOMAN'S TALE, PART I

720-749

For 7 years I have worked with this Canon, till my face is scorched and eyes bleared. Alchemy is a hopeless gamble and has left me and others deep in debt.

36	*quite* pay back	45	*lesen* lose
39	*thrift* prosperity. *ydo* ended	49	*of that no charge* that
43	*jupartye* taking chances		doesn't matter

30 Baum, *PMLA:* pun on *blered is myn ye* (bleared and "fooled").

750-829

I shall now tell you about the materials, apparatus, and methods of this mysterious science, the processes we have tried, the ingredients we mix together and heat with slow or fast fires.

51	*elvysshe* mysterious	70	*sublymyng* sublimating,
52	*clergial* learned		changing solid matter into
59	*iren squames* iron scales		gas by heating
62	*papeer* pepper	71	*calcenyng* calcination, reduc-
64	*lampe* plate		ing a metal to an oxide by
66	*enlutyng* daubing with clay		heating

75 *porfurie* porphyry

78 *spirites ascencioun* rising of gases

82 *twenty devel waye* confound it!

90 *boole armonyak* Armenian clay

93 *violes* vials. *crosletz* crucibles

94 *cucurbites* cucurbits (gourd-like flasks for distillation)

05 *albificacioun* whitening

06 *gleyre of ey* white of egg

08 *cered pokkets* little bags closed with wax

10 *sal preparat* prepared (common) salt

13 *berme* yeast. *wort* unfermented beer. *argoille* crude tartar

14 *resalgar* disulphide of arsenic

16 *citrinacioun* turning to citron color

18 *testes* vessels for assaying metals

74, 98 Aiken: Ch was apparently unaware that *orpyment* and *arsenyk* are same thing, native yellow trisulphide of arsenic.

84-18 Mus 219-20: "solid unspiritual mass of *realism*" unparalleled elsewhere in Ch.

90 Aiken: *boole armonyak* is error for "bolus Armenius" or Armenian clay.

04-8 Cog 173: confusion blended with anger and disappointment in Yeoman's mind (see also 830-1).

13-4 Aiken: 4 of these terms—*berme, wort, argoille, resalgar* (red orpiment)—are connected with wine or beer making or storing; Ch may well have known them through his father's wine business.

830-897

Alchemists are misguided fools; no one, learned or ignorant, will ever find the secret. The search for philosopher's stone is like a compulsion: once started, one lives on false hopes and can never give up. You can tell an alchemist by his foul smell and shabbiness.

34 *outen* show

38 *ascaunce* perhaps

46 *letterure* booklearning

53 *lymaille* metal filings

54 *mollificacioun* softening

55 *induracioun* hardening

61 *rowe* rough

81 *brat* cloth cloak

94 *rownen* whisper

79-83 Sp 197: describes obsession growing into "unworldly frenzy."
84-6 Sp 197: smelly alchemists "are farcically distorted into carica-
tures."

898-971

Often my master mixes metals carefully, but the pot breaks or explodes, scattering the costly ingredients. Then follows a bitter argument over what went wrong. We sift the straw on floor to recover
as much metal as possible, and then start over. This madness has no
end.

04	*algate* anyhow	34	*crased* cracked
21	*chit* chides. *halt hym yvele*	40	*syve* sieve
	apayd thinks himself dis-	41	*throwe* time
	pleased	53	*wite* blame
29	*so thee'ch* so may I prosper	68	*preef* proof

59-68 Sp 198: "externalized confusion projects an original moral
confusion and spectacularly exposes it."

PART II

972-1011

I will tell of a canon who is a clever cheat. Canons should beware
of harboring such scoundrels in their convents.

84	*but* unless	97	*singuleer* individual
95	*shrewe* rascal. *pardee* by	99	*mys* amiss
	God (Fr., par Dieu)		

1012-1101

One day this fraudulent canon comes to visit a priest in London to
borrow some money which he promptly repays. To show thanks for
loan, canon offers to reveal alchemical secret to priest.

12	*annueleer* priest who sings	19	*no fors* no matter
	annual masses for dead	29	*hals* neck
15	*at table* boarding	30	*as swithe* immediately

31	*sithe* times	65	*beede* offer
49	*yvele apayd* ill pleased	77	*blent* blinded
54	*kithed* showed	81	*wrenches* tricks
60	*maistrie* masterpiece	85	*unwit* stupidity

12-9 Lum 232: since Yeoman aims to stress evil of canon, he brushes lightly over greed of priest who is dupe like himself.

1102-1143

At canon's request, priest sends out for 3 ounces of mercury and some coals. Canon promises to show how to change ounce of mercury to silver by means of magic powder sprinkled over it.

03	*quyksilver* mercury	26	*mortifye* transmute
16	*yfet* fetched	36	*voyde* get rid of
17	*crosselet* crucible	41	*yede* went

1144-1203

Priest heats crucible over fire, then puts hot coals on top of it. In rearranging coals, canon secretly inserts a hollow coal filled with silver directly over crucible. Silver melts and drops unnoticed into crucible.

49	*outher* either	70	*at wynne* apart
60	*bechen cole* charcoal of beechwood	71	*terved* fleeced. *blynne* cease
62	*lemaille* filings	73	*wreke* avenge
65	*gyn* device	75	*abit* abides
		02	*yliche* equally

73-5 Hamilton: since alchemist canon had no fixed abode he was either an apostate or guilty of violating monastic rules against wandering about.

76-03 Mus 217-8: Yeoman's style is "ruggedly dramatic."

1204-1248

Canon goes out with priest to obtain piece of chalk for mold and pan of water. Canon privately slips silver plate from his sleeve, cuts mold to same shape, and hides plate again. He then pours crucible

into mold and plunges it in water. Priest reaches in pan and joyfully
pulls out silver plate.

09	*ingot* mold. *hap* luck	44	*halwes* saints
10	*bolle* bowl	45	*malisoun* curse
12	*preeve* succeed		
25	*tyne* thin plate. *cheeve* thrive		

1249-1282

Canon then insists on a second experiment. This time he slips silver in
crucible by means of hollow stick used to stir coals.

65	*kep* heed	77	*jet* contrivance
71	*gan hym dresse to hym* went up to him		

1283-1329

Priest offers to buy secret, but canon makes third experiment, this
time with an ounce of copper. When mold is plunged in water, canon
reaches in and slyly substitutes silver plate from his sleeve for copper
plate. Priest then finds silver plate.

83	*bet* better	13	*ape* fool
90	*crafty* skillful	19	*heyne* wretch
97	*nam* seized	22	*rombled* fumbled
12	*er* before. *jape* hoax	28	*whileer* before

1330-1340

Canon takes priest to goldsmith to have silver tested. Silver is pronounced pure.

33	*been oght* are worth anything	36	*as swithe* immediately

1341-1387

Priest asks price of recipe for magic powder, and buys it for 40 pounds, promising to keep it a close secret. Canon leaves and is never seen again. Priest has been swindled.

41	*sotted* stupid
53	*receite* recipe
68	*kepe han no loos* care to have no praise

79	*preef* success
81	*sy* saw

1388-1481

This cursed alchemy has caused the scarcity of gold, and brings sorrow to all who dabble in it. Stay away from it; the secret will never be found, as Plato explains, except by certain philosophers chosen by God.

97	*chiteren* chatter
03	*grame* grief
09	*leete* let alone
12	*prolle* prowl about
14	*peril casteth noon* has no thought of danger
21	*chaffare* trade
22	*rape and renne* seize and lay hold of

32	*brother* (of Mercury = sulphur)
40	*Sol* (gold). *Luna* (silver)
70	*deffende* forbid
73	*nevene* tell
80	*poynt* full stop
81	*bale* ills

88-81 Lum 232-3: Yeoman is no fool as some argue (Man 239), but shows real knowledge of alchemy; his whole performance "aimed at shifting the responsibility for his own connection with alchemy."

13-4 Pres 283: notable alliterative passage suggests Ch "was alluding, and paying homage, to a lower level of culture than his own."

28-81 Damon: passage suggests Ch was serious student of alchemy since he here goes out of his way to defend it.

72-81 Lum 233: passage has a "definitely uncalled-for moral smugness about it." Mus 215: philosophical postscript expressing "ruling attitude toward alchemy" in tale.

80 Baum, *PMLA:* pun on *poynt* (point and full stop, period).

81 Pres 283: Yeoman here "contributes to the literature of complaint, not of revolution."

The Manciple's Tale

COMMENTARIES: Gr 243-4; Ham 317-8;/ Don 911, 946-7; ManCT 654-5; Rob 762-5; Sk 5, 435-43;/ Bald 46; Baum 174; Brew 176-7; Cow 178; Ev 158, 172; Fr 333-4; Law 147-8; Lum 235-9; Man 257-8; Mus 238; Pres 206, 282, 284-5; Shan 324; Shel 208-10, 289; Sp 199; Tup 99-103;/ Baum, *PMLA,* 58, 167-70; Donner, *MLN,* 55, 245-9; Elliott, *N&Q,* 54, 511-2; Lumiansky, *MS,* 55, 208-9; Manly, *PBA,* 26, 95-113 (ST); Root, *MLN,* 29, 493-6; Schlauch, *ELH,* 37, 201-12; Severs, *JEGP,* 52, 1-16; Shumaker, *UTQ,* 53, 147-56; Spector, *N&Q,* 57, 26; Stillwell, *PQ,* 40, 133-8; Tatlock, *MLN,* 35, 277-96; Tupper, *JEGP,* 14, 553-65, and 15, 256-70; Work, *SP,* 32, 11-4, and *JEGP,* 32, 62-5, and *SA,* 699-722.

GENRE: Folk tale of the Tell-Tale Bird, used as exemplum.

SOURCE: story of Phoebus and Coronis in Ovid's *Metamorphoses,* or a medieval version thereof (possibly the French *Ovide Moralisé*); for digressive material, philosophic comments, etc., Ch was indebted to *RR* and Boethius.

DATE: Uncertain, but probably early.

GENERAL CRITICISM: Tupper, *JEGP,* 15: Ch's masterly irony in contrast between Manciple's chiding tongue in Prologue and his own counsel against this vice in Tale (see also *ParsT* 623 f.). Man 257: after Second Nun, Manciple is most thinly drawn of pilgrims who tell tales. Manly: one of least interesting tales, not especially suited to teller, with unreal characters, mechanical composition, developed rhetorically, not imaginatively. Cow 178: a "spirited little tale" on age-old theme. Stillwell: French *Ovide Moralisé* and Machaut's *Livre du Voir-dit* are both closer to Ch's tale than Ovid and are possible sources. Law 147: tale is conventional, unimpressive, not especially fitted to thieving Manciple; but Prologue is "one of the most delightful of all the interludes." Sp 199: tale shows "formal, almost mannered, wit." Severs: effective exemplum, with everything subordinated to thesis; Ch drastically changes stress in analogues which show wife sympathetically; he blackens her by praising Phoebus, degrading paramour, omitting dying wife's pitiful confession, minimizing crow's blame—all to emphasize warning against jangling; moral seems unfair to good crow, but this is because Manciple shifts ground at 307 from morality to expediency—this fits his dishonest character (*Gen Prol*), as do traces of ignorance, rudeness, quarrel with Cook. Pres 206, 282: Manciple's digressions are amusing; tale "looks like a leftover from the marriage-feast." Shumaker: central warning is not against false gossip (since crow told truth), but against *all* loose talk; extended discourse is advisable *only* in praise of God (329-31), as shown also in Parson's Prologue and in Retractions; thus *MancT, ParsT,* and Retractions all fit together, unified by theme in *MancT.* Brew 176: treatment of tale is "somewhat mechanical." Ev 172: in rhetorical method only, tale resembles *PardT* and (more closely) *NPT.* Lum 237 (also Donner): Manciple wants to show by his tale that he has learned lesson about excessive talk (to Cook). Mus 238: tale is "creditable example" of Ch's ability to adapt a moral fable. Don 947: tale fits practical Manciple who cares little for moral values; crow deserved punishment because it was foolish, even though it told truth; point against Manciple's own loose mouth is new variation on tales rising out of quarrels in *CT.*

THE MANCIPLE'S PROLOGUE

IX, 1-24

Host awakens sleepy Cook and asks for a tale. Cook is drunk and wants only to sleep.

5	*Dun is in the myre!* horse stuck in mud (refers to a game)	14	*botel* bundle
		16	*by the morwe* in morning
9	*nappeth* nods. *cokkes =* Goddes (oath)	17	*fleen* fleas
		18	*quene* wench

1-104 Tupper, *JEGP,* 14: in medieval mind cooks were traditionally drunken types, gluttons and rioters; dishonest Manciple would have many dealings with cooks; thus Cook-Manciple antagonism is natural. ManCT 654: "highly dramatic episode is in Ch's best realistic manner"; Host is apparently calling on Cook for second tale (see *Gen Prol*). Shel 208-10: a "realistic bit of low life." Law 147-8: Host takes opportunity to persecute drunken Cook by asking for tale with threat of heavy penalty if he refuses; whole Prologue in Ch's best vein, "rollicking, dramatic, vivid."

1-3 Root: since Harbledown (*Bobbe-up-and-doun*) is only 15 minutes' ride out of Canterbury, Ch probably planned *MancT* as first tale of return trip (*by the morwe* in 16 suggests early morning), and *ParsT* as last of return trip.

5-19 Work, *SP:* because of trade rivalry, Host calls on drunken Cook to shame and frighten him and amuse pilgrims, does not really expect tale; "the Host's triumph over the contentious Cook is complete." Don 911: lack of reference to earlier action of Cook shows "imperfect state" of *CT*.

11 Law 148: Host implies drunken Cook is hardly recognizable.

25-55

Manciple offers to tell tale in Cook's place, then jokes about Cook's drunken condition. Cook takes offense, threatens Manciple, falls off horse, and has to be lifted back into saddle.

31	*daswen* are glazed		44	*wyn ape* ape-wine	
34	*yglosed* flattered		46	*wraw* peevish	
35	*ganeth* yawns		50	*chyvachee* feat of horseman-	
42	*atte fan* at the vane (refers to a jousting game)			ship	

25-50 Tupper, *JEGP,* 15: Manciple "assails the enemy of his class with the weapon of an ancient tradition" (intemperance of cooks). 37-4 Shel 289: "plain and homely and Saxon as can be."

56-104

Host orders Manciple to proceed, but warns him against talking too much and making enemies. Manciple agrees, gives Cook a drink of wine to make peace, and is ready to tell tale.

62 *fneseth* wheezes. *pose* head   75 *preef* the proof
   cold   81 *bourde* jest
64 *capul* nag   90 *pouped* blown
74 *pynchen at* find fault with

56-75 Lumiansky: in warning Manciple against antagonizing Cook, Host is recalling his own rashness in jeering at Cook (*CkT* 4345-55) who then threatened to expose his shady dealing as innkeeper. Lum 237: Host knows Manciple cheats lawyers and he also knows Cook is aware of this—"a tightly knit group of city businessmen."

71-2 Sk 5, 439: to *reclayme* a hawk is to bring it back by lure; thus Host means Cook will some day snare Manciple for dishonest dealings; in 76-80 Manciple admits "in all good humour" that this is quite possible.

82-93 Man 258: this is "only time the Manciple exhibits any trait of humanity."

90 Baum: puns on *horn* (drinking horn and wind instrument) and possibly on *poup* (blow and gulp—Cook may have belched and gulped).

99-00 Baum 174: example of Ch's "almost habitual blend of grave and gay."

THE MANCIPLE'S TALE

105-144

When the god Phoebus lived on earth he was a wonderful archer, musician, and singer. In his house he had a white crow in cage who could talk and sing beautifully. He also had a wife of whom he was very jealous.

09 *Phitoun* Python   22 *on-lyve* alive (petrified dative)

23-6 Shan 324: classical god Phoebus is "after all a medieval knight."

145-202

It is foolish to keep close watch on a wife, or to try to restrain any creature. A caged bird, though pampered, prefers freedom. A cat, though well fed, will chase a mouse. Thus, Phoebus's wife, despite all, deceived him with a man of low reputation.

45	*byjaped* deceived		82	*fleemeth* drives out
49	*awayt* surveillance		83	*vileyns kynde* base nature
61	*destreyne* constrain		86	*make* mate
78	*weyveth* abandons		93	*newefangel* fond of novelty

203-239

There is no moral difference between aristocratic and low class adulteresses, though one is called lady and other wench. Similarly, a tyrannical conqueror is morally equal to outlaw or thief.

04	*lemman* lover		29	*playn* flat
11	*boystous* plain		35	*textueel* learned
24	*erraunt* wandering		39	*volage* wanton
28	*meynee* army, following			

05-6 Donner: Manciple apologizes, remembering that Host feared Cook would tell his tale coarsely (see 59) and called on him instead. Lum 239: *lemman* was *not* generally considered a shocking word by Ch's audience.

07-34 Pres 284-5: same argument Ch used in *Gen Prol* 725-46 to justify accurate reporting of details which might be offensive.

11-22 Schlauch: a clear negation of standards of courtly love, a system which Ch turned against in his later years, as in his devastating burlesque in *MerchT*. Brew 176: "Ch, who never approved adultery or promiscuity, may be taken to agree with his mouthpiece."

240-308

When Phoebus returns home one day, crow tells him of wife's adultery. Phoebus shoots wife dead with arrow, breaks his bow and musical instruments, then angrily attacks crow. Phoebus imagines wife to have been innocent and blames crow. He takes away crow's fine voice and white feathers. Since then all crows have been black.

52	*waityng* watching		56	*swyve* have sexual inter-
55	*montance* value			course with

58	*sadde tokenes* sure signs	74	*lustiheed* delight
62	*gan wryen* turned away	78	*rakel* reckless
64	*flo* arrow	81	*wantrust* distrust
68	*gyterne* guitar. *sautrie* psal-tery	98	*awreke* avenged

309-362

Be warned by this, and never tell a man of his wife's infidelity. My mother advised me always to keep my mouth shut, to speak only when necessary. Gossiping always leads to trouble; a word spoken can never be recalled.

10	*kep* care	43	*jangler* gossip
12	*dight* dishonored	46	*bekke* nod
26	*spilt* ruined	58	*yvele apayd* sorry
28	*shent* injured		
40	*forkutteth* cuts. *forkerveth* hews		

09-62 Elliott: long, repetitious moral aimed at drunken Cook; Manciple's fiction that he is repeating mother's advice enables him to use *my sone* 10 times to recall Cook's wandering attention. Spector disagrees with argument (Tupper, *JEGP,* 15) that moral passages are reply to Cook; rather they may be rebuttal to *CYT,* advice to Yeoman (357-60 is appraisal of *CYT*); also, Manciple's use of authorities after saying he knows none (316) is parody of Yeoman's claim that he does not know alchemy. Brew 177: repetitious lines are "hardly poetry."

18-9 Tatlock: repetitions of *my sone* (see also 321-2, 325, etc.) probably not due especially to Solomon's Proverbs but to many collections of gnomic sayings and to oral folklore.

The Parson's Tale

COMMENTARIES: Gr 244-7; Ham 318-22;/ Don 947-50; ManCT 655-8; Rob 765-73; Sk 5, 444-76;/ Bald 83-110 (ST); Bloomfield, *Seven Deadly Sins* (Mich. State Coll. Press, 1952), 191-2; Brew 177-8; Ches 55, 109; Cog 179; Cow 178; Fr 334-8; Ger 99; Law 147; Lum 239-45; Mad 63-79, 103-15; Pat 193; Petersen, *Sources of ParsT* (Boston, 1901); Pres 294-302; Root 284-8; Shel 44; Tho 97-100; Tup 68;/ Chapman, *MLN*, 28, 229-34; Dempster, *SA*, 722-60; Fox, *N&Q*, 58, 523-4, and *MLN*, 60, 101-2; Friend, *MP*, 48, 117-21; Gordon, *Baugh*, 81-96; Hammond, *MLN*, 33, 514-6; Heninger, *JEGP*, 57, 382-95; Homans, *RES*, 38, 447-9; Immaculate, *MLQ*, 41, 59-66; Johnson, *PMLA*, 42, 51-6; Landrum, *PMLA*, 24, 75-100; Langhans, *Anglia*, 29, 235-68; Lumiansky, *TSE*, 56, 5-13; Mariella, *N&Q*, 36, 119, and *MLN*, 38, 251-6; Maxfield, *PMLA*, 24, 64-74; Owen, *JEGP*, 58, 449-76; Pfander, *JEGP*, 36, 243-58; Shain, *MLN*, 55, 235-45; Swart, *Neophil*, 52, 45-50; Tatlock, *PMLA*, 13, 521-9; Work, *MLN*, 32, 257-9.

GENRE: Prose manual on Penitence, into which is inserted long treatise on Seven Deadly Sins.

SOURCES: Material on Penitence from 13th-century *Summa* by St. Raymund of Pennaforte, on Sins from 13th-century *Summa vitiorum* by Guilielmus Peraldus; Ch follows Pennaforte closely, but makes extensive omissions from and additions to Peraldus; neither was his direct source, which must have been French or Latin religious manual (or manuals) derived from Pennaforte and Peraldus, either separately or combined.

DATE: Very uncertain; no positive evidence.

GENERAL CRITICISM: Root 286: "interminably long" and "intolerably dull," inferior to brilliant sermon of Pardoner; digression on Sins destroys unity; orthodoxy disproves that Ch had Wycliffite sympathies or that Parson is Wycliffite. Landrum disagrees with TatDC 202 that Ch's knowledge of Bible was mostly second hand;

tale and other writings show Ch knew Vulgate Bible directly, thoroughly; of some 700 Biblical references in Ch, about 275 come directly from Vulgate. Maxfield distinguishes between Wycliffe's ideas (conservative) and those of more extreme followers (Lollards); *ParsT* gives no sign of Wycliffite tendency. Mad 75-9: "every page is a chronicle of life actual and contemporary, in all its moral phases, from sanctity to superstition"; whole treatise in spirit of love, sweetened with humor, recording common interest of Ch's age in spiritual life and literature. Tup 68: "prosaic journey along the weary levels of theological commonplaces." Cow 78: a compilation of scholastic theology, yet style is too easy and vivacious for a translation. Chapman: a homily or medieval sermon, adhering strictly to principles of medieval sermon writing. Pfander doubts tale is (as Petersen says) an unhappy piecing together of Pennaforte and Peraldus; it has same combination and order of materials as many confessional manuals of the age and is probably direct translation of one of these in French. Pat 193: if Ch sympathized with Wycliffites, it was not for their heresy but for their moral sincerity. Shel 44: tale is dramatic in intention, must be viewed as part of *CT* as a whole. Ches 109: "almost excessive devotionalism." Cog 179: main interest revelation of Ch's mind. Law 147: Prologue, Tale, Retractions all connected by echoes and references. Ger 99: prose pleasant to ear if read aloud, but lacks elegance of Ch's poems. Pres 294-301: tale is "attempt to improve sinners," the pilgrims; it is uncompromising "reality after the illusion" of *CT,* in which Parson tries to "wash the dirty linen that has accumulated." Brew 177-8: sermon is voice of the age whose philosophy Ch shared; it is brave, honest, too long, but commands respect. Bald 98-105: orthodox, dull only to moderns, tale may well have seemed to Ch most meaningful of *CT,* recapitulating all the rest, as Parson combats sins not only in abstract, but speaks "more specifically, and dramatically, against the weaknesses and sins which have been displayed *en route*" in earlier tales and tellers. Shain: genre of tale is religious manual, not sermon. Owen: influence of tale on later *CT* suggests it was written midway in *CT* period (1391-3) during period of penitence and religious mood, before resumption of tales with Marriage Group (1394-8) and final expansion of plan to 4 tales each with Fragment I (1399-1400).

THE PARSON'S PROLOGUE
X, 1-74
As Manciple finishes, pilgrims enter village at 4 p.m. Host calls on Parson for final tale. Parson refuses to tell fable or alliterative tale, but agrees to give prose sermon. Host accepts, urges brevity.

26 *male* bag
33 *weyven* set aside
35 *draf* chaff. *fest* fist
41 *leefful* lawful
43 *geeste* tell in alliterative verse

45 *glose* deceive you
57 *textueel* learned
71 *fructuous* fruitful

17 Lumiansky: line suggests a second change in Ch's plan—from 4 tales each (*Gen Prol*), to 1 or 2 tales each (Franklin's Prologue), now to a tale at least from each *rank,* thus allowing for absence of tales by Yeoman, Plowman, Guildsmen; Ch may well have considered book almost complete with *ParsT,* and intended to revise *Gen Prol* to agree with final plan.

45-60 Lum 244: Parson's strategy to keep Host and others from thinking he will give long sermon—revenge against Host for blasphemous condescension.

61-6 Bald 83-95: ending with Parson's sermon was recognized as fitting by pilgrims and Ch's audience as climax of pilgrimage to Canterbury (analogous to man's pilgrimage to City of God); Parson, as spiritual guide, replaces Host (worldly guide), with full consent of pilgrims (65-6).

THE PARSON'S TALE
THE FIRST PART OF PENITENCE (Contrition)
75-112
Penitence is one of many paths to Christ; it is the sorrowing of a man for his sins. There are 3 kinds of penitence: solemn or open public penance, common penance enjoined on a group, and private penance for private sins. There are 3 parts or steps in penitence: contrition of heart, confession of mouth, and satisfaction or expiation.

75 *perdurable* everlasting
76 *amonesteth* admonishes
80 *covenable* fitting
84 *pleynynge* sorrowing
85 *waymentynge* lamenting.
    pyneth punishes

93 *forlete* forsake
04 *destreyneth* constrains,
    requires
05 *naked* thinly clad
07 *bihovely* helpful
10 *wratthe* anger, offend

80 Owen: passage may have suggested Parson's Prologue 51 (written later).

113-132

Contrition defined: it is the true grief of a man in his heart for his sins, leading to confession, penance, and resolution to sin no more.

22 *medled* mixed
24 *sadly* earnestly

31 *agilt* offended

133-291

Six causes ought to move a man to contrition: (1) remembrance of and shame for sins; (2) disgust at idea of sins which have enslaved him; (3) fear of God's judgment and of everlasting pains of hell; (4) memory of good works he has failed to do or has spoiled by deadly sin; (5) memory of how Christ suffered for us; and (6) hope for forgiveness, grace to live well, and rewards of heaven.

51 *tak reward of* have regard to
57 *wroteth* roots, digs with
    snout
64 *essoyne* excuse
67 *meede* bribe
70 *biknowen* acknowledge
77 *mysese* discomfort
80 *at regard of* in comparison
    with
85 *destourben* hinder
86 *agayn (agayns)* in place of

91 *abated* put down. *defouled*
    trampled upon
93 *oneden . . . to* united to,
    centered upon
96 *forther over* moreover
98 *strawed* strewn
07 *wittes* senses
25 *halwes* saints
28 *talent* desire

48   *Jay tout,* etc. (trans: "I have   69   *brast* burst
     wholly wasted my time and   73   *forfeted* did wrong
     labor")   76   *bispet* spit upon
58   *mowes* grimaces   91   *bihooteth* promises

18 Heninger: echoes Boethius' concept of order as foundation of universe.

47-8 Mad 77: use of popular song here is "about the most deliciously funny thing in Ch"; it may have been in source, but sounds more like Ch's own "pertinent impertinence."

292-315

Contrition should be sincere and total, for evil thoughts as well as for evil speech and deeds. It is first step in cleansing of sins.

94   *apertly* openly
04   *angwissous* causing of feel-
     ing distress

THE SECOND PART OF PENITENCE (Confession)
316-357

Confession, sign of contrition, must be complete and frank. Ever since corruption through original sin of Adam and Eve, all men have been beset by fleshly desire or concupiscence which is hard to subdue (witness Saints Paul, Jerome, etc.), and is encouraged by entice- ments of devil.

19   *as ferforth as* insofar as   41   *malefice* maleficent act or de-
20   *noght avaunte thee* he must   vice
     not boast (shift in subject)   51   *subjeccioun* suggestion,
31   *naddre* adder, serpent   temptation
32   *defended* forbidden   53   *weyve* put aside
34   *contract* contracted   55   *departe* pick out, separate
35   *bynymeth us the culpe*
     takes away the guilt from us

358-386
There are 2 kinds of sins, venial and deadly. It is deadly sin to love
something more than God, venial to love God less than one should.
Venial sins (several examples), if unrepented, may lead to deadly
sins.

59	*amenuse* diminishes	69	*bireveth* takes away
63	*thurrok* sink (in ship's hull), bilges	74	*enchesoun* reason
64	*algates* nevertheless. *dreynt* sunk	79	*biheteth* promises

THE SEVEN DEADLY SINS, THEIR BRANCHES, CIRCUMSTANCES, AND KINDS

387-389
Pride is chief of deadly sins, and from it come the others—Envy,
Wrath, Sloth, Avarice, Gluttony, and Lechery, with their branches
and twigs.

87 *lees* leash

PRIDE (Superbia)

390-483
From Pride comes disobedience, boasting, hypocrisy, arrogance, impudence, swelling of heart, impatience, contumacy, irreverence, vain
glory, etc. Signs of Pride are extravagant and immodest clothing,
retaining of excessive and unruly servants, and extravagant eating.
Pride springs from self-satisfaction in gifts of nature (health, etc.),
gifts of fortune (wealth, social position, etc.), and gifts of grace
(spiritual and moral strength). The remedy against Pride is humility in heart, speech, and actions.

92	*goostly* spiritual	07	*pax* small piece of wood or metal used at Mass for "kiss of peace"
01	*undernome* reproved. *werreieth* makes war on		
03	*Surquidrie* arrogance	11	*leefsel* arbor

14 *cowpable for* reprehensible because of. *degisynesse* elaborateness

15 *costlewe* costly

17 *degise endentynge* elaborate heraldic indentation. *owndynge* adornment with waved lines. *palynge* adorning with heraldic stripes

18 *pownsonynge* piercing. *daggynge* cutting into tags

21 *beete* remedy

22 *kutted sloppes* curtailed garments. *haynselyns* short jackets

23 *boce* protuberance

25 *flayne* flayed

27 *fir of seint Antony* erysipelas

30 *atyr* attire

33 *peytrels* collars for horses

48 *sourden* arise, originate

52 *gentrice* gentility. *franchise* nobility

53 *engyn* skill

61 *binymeth* takes away

73 *brotel* fickle

91-06 Swart: exposition of Pride "reads like an exposition of the Pardoner's characteristic qualities."

07 Owen: passage perhaps suggested *Gen Prol* 449-52 (theory that *Gen Prol* was written after *ParsT*).

07-8 Bald 102: Wife of Bath is clearly target of Parson's words here, as also in 927.

25-7 Ches 55: Parson here attacks "motley figures of contemporary fops."

58-60 Bald 102-3: Parson may here be rebuking Monk, as also in 432-4.

ENVY (Invidia)

484-532

Envy is sorrow at others' prosperity, sin against Holy Ghost, bitter malice toward God's grace to one's neighbor. Unlike other sins, Envy gives no pleasure. It results in backbiting, detraction, malicious gossip, grumbling at one's lot, impatience against God, false accusations, and secret hate. Best remedy against Envy is love of God and of man, including enemies as well as friends and neighbors.

85 *platly* plainly

90 *unnethe* hardly

91 *kyndely* by nature

00 *catel* goods, property

02 *heved* head

06 *leveful* lawful

07 *withseye* refuse

14 *algate* nevertheless. *sembla-ble* similar

18 *amonestynge* admonishing

32 *speces of this paas* kinds of this grade or degree

84 Fox, *N&Q:* *the philosophre* is Aristotle who has a similar defini-tion of envy. Owen: passage may have suggested *PhysT* 114-8 (writ-ten later).

WRATH (Ira)

533-676

Wrath, the evil passion for violence, comes from Envy and Pride, is different from virtuous anger at wickedness. The 2 kinds of Wrath (sudden and premeditated) take away man's reason and alienate him from God. From Wrath come hate, discord, war, homicide, fraud, etc. They are guilty of Wrath who blame or despise God or reject penitence. Other branches of Wrath are blasphemy, swearing falsely, lying, cursing, chiding, scorning, giving evil advice, sowing discord, etc. The remedies against Wrath are meekness, patience in face of evil words or deeds, and obedience to God.

37 *eschawfynge* heating. *trou-ble* troubled (adj.)

40 *debonairetee* humility. *Iras-cimini,* etc. Be ye angered and sin not

48 *gleedes* coals

52 *Estre* (allusion to custom of kindling Easter fire on Holy Saturday)

56 *cheeste* quarreling

59 *halwes* saints

61 *reveth hym* robs him of

65 *sixe* (error for 3)

67 *areysen* raise. *custumes* cus-toms duties. *taillages* taxes

68 *shepe* reward

72 *defendaunt* own defense

80 *arretteth* imputes. *hasar-dours* gamblers

82 *auter* altar

83 *attry* venomous

84 *hokerly* scornfully

85 *compleccioun* temperament. *corageous* high-spirited

86 *biknoweth* acknowledges

92 *quarto capitulo* in 4th chap-ter. *doom* judgment

95 *evene-Cristene* fellow Chris-tian

97 *Actuum, quarto* Acts, in 4th (chapter)

98 *ad Philipenses, secundo* Phi-lippians, in 2nd (chapter). *ynempned* named

03 *nigromanciens* necroman-cers

05 *divynailes* divinations
06 *deffended* forbidden
13 *losengerie* flattery
17 *Placebo* I shall please
21 *as ferforth as in hem is* insofar as they can
24 *mesel* leper
25 *rightwys sonde* righteous sending. *maheym* maiming
26 *holour* lecher
29 *deslavee* immoderate
31 *uncovenable* unfitting
34 *Ad Colossenses, tertio* Colossians, in 3rd (chapter)
39 *ut Achitofel ad Absolonem* as Achitophel to Absalom (II Sam. xvii, 1)
49 *apert* open
52 *knakkes* tricks
54 *Mansuetude* meekness
70 *yerde* stick. *scoure* scourge, beat

556-7 Bald 103: applies to quarrelsomeness of Miller and Reeve, Friar and Summoner.

64-79 Johnson: for homicide passage Ch abandoned Peraldus, drew on Pennaforte; *sixe thynges* in 565, believed to be error, includes 3 more evils listed in 568 (withholding wages, usury, withdrawal of alms), as comparison of Pennaforte with Peraldus shows, with only usury lacking in sources, perhaps added by Ch; 571 promises 4 *maneres* of manslaughter, but Ch gives only 3—by law (571), by necessity (572), by carelessness (574); perhaps Ch's direct source, combining Peraldus and Pennaforte, contained these errors.

91 Bald 103: here Parson rebukes Host for swearing, as he had done earlier (*MLT* 1170-1).

SLOTH (Accidia)

677-738

Bitterness from Envy and Ire leads to Sloth, indifference to and neglect of goodness. Sloth makes a man reject penance and good words, despair of God's mercy, and sink into laziness, idleness, procrastination, and laxity. Remedies against Sloth are fortitude, faith, hope, constancy, etc.

77 *wraw* fretful, angry
80 *unlust* disinclination
82 *heriynge* praising. *adowrynge* adoration
85 *liflode* means of support. *purveaunce* provision. *forsleweth* wastes by sloth. *forsluggeth* spoils. *reccheleesnesse* carelessness

88 *shendeth* ruins
92 *chargeaunt* burdensome
93 *wanhope* hopelessness
96 *douteth* fears
98 *seith "creant"* acknowledges
defeat. *recreant* cowardly
11 *dooth no fors* does not care
14 *yate* gate

15 *thurrok* sink. *trufles* trifles
18 *tarditas* lateness. *laterede*
slow
20 *lachesse* indolence
21 *breres* briars
23 *blent* blinded
33 *queyntise* cunning

21 Owen: passage perhaps suggested use of proverb in *PhysT* 102.

AVARICE (Avaricia)

739-817

Avarice, the lust for worldly treasure, robs Christ of love due Him, results in idolatry of wealth, merciless exploitation of bondmen by lords. Natural order requires subordination in state and church, but lords should be benevolent. Avarice in church leads to degrading simony (selling of offices) which destroys respect for sacraments. Other results of Avarice are gambling, lying, theft, false witness. Remedies against Avarice are compassion and reasonable generosity.

39 *Ad Thimotheum Sexto* (I) Timothy, in 6th (chapter)
42 *purchacen* acquire
48 *ad Ephesios, quinto* Ephesians, in 5th (chapter)
49 *mawmet* idol (corruption of "Mahomet")
50 *Exodi capitulo vicesimo* in 20th Chapter of Exodus
52 *cariages* services of carrying or payments in lieu of same. *amercimentz* fines exacted "at mercy" of lord
53 *stywardes* stewards
54 *Augustinus,* etc. St. Augustine, *City of God,* in 9th Book

55 *Genesis, nono* Genesis, in 9th (chapter)
60 *contubernyal* familiar
64 *skile* reason. *devoir* duty
66 *kowth* known
67 *pilen* rob, pillage
82 *ordred* ordained in holy orders
88 *at regard of* in comparison with
93 *ravynes* plunderings. *reneiynge* denying
96 *meede* bribe
97 *questemongeres* jurymen
99 *met* measure of capacity. *mesure* moderation
01 *chirche-hawes* churchyards

04 *misericorde* mercy   16 *drovy* muddy
06 *mysese* distress

77-80 Bald 103: Parson here rebukes Merchant's sharp practices.

GLUTTONY (Gula)
818-835

Gluttony, excessive appetite for eating and drinking, leads to other sins. Branches of Gluttony are drunkenness by which man loses reason, and greed for too much and too luxurious food. Remedies are abstinence and temperance.

18 *expres* clearly. *desordeynee*   27 *foryetelnesse* forgetfulness
    inordinate   34 *deslavee* immoderate
20 *wombe* belly

28-9 Bald 103: passage applies to gluttony of Franklin.

LECHERY (Luxuria)
836-957

Lechery, cousin to Gluttony, includes adultery. Five fingers of Lechery are looking, touching, speaking, kissing, and copulating. Other branches are fornication and deflowering of virgins. Adultery is breaking of faith and sin against God who made marriage. From it often comes prostitution and lechery by clergy which degrades God and church and poisons whole parishes. Other kinds of Lechery are excessive indulgence between man and wife, incest, unnatural relations, etc. Remedies are chastity, continence, and virtuous marriage. God made Eve not of Adam's head (too high—master), nor of foot (too low—servant), but of rib as companion. Wife should be obedient, modest in dress and action. Chaste widowhood and, above all, virginity are holy states. Avoid temptations to Lechery. Now I have ended treatise on 7 Deadly Sins.

36 *departe* separate   41 *stank* pool
39 *thonder-leyt* thunder-bolt   51 *chaffare* trafficking
40 *avowtrie* adultery

53 *basilicok* basilisk or cocka-trice (supposed to kill by a glance)
57 *smatre* defile
58 *roser* rose-bush
59 *tonne* wine cask
63 *reynes* loins
64 *totrede* trample under foot
80 *douted* feared
85 *gong* latrine, privy
86 *putours* procurers
87 *gladly* by preference
90 *destourbed* hindered
92 *agreggen* aggravate
94 *meignee* retinue, company

00 *soden* boiled, seethed
04 *take no reward* have no re-gard
08 *parentele* kinship
11 *mixne* dunghill
15 *talentes* desires
16 *eschawfynges* heatings
19 *halwen* sanctify
21 *in right poynt* in good con-dition
27 *desray* disorder
33 *purpre* purple
47 *boyste* box
54 *leyt* flame

97-9 Homans: *free bole* was technical term for bull who ran with and serviced cows of whole village herd; normally lord of manor owned bull and peasants made some sort of payments for his use.
25-8 Mariella, *N&Q:* use of head, foot, and rib in treating headship of husband or wife was a commonplace in medieval literature. Mariella, *MLN:* passage sums up whole argument of Marriage Group, probably expresses Ch's own opinion.
36 Fox, *MLN: the philosophre* is probably Seneca.
48 Immaculate: *lyf* is perhaps scribal error for *lyk*—"she is like the angels."
55 Friend: Ch here uses rhetorical device of proverb for closing a section, as recommended by Geoffrey de Vinsauf.

THE SECOND PART OF PENITENCE (Continued)
958-1028

The 7 circumstances which aggravate sins (who, what, where, with whose help, how often, why, in what manner) must be fully confessed. Four conditions are needed for true confession: (1) sincere sorrow, shame, and humility; (2) promptness in confessing fully and to one priest soon after sin; (3) willingness to confess voluntarily; (4) complete truthfulness and frankness.

59   *wittes* senses
60   *agreggen* aggravate
62   *goostly* spiritually
65   *spille his kynde* spills his seed. *entredited* interdicted
68   *eggen* incite
71   *eschew* reluctant
74   *harneys* details
79   *engreggen* weigh down, burden
86   *heven* lift
98   *warisshe* cure

03   *purveyed* foreseen, prepared for
05   *eft* afterwards. *countrewaite* watch over
13   *nayte* deny. *lete* give up, leave off
16   *wyten* blame, accuse
23   *doute* fear
27   *housled* houseled, have eucharist administered. *renovellen* renew

THE THIRD PART OF PENITENCE (Satisfaction)
1029-1056

Third step in penitence is satisfaction or expiation through alms or bodily pain. Charitable works should be done for Christ's sake, not for the world's thanks. Bodily penance may consist of prayers (especially Pater Noster), fasting, waking, wearing of hair-shirt, scourging, etc.

36   *capitulo quinto* in 5th chapter
39   *redresseth it* reforms itself, rises again
41   *koud* known
43   *bitake* entrust
51   *in untyme* out of season

52   *heyres* hair-shirts. *stamyn tamine*, coarse wool cloth. *haubergeons* coats of mail, hauberks
54   *apayed* pleased
55   *yerdes* sticks

1057-1080

Four things hinder penance: (1) fear of bodily pain, (2) shame at revealing sins, (3) hope for long life leading to delay of penitence, (4) despair of Christ's mercy and of one's own strength to refrain from sin. The fruit of penance is the bliss of heaven.

57 *wanhope* despair 69 *hir thankes* willingly
64 *apertly* openly 78 *apeyren* injure
67 *surquidrie* presumption

76-80 Bald 105: "a remarkable summary paragraph, that points up the whole Tale, and tales, and pilgrimage, and Pilgrimage" (of man).

CHAUCER'S RETRACTIONS
1081-1092
Whoever likes this sermon should thank Christ; any faults in it are my own. I ask forgiveness for my writings of worldly vanity and revoke them: namely *Troilus, The House of Fame, Legend of Good Women, Book of the Duchess, Parliament of Fowls,* those of *Canterbury Tales* that tend to sin, *The Book of the Lion* [unidentified], etc. I thank Christ for my good works: translation of Boethius, saints' legends, sermons, etc. May Christ help me to penitence for my sins so that I may be saved at the Day of Judgment. Amen.

82 *arrette* impute
92 *Qui cum patre,* etc. Who
   with the Father and Holy
   Ghost lives and reigns as
   God through all ages.

81-92 Tatlock: Retractions result of "narrowly pious impulse in the sick or aging Ch," following convention also used by later writers (Spenser, Dryden, Herrick, etc.); but Ch's otherworldliness not strong enough to make him suppress or change *CT* to which Retractions are appended. Root 288: unquestionably sincere; in last days Ch's conscience "was seized upon by the tenets of a narrow creed, which in the days of his strength he had known how to transmute into something better and truer." Mad 105-15: Ch's judgment of his poems not as art, but as moral acts; Retractions are uncompromising and utterly sincere evaluations based on presence or absence of positive spiritual values; "he had reached Canterbury; he would reach Christ." Work: tale and Retractions not intended as part of *CT* (see

ManCT 656); casual mention of *CT* in Retractions and use of phrase *litel tretis* (which fits *ParsT* but not *CT*) suggest tale was composed as separate work. Tho 100: tone of "sincere Christian repentance" from man who has shown sensitivity to spiritual values. Bald 107-10: here Ch the man regrets sins of Ch the artist and recants in a general and public confession (see 103), with note of strong and sincere conviction. Owen: Ch viewed Retractions as conclusion of separate treatise on penitence, not part of *CT;* last lines sound more like resolution to live better than death-bed confession.

86 Hammond: most MSS read 25 ladies; Retractions written to end tale, and whole (tale and Retractions) planned as conclusion to *CT* while work still in progress—not a final or death-bed production.